# HISTORY OF CHRISTIAN ETHICS

George Wolfgang Forell

# HISTORY OF CHRISTIAN ETHICS

## VOLUME I
From the New Testament to Augustine

**AUGSBURG** Publishing House • Minneapolis

241.09
F 71 h
V. 1

# Contents

# Preface

**I**T HAS BEEN A VERY LONG TIME since the last attempt was made to present a history of Christian ethics to the English reading public. The reasons for this state of affairs are both numerous and obvious. Two deserve some special comment. First of all, the vast secondary literature produced by the knowledge explosion has accumulated a library of books around every major topic which such a "history" would have to examine and this development makes it foolhardy to engage in such an effort. Secondly, the community of men and women who are engaged in the study of ethics has shown an almost exclusive interest in the very real and overwhelming ethical problems of the day.

This preoccupation with contemporary moral issues makes interest in the history of Christian ethics seem to many antiquarian if not frivolous. If the following pages are nevertheless offered to the readers for their examination it is because the author became convinced that the difficulties while real are not insuperable. The vast and virtually unmanageable secondary literature poses less of a threat to understanding if one approaches the subject with a basic commitment to the primary sources. This approach characterizes the ensuing description and analysis. And even when secondary sources are occasionally brought into the discussion the emphasis is always clearly and intentionally on the original texts themselves. They are extensively quoted, and occasionally sources not available in translation are presented here for the first time in English. Available translations are frequently modified if they obscure the intent of the original text or confuse the modern reader as to the meaning of the original word. Some readers may find these sometimes lengthy quotations burdensome and they often seem quite inelegant, but comments on Christian ethics that are only vaguely related to what the early writers actually wrote or based on quotations nobody has ever been able to locate are unhelpful if not dangerous. In a number of instances (e.g. Tertullian) some of the discussion in the secondary literature has simply ignored the sources or especially in the case of Augustine significantly distorted them.

Another reason for offering a history of Christian ethics toward the end of the 20th century to those interested in this subject is the conviction that especially in the area of Christian ethics one may learn a great deal from the insights and errors of the past. For example, the study of the development and abandonment of a "civil religion" in the years between Tertullian's *Apology* and Augustine's *City of God* may add depth and perspective to the discussion of the varieties of civil religion which are being developed by people all across the *oikumene*, the inhabited world, at this particular time. Likewise, looking at the serious efforts of the past to steer the church on a precarious course between legalism and antinomianism may throw some light on similar efforts in our day. Thus it is hoped that this is indeed not merely an antiquarian effort but a means of enriching the ethical debate in this age. In the preparation of these pages it soon became obvious that the task was much larger than was first anticipated, even if one concentrated on the primary material and did not try to listen to every voice. Thus the present volume takes us only from the New Testament to Augustine.

A second volume will deal with the Middle Ages and the Reformation and its aftermath, to be concluded eventually with a third volume describing Christian ethics after first the *de facto* and then the *de jure* collapse of the Constantinian arrangement and the resulting preoccupation with ethics in our time. Ethics has become the concern of everybody precisely because the ethical consensus which supported previous ages has dissolved even among Christians.

In the resulting pervasive and often superficial concern with ethics those interested in Christian ethics might be helped if they were to see the present turmoil in the context of history and learn from the serious efforts of the past how a way of living responsibly in a changing world might be found. The people with whom this volume deals did this with imagination and fervor.

I am indebted to many people: The taxpayers of the state of Iowa who have established a first-rate research library at the University of Iowa deserve special thanks; Augsburg Publishing House whose administrators and staff encouraged and supported this venture; many individuals who helped with the details of the work, among them my former research assistants Joan Mau, Paul Spalding, Leonard Allen, Ann Swaner and secretaries Carol Hines Casebolt, Gary Taylor and Rachel Mithelman. Above all, my wife Elizabeth who helped and encouraged me along the way.
S.D.G.

GEORGE WOLFGANG FORELL
Iowa City, Iowa

# Introduction

**F**OR MOST PEOPLE inside as well as outside Christendom, Christianity is a body of beliefs based more or less closely on the teachings of Jesus, the Christ. Those who are aware of the fact that Jesus' teachings have come to us by way of "apostles" and "evangelists" and that we have to depend on the witness of generations of disciples for our view of his life and teaching may claim that Christianity is a growing and changing body of beliefs held by the followers of Jesus of Nazareth and developing over a period of approximately two thousand years into the complex system of beliefs associated with Christianity in our age. An avalanche of learned books dealing with the history of Christian doctrine supports this latter view.

As a result, an interested observer would come to the conclusion that Christianity is essentially a system of doctrines, a body of intellectual principles, that one accepts or rejects. The difference between Christians and non-Christians is apparently that the former assent to certain propositions which the latter reject. Similarly, the variety of Christian denominations or sects evidently depends on the doctrines that one group or the other emphasizes or sets aside.

This understanding of the phenomenon of Christianity supposes that religion in general and Christianity in particular are cognitive systems. People are religious because they want to know things and the several religions are different ways of knowing. Christianity is true because it gives us the most reliable information about God, the world, and ourselves. Other religions are less true because the information they convey is less reliable.

The obvious concern with correct knowledge which has characterized Christian leaders through the ages supports this impression. The bitter controversy in the fourth century about the relationship of Jesus the Christ to God the Father that helped to shape the Nicene Creed, seemed to revolve around a piece of knowledge; namely, is the Son "of the same substance" with the Father or is he not? In more recent years the celebrated debate between the two distinguished Swiss theologians Karl Barth and Emil Brunner focused on the proposition that God can be *known* only through the Word as found in the Bible. Barth seemed to insist that apart from the Word there is no *knowledge* of God. Closer at hand, much of the fundamentalist-modernist controversy in its ever-recurring variations seems to revolve around the accuracy of the *knowledge* conveyed to us in the Bible.

In view of this two-thousand-year-old concern with Christian knowledge it may seem foolhardy to suggest that the reality of the Christian movement includes a great deal more than information and that it could be more adequately explained if other aspects of this complex phenomenon were taken seriously. It is true, of course, that Christianity, like any religion, does have a concern with certain propositions and that it claims to convey some knowledge, but the universal obsession with this cognitive aspect of Christendom may have obstructed a comprehensive and adequate understanding of the Christian movement in its entirety. The fact that almost all of the important and eloquent defenders and foes of this movement were principally concerned with Christianity as an intellectual system has certainly tended to suppress its moral, emotional and communal dimensions. But it would be difficult to do justice to the reality "Christendom" if one excluded these dimensions from the investigation.

A more inclusive approach is especially important since the cognitive dimension is of more interest to the professional religionist, the scholar or the theologian, than to the ordinary participant in the movement. It is indeed the very fact that the theoretically most sophisticated tend to write the history of the movement that has caused the rather skewed interpretation of Christianity in predominantly intellectual terms. This, however, tells us more about the paramount interests of the interpreters than about those whose life-style they have tried to interpret. It has obscured what has been called "the rootedness of religion in the practical concerns of everyday life." [1] Yet the New Testament suggests that the proclamation of the Gospel, the good news of God's action in Jesus as the Christ, provoked the question, "What shall we do?" (Acts 2:37).

Faith in Jesus as the Christ resulted in the demand for a life-style reflecting the new situation that God's action had brought about. Similarly every major development in the history of Christendom, from the time of the Apostles to the present, has involved a change in the life-style; that is, it implies moral, emotional and communal modification. The question, "What shall we do?" appears to be the permanently appropriate response of human beings whom the Christian Gospel has reached in some way. This observation assumes that it is the nature of the Gospel to demand a response, that it is the word that "shall not return to me empty" (Isa. 55:11), a creative word which has the power to change human beings and their world.

It is with this in mind that we shall look at the history of the Christian movement as a varied and complex response to the Christian message which not only words express but also attitudes and feelings, a sense of community and a life-style. What impressed the non-Christian world when it encountered Christians was rarely the plausibility or cogency of their theoretical formulations but rather the obvious and impressive new life. It is this new life-style in its polymorphous development which is the subject of the following pages.

# I

# New Testament Ethics

**H**

### 1. *The Centrality of the Encounter with Jesus as the Christ*

ARDLY ANY MORAL, METAPHYSICAL, PSYCHOLOGI-
cal or social idea or approach to life in the New Testament is
without some parallel in the world into which Christianity came.
It is this fact which has led novelists, journalists and even scholars
to the conclusion that "Christendom" is the result of combining the
dominant religious ideas of the time into a popular religious movement. These ideas abroad in the cultural atmosphere of the first
and second centuries crystallized around the person of Jesus of Nazareth, whose historical existence some will deny and others will consider of marginal importance for the movement which was named
after him. But this analysis obscures what is obvious to any reader
of the New Testament, that the life of Jesus of Nazareth and especially particular events in that life, however imprecisely known, are
overwhelmingly significant for the self-understanding of the Christian movement.

A reader of the Hebrew Bible would hardly conclude that the
death and resurrection of the coming Messiah is of central importance to its messianic expectations. One might anticipate a mes-

13

sianic king, a messianic realm, a messianic style of life, all of which
could be described without any reference to the death and resurrection of the Messiah so central in the Christian tradition. Indeed,
the death and resurrection story seems almost an embarrassment
against the background of the conventional messianic expectations.
In the Shemoneh Esrah, the godly Jew extolls God's mercy and
prays,

> And to Jerusalem, thy city, return in mercy, and dwell there as thou
> has spoken; rebuild it soon in our days as an everlasting building, and
> speedily set up therein the throne of David. Blessed art thou, O Lord,
> who rebuildest Jerusalem. Speedily cause the offspring of David, thy
> servant, to flourish, and lift up his glory by thy divine help because we
> wait for thy salvation all the day. Blessed art thou, O Lord, who causeth
> the strength of salvation to flourish.[1]

He prays clearly for a triumphant being, not for a suffering servant.
Thus Bultmann can say, "In its traditional form the hope of Israel
was nationalistic in character. It looked for a restoration of the
Davidic kingdom under a Davidic king, the 'Messiah.' " [2] The interpretation of the messianic hope in 2 Esdras 12:31-33, illustrates the
conventional expectation:

> As for the lion which you saw coming from the forest, roused from
> sleep and roaring, which you heard addressing the eagle, taxing with its
> wicked deeds and words, this is the Messiah whom the Most High has
> kept back until the end. He will address those rulers, taxing them openly
> with their sins, their crimes, and their defiance. He will bring them alive
> to judgment; he will convict them and then destroy them (NEB).[3]

While there were variations in these hopes, since only obedience
to the law is obligatory for the Jew and not any particular form of
eschatological expectation, none of these prospects included a suffering Messiah who would die for the sins of the people.[4] It is therefore strange and surprising that the Christians use Jesus' passion as
the evidence of his messiahship. Luke 24:25-31 attributes this unex-
pected view to the risen Christ himself. According to Acts 17:2ff.,
Paul uses this approach in the Jewish synagogue in Thessalonica.
And Paul summarizes his gospel in 1 Corinthians 15:3-4, "that
Christ, [the Messiah] died for our sins, *in accordance with the scriptures,* that he was buried; that he was raised to life on the third
day, *according to the scriptures . . ."* (NEB). Not the conventional

messianic expectation but a uniquely Jesus-centered interpretation characterizes the early Christian church.[5]

Similarly, the significance of the earthly life of Jesus constitutes the obvious uniqueness of Christendom in relationship to the prevalent and powerful mystery religions in its Hellenistic environment. While knowledge of these cults is fragmentary because of the rigidly enforced obligation of secrecy imposed on all adherents, they can be described as "cultic rites in which the destinies of a god are portrayed by sacred actions before a circle of devotees in such a way as to give them a part in the fate of the god." [6] All mysteries offered the participants salvation by giving them a share in cosmic life. The deities were personalized forces of nature, of life, death and fertility. Their rituals were closely related to the changing seasons and the natural cycles of life.

Lucius, the hero of Apuleius' novel *The Golden Ass*, describes his initiation into the mysteries of Isis in the following words: "Then was all the laity and profane people commanded to depart, and when they had put on my back a new linen robe, the priest took my hand and brought me to the most secret and sacred place of the temple. Thou wouldest peradventure demand, thou studious reader, what was said and done there: verily I would tell thee if it were lawful for me to tell, thou wouldest know if it were convenient for thee to hear . . ." [7] But after this reference to the secrecy of the ritual he summarizes his experience by saying, "Thou shalt understand that I approached near unto hell, even to the gates of Proserpine, and after that I was ravished throughout all the elements, I returned to my proper place: about midnight I saw the sun brightly shine, I saw likewise the gods celestial and the gods infernal, before whom I presented myself and worshiped them." [8] In his final prayer Lucius extolls the power of Isis as a nature-goddess in this prayer:

O holy and blessed dame, the perpetual comfort of human kind, who by thy bounty and grace nourishest all the world and bearest great affection to the adversities of the miserable as a loving mother. . . . Thou art she that puttest away all storms and dangers from man's life by stretching forth Thy right hand, whereby likewise Thou dost unweave even the inextricable and entangled web of fate, and appeasest the great tempest of fortune and keepest back the harmful course of the stars. . . . Thou dost make all the earth to turn, Thou givest light to the sun, Thou governest the world. Thou treadest down the power of hell. . . . At thy commandment the winds blow, the clouds nourish the earth, the seeds prosper, and the fruits do grow. . . .[9]

The notion of a dying and rising god was an important part of the mystery religions. They saw death and resurrection as part of the ever-recurring cycles of nature, following each other as spring does winter. In the words of Sir James Frazer, "Under the names of Osiris, Tammuz, Adonis, and Attis, the peoples of Egypt and Western Asia represented the yearly decay and revival of life, especially of vegetable life, which they personified as a god who annually died and rose again from the dead." [10] An idyll of Theocritus contains a description of the cult of Adonis as Queen Arsinoe II celebrated it publicly around 272 B.C. Here the singer described the scene which re-enacts the annually recurring death of Adonis in the arms of Aphrodite: "In Adonis' rosy arms the Cyprian [Aphrodite] lies, and he in hers . . . Thou dear Adonis, alone of demigods, as they tell, dost visit both earth and Acheron. . . . Look on us with favour next year, too, dear Adonis. Happy has thy coming found us now, Adonis, and when thou comest again, dear will be thy return." [11]

The Adonis cult and others with similar resurrection stories were prevalent in New Testament times.[12] But the striking difference between the recurrent resurrections in these fertility cults and the story of Jesus is the Christian emphasis on the man Jesus and the once and for all significance of his death. It seems as if Paul were arguing against the mystery cults when he writes in Romans 6:9ff., "We know that Christ, once raised from the dead, is never to die again: he is no longer under the dominion of death. For in dying as he died, he died to sin, *once for all*, and in living as he lives, he lives to God" (NEB). The author of Hebrews makes the same point: "And as it is the lot of men to die once, and after death comes judgment, so Christ was offered once to bear the burden of men's sins . . ." (Heb. 9:27-28, NEB). 1 Peter declares, "For Christ also died for our sins once and for all. He, the just, suffered for the unjust, to bring us to God" (1 Peter 3:18, NEB).[13]

Thus while the analogies with the religious movements in the environment of New Testament Christianity are striking and important, the differences seem even more impressive. These revolve around the centrality of Jesus as the Christ. The life of this particular person is decisive not only for the faith of Christians but also for what is interwoven with and dependent on their faith: their life in discipleship to this man.

Jesus the Christ has many titles in the New Testament. "Jesus, the Word" and "Jesus, the Son of God" refer to his preexistence; "Prophet," "Suffering Servant of God" and "High Priest" to his earthly work; "Lord" and "Savior" to his present work; and "Messiah" and "Son of Man" to his unfinished work.[14] But the person whom all these titles describe is the ethical norm of his people's life precisely because of all he represents in their faith. This is not only the message of the Synoptics, which quote Jesus as saying, "Anyone who wishes to be a follower of mine must leave self behind; he must take up his cross, and come with me" (Mark 8:35, NEB) and "Come to me, all whose work is hard, whose load is heavy; and I will give you relief. Bend your necks to my yoke, and learn from me, for I am gentle and humble-hearted; and your souls will find relief" (Matt. 11:28-30, NEB). It is also the message of John: "I give you a new commandment: love one another; as I have loved you . . . then all will know that you are my disciples" (John 13:34-35, NEB). And Paul, who tells us relatively little about the life of Jesus nevertheless insists, "Follow my example as I follow Christ's" (1 Cor. 11:1, NEB). To subdue the quarrelsome spirit of the Philippians he gives for their emulation the example of Jesus who "did not think to snatch at equality with God, but made himself nothing, assuming the nature of a slave" (Phil. 2:6-7, NEB). And the author of 1 Peter insists to his Christian audience that ". . . Christ suffered on your behalf, and thereby left you an example; it is for you to follow in his steps" (1 Peter 2:21, NEB). Here it is very clear that the ethics of the New Testament is based on what this Jesus has done, not only obtaining for us freedom from the power of sin but continually supplying the strength to live healed lives in conformity with his life (1 Peter 2:22-25).

## 2. The Eschatological Character of New Testament Ethics

Besides the centrality of the encounter with Jesus as the Christ, the conviction that the times are rapidly changing and that human life has to be lived in the presence of the realm of God dominates the New Testament ethic. This, again, is similar to the belief in intertestamental Judaism that "this present age is quickly passing away" (2 Esdras 4:27). The dynamics of the Christian life is movement into God's future. In Paul's words, ". . . Forgetting what is behind me, and reaching out for that which lies ahead, I press towards the goal to win the prize which is God's call to the life above, in Christ Jesus" (Phil. 3:13-14, NEB). Eschatology in this sense is orientation toward the future. William Lillie has pointed out, "The Bible has a myth of a perfect natural order in the garden of Eden before the Fall, not unlike the Stoic myth of a primeval Golden Age found in Seneca, but the New Testament writers look forward to a heavenly city rather than backward to a garden of Eden." [15]

But this heavenly city that lies ahead is also already present in the faith of the people of God who are a colony of heaven in and for this world. Unlike the essentially futuristic beliefs of their Jewish neighbors, who see these events as entirely impending, the New Testament churches also assume a kind of "realized eschatology," that the coming rule of God has already begun and that this rule is the key to all life now and forever and thus to all Christian ethics.[16] Christians are in a somewhat ambiguous position, for they are citizens of an earthly government with all the rights and duties of such citizenship, and simultaneously citizens of heaven, with all that this new status implies. Thus Paul can write from Rome, where he was taken because of his appeal to the rights which his Roman citizenship conferred on him, that "we are citizens of heaven, and from heaven we expect our deliverer to come" (Phil. 3:20, NEB).

To make into alternative claims realized eschatology which sees the realm of God in the present, and orthodox eschatology which sees it in the future would falsify the complexity of the New Testament vision. According to Mark, Jesus' proclamation begins with the announcement: "The time is fulfilled, and the kingdom of God is at hand; repent, and believe in the gospel" (Mark 1:15). But the New Testament closes with the vision of the author of the book of Revelation: "Then I saw a new heaven and a new earth; for the first heaven and the first earth had passed away, and the sea was no more. And I saw the holy city, new Jerusalem, coming down out of heaven from God . . . (Rev. 21:1-2). The power of both com-

ponents of this vision gives the New Testament its ethical thrust.
And it is eschatology, the simultaneous presence and future of God's
kingdom, which is at the very basis of New Testament ethics.[17] It
is because the kingdom of God is upon them that those who hear
this message must "repent" or, more accurately, turn around. The
dawn of the kingdom Jesus Christ has brought about and made
manifest is the turning point of world history. That mankind is
now in a totally new situation is reason to rejoice: "How blest are
those who know their need of God; the kingdom of heaven is theirs"
(Matt. 5:3, NEB). In the words of Paul: "The hour of favor has come;
now, I say, has the day of deliverance dawned" (2 Cor. 6:2, NEB).

Out of this new situation a new life-style develops. Jesus does
not abolish the law, he reaffirms it. But it is fulfilled in the light of
the new situation. This means it is interpreted not according to its
form (letter) but rather its intention (spirit). He accuses the religious leaders of his people of having set aside the commandments
of God by the very traditions that were supposed to uphold them
(cf. Mark 7:1-15). It is because God created the Sabbath for the
sake of man and not man for the sake of the Sabbath (Mark 2:27)
that Jesus heals the man with the withered arm on the Sabbath
(Mark 3:1ff.; cf. Luke 13:10ff.). And the eschatological dimension
of the new ethical situation is stated very clearly when Jesus gives
as a reason for the neglect of fasting by his disciples the new circumstances his presence has created: "Can you expect the bridegroom's friends to fast while the bridegroom is with them?" (Mark
2:19, NEB).

The ethical emphasis is always that the law has now to be seen
from its intention. Purity is not the result of ritual washing but
rather the purity of heart: "Nothing that goes into a man from outside can defile him; no, it is the things that come out of him that
defile a man" (Mark 7:15, NEB). And then Jesus offers a list of such
defiling actions that come from an impure heart (Mark 7:22-23).
This new way of seeing the human response in the light of the
changed eschatological situation generates a new kind of responsibility.[18] Because his followers are the friends of the bridegroom
they will live lives of joyful celebration, for the kingdom of God is
both present and coming, and it is the Christian's responsibility to
live as followers of Jesus the Christ, proclaiming the reign of God.

Other obligations, even the universally respected duty of a son to bury his father, have only secondary importance in the presence of the kingdom. "Leave the dead to bury their dead; you must go and announce the kingdom of God" (Luke 9:60, NEB).

But the eschatological character of New Testament ethics calls also any mere individualistic interpretation into question. It is not only the individual for whom the arrival of Jesus and the breaking in of the kingdom of God has changed everything; the new situation affects all the powerful institutions of society, however the various contemporary philosophers might have interpreted them. It challenges business as usual which the Roman Empire, Hellenistic culture, and Jewish society represented. It is this attitude which enraged all the representatives of the powers of the time, who understood the "dealienating" (Berger) emphasis of even those sayings of Jesus which have been conservatively interpreted through the centuries. While he granted Caesar's right to the coin that bore the emperor's image, he claimed for God all human beings, created in the divine image (Mark 12:14ff.).

The enmity of the powerful of the time against the Christians was well deserved, not because the Christians were about to start a revolution to substitute their power for the existing powers; rather because the kingdom of God whose arrival they announced undermined all absolute claims of sex, marriage and family as well as society, culture and religion, the profane and the sacred. This was as true for Paul as it was for Jesus. "For upon us the fulfillment of the ages has come" (1 Cor. 10:11, NEB). "When anyone is united to Christ, there is a new world; the old order has gone, and a new order has already begun" (2 Cor. 5:17, NEB). Paul's tolerance for the remnants of the existing order grows out of his awareness of the new situation which makes the glorification of the existing institutions as irrelevant as their defamation.

## 3. *The Paranetic Emphasis in New Testament Ethics*

In view of the overriding orientation toward the future characterizing New Testament ethics, the question arises whether it offers any concrete guidelines for the present. This question may seem perverse, since it is apparent that Christians through the ages have been convinced that the Bible and particularly the New Testament supplies answers to all ethical problems. Yet in more recent years the opinion Rudolf Bultmann expressed as early as 1930 has become generally accepted, namely, that any ethics that hopes to answer the question, "What must I do?" is based on a misunderstanding of the human situation.[19] Discussing the "great commandment" he insisted that loving the neighbor does not tell you what to do but only how to do it.[20]

Bultmann's observation has become a cliché in Christian ethics. Christians allegedly know intuitively what to do if they stand under the power of love. As Herbert Preisker states it: "It is of the essence as far as the original attitude of early Christianity is concerned that love says everything that God does, and gives to people what they in turn have to show to their neighbors." [21] Paul Lehmann describes the Christian ethic as follows: " 'I am to do what I am!' To do what I am is to act in every situation in accordance with what it has been given to me to be. Doing the will of God is doing what I am." [22] And he attributes this ethical insight directly to the New Testament when he continues, "If this sounds like double-talk, then the Johannine literature is also engaged in double-talk." [23]

Similarly, Joseph Fletcher says, "No law or principle or value is good as such—not life or truth or chastity or property or marriage or anything but love. *Only one thing is intrinsically good, namely, love: nothing else at all.*" [24] Eric H. Wahlstrom describes Pauline ethics by saying, "What the Christian does is God's work. The Christian is free, independent, and sovereign." [25] Wolfgang Schrage has summarized this approach as saying: "Freedom from the law means here not only freedom from the law as road to salvation or freedom from the content of the nomos of Moses, but, beyond all this, freedom from all demands and commands except the command to love." [26]

Yet it is quite apparent that the New Testament and especially Paul propose concrete and specific standards for the Christian life.[27] Paul says in the epistle to the Galatians, the very charter of salvation by grace alone,

Now the works of the flesh are plain: immorality, impurity, licentiousness, idolatry, sorcery, enmity, strife, jealousy, carousing, and the like. I warn you, as I warned you before, that those who do such things shall not inherit the kingdom of God. But the fruit of the Spirit is love, joy, peace, patience, kindness, goodness, faithfulness, gentleness, self-control; against such there is no law. And those who belong to Christ Jesus have crucified the flesh with its passions and desires (Gal. 5:19-24).

This is a most specific list of sins and virtues and Paul's approach seems to try very hard to help his Galatian readers to discover precisely what they should not do and what they should do. Paul is clearly willing to answer the question "What must I do?", and with considerable specificity.

This concreteness of the New Testament has been explained in various ways. Some have suggested that it is the result of the decline of the fervor of Paul's eschatological expectations. He developed these concrete prohibitions and recommendations after his hope for an immediate return of Christ had grown dim.[28] Schrage has shown that such an explanation simply will not do. Paul's eschatological point of view does determine all of his thinking, but it does not weaken his commitment to specific Christian obligations. When writing to the Thessalonians about the "Day of the Lord" which will come "like a thief in the night" (1 Thess. 5:2) he continues by exhorting his readers to "admonish the idle, encourage the faint-hearted, help the weak . . ." (1 Thess. 5:14). For him there seems to be no contradiction between high eschatological expectation and very specific moral admonition.

Indeed it is apparent that Paul believes that there is specifically Christian behavior that is definably different from the behavior customary in this world which is "passing away" (1 Cor. 7:31). "For the wisdom of this world is folly with God" (1 Cor. 3:19; 7:31), and Christians should not behave "like ordinary men" (1 Cor. 3:3), although they frequently do. He tells them to put away "anger, wrath, malice, slander, and foul talk from your mouth. Do not lie to one another, seeing that you have put off the old nature with its practices and have put on the new nature, which is being renewed in knowledge after the image of its creator" (Col. 3:8-10). This means a different attitude toward women, who can be "fellow workers" (Rom. 16:3), who as wives are to be loved (Col. 3:19). It means also a different attitude toward manual work, which Paul sees as a positive good rather than, as many of his Gentile contemporaries saw it, a necessary evil that "belonged to sickness, misfortune and being despised." [29] For the Christian work was an appropriate and blessed activity, because Jesus, the Lord, had himself been a manual laborer (cf. Mark 6:3) and Paul, the apostle to the Gentiles, continued during his ministry to support himself by manual work and considered this an important example for his followers:

> For you yourselves know how you ought to imitate us; we were not idle when we were with you, we did not eat anyone's bread without paying, but with toil and labor we worked night and day, that we might not burden any of you. It was not because we have not that right, but to give you in our conduct an example to imitate. For even when we were with you, we gave you this command: If anyone will not work, let him not eat" (2 Thess. 3:7-10).

Here again Paul does not hesitate to give specific commands for the behavior of those who want to be Christians. In the light of these observations a fairly clear bridge becomes visible between the moral behavior Paul advocates and the detailed ethical advice in the letter of James. The theological reasons given in this epistle to support the behavior it recommends may not be adequate, but the actual advice is very similar indeed. The Christian life-style it proposes seems to be closer to Paul's position than the theology it articulates. Paul would have no trouble understanding James' cry, "Behold, the wages of the laborers who mowed your fields, which you kept back by fraud, cry out; and the cries of the harvesters have reached the ears of the Lord of hosts. . . . Be patient, therefore, brethren, until the coming of the Lord. . . . For the coming of the Lord is at hand" (James 5:4ff.).

Eschatological expectation and specific social criticism and moral counsel go together in the New Testament. This appears clearly in the parable of the Good Samaritan, which both criticizes the hypocrisy of the religious establishment and advocates specific acts of love. To be a Christian implies a very specific life-style in all the writings of the New Testament.

Certain basic beliefs undergird the concrete standards the New Testament puts forth to guide the behavior of the increasingly polymorphous Christian community. These are:

1) *Creation reflects the Creator.* "Ever since the creation of the world his invisible nature, namely, his eternal power and deity,

have been clearly perceived in the things that have been made"
(Rom. 1:20, compare Ps. 19:1-4). This is the reason that some "Gen-
tiles who have not the law do by nature what the law requires . . ."
(Rom. 2:14). If people act counter to nature, they demonstrate the
effect of their basic unnatural act, namely, idolatry, the worship as
God of things which are not God. This results in all kinds of asocial
behavior, homosexuality being for Paul the most drastic example
(Cf. Rom. 1:21-32).

But while nature is authoritative, it is not the final authority. For
example, "nature" would demand that the apostle receive his support from the congregation: "Who serves as a soldier at his own
expense? Who plants a vineyard without eating any of its fruit?
Who tends a flock without getting some of the milk?" (1 Cor. 9:7).
Nevertheless Paul has not made use of this natural right because
it might "put an obstacle in the way of the gospel of Christ" (1 Cor.
9:12). The decisive concern is always the proclamation of the
gospel of Christ.

2) *The Old Testament is authoritative.* It is very obvious in the
Gospels that the Mosaic law in its ethical intention continues to
be authoritative for the people of the New Testament. To the man
who asks Jesus, "What must I do to inherit eternal life?" he answers,
"You know the commandments: 'Do not kill, Do not commit adultery, Do not steal, Do not bear false witness, Do not defraud, Honor
your father and mother'" (Mark 10:17ff.; cf. Matt. 19:16-30; Luke
18:18-30).

If there is a change it is in the direction of a more radical interpretation of the law in the light of its basic intention. So we read:
"You have heard that it was said to the men of old, 'You shall not
kill; and whoever kills shall be liable to judgement.' But I say to
you that every one who is angry with his brother shall be liable to
judgement; whoever insults his brother shall be liable to the council, and whoever says 'you fool!' shall be liable to the hell of fire"
(Matt. 5:21ff.).

Even Paul the apostle to the Gentiles insists, "The law is holy,
and the commandment is holy and just and good" (Rom. 7:12).
While the law in all its forms does not save man, it is a help for
the guidance of the Christian. In his exhortations to a responsible

Christian life Paul frequently refers to the Old Testament, e.g., "Beloved, never avenge yourselves, but leave it to the wrath of God; for it is written, 'Vengeance is mine, I will repay says the Lord'" (Rom. 12:19; cf. Lev. 19:18; Deut. 32:35. See also 1 Cor. 9:9; 10:1; 14:34; also 2 Cor. 8:15; 9:9, etc.).

But in his Gentile environment Paul does make a distinction between the ceremonial law and the moral law of the Old Testament. Ritual concerns about "clean" and "unclean" are irrelevant for the Christian: "I know and am persuaded in the Lord Jesus that nothing is unclean in itself . . ." (Rom. 14:14). Circumcision is a physiological operation of no consequence (cf. Rom. 2:25ff.). In response to the Galatian desire to be under the law of circumcision Paul writes, "For freedom Christ has set us free; stand fast therefore, and do not submit again to the yoke of slavery" (Gal. 5:1).

The New Testament use of the Mosaic law is positive and constructive. "Freedom from the law as the road to salvation is simultaneously freedom for the law as a commandment with a specific content." [30] While by no means the only source of New Testament ethics, it is an important and respected source.

3) *Love is the central norm.* In the Gospels as well as the Epistles love is the absolute ethical norm (Mark 12:28ff.). This love is the hallmark of the children of God: "Love your enemies and pray for those who persecute you, so that you may be sons of your Father who is in heaven; for he makes his sun rise on the evil and on the good, and sends rain on the just and on the unjust" (Matt. 5:44ff.). This is the message of the Synoptics (cf. Luke 6:27ff.) as well as of John. "A new commandment I give to you, that you love one another; even as I have loved you, that you also love one another. By this all men will know that you are my disciples, if you have love for one another" (John 13:34-35). And Paul insists that "he who loves his neighbor has fulfilled the law."

All the important commandments of the Mosaic law are summed up in the sentence "You shall love your neighbor as yourself" (Rom. 13:8-9). Without love any deed is worthless, even such special gifts of Christians as the ability to speak in tongues or the gifts of prophecy, faith and knowledge (1 Cor. 13:1-3). "Let all that you do be done in love," Paul writes to the Corinthians (1 Cor. 16:14). Love, which God originates and the Christian serves as a vehicle and instrument, must permeate every human relationship in the public and private sphere. For the New Testament, all commandments of the law are in the service of love, are aids to love and under its control. James is as insistent on the royal law of love as Paul (James 2:8), and Wendland says rightly about the writings of the Johannine corpus, "Here every separation between salvation and commandment, Christology and ethics is suspended. The new being is love." [31]

This love is not some amorphous sentimental feeling; it finds its structure by the law which calls Christians to love God and the neighbor. Thus they know that "love is patient and kind; love is not jealous or boastful; it is not arrogant or rude. Love does not insist on its own way; it is not irritable or resentful; it does not rejoice at wrong, but rejoices in the right. Love bears all things, believes all things, hopes all things, endures all things. Love never ends . . ." (1 Cor. 13:4-8).

The New Testament sees the specific commandments not in opposition to love but in the service of love, enabling the believer to love in conformity with Christ. Through Christ's love Christians are to permeate the entire world with their love. New Testament ethics does not hesitate to be specific: it answers for its time very clearly the question, "What must I do?"

## 4. The Servant Function of the Mind

Granting the concreteness of the moral advice of the New Testament, the question remains how this specific counsel applies to the ever-changing situations in which Christians find themselves. It is apparent that in the New Testament the "mind" and "practical reason" play an important part in the guidance of one's moral life. Jesus, for example, opens the mind of his disciples and leads them to understand the Scriptures (Luke 24:45). Paul writes to the Romans, "Do not be conformed to this world but be transformed by the renewal of your mind, that you may prove what is the will of God, what is good and acceptable and perfect" (Rom. 12:2; cf. Eph. 4:23).

The Greek word *nous* translated here as "mind" is used to describe a resource for the formation of the new life of the Christian.

And this same word *nous* describes the way in which we discover the law in our inmost self which urges us to serve God (cf. Rom. 7:21-23). In Mark 12:34 the scribe who correctly answered the basic ethical question confronting humanity is called "wise," a term that refers to the possession of *nous*. Responsible behavior demands that "every one be fully convinced in his own mind" (Rom. 14:5), a Pauline phrase which has a clear analogy in Ecclesiastes 5:10.

Ignorance is considered something to be overcome (Acts 17:30), and Paul can write to the Corinthians, "Come to your right mind, and sin no more" (1 Cor. 15:34). He seems to regard ignorance as contributing to the alienation of the Gentiles. The servant function of the mind in the task of Christian ethics clearly appears in Ephesians 4:17ff.: "Now this I affirm and testify in the Lord, that you must no longer live as the Gentiles do, in the futility of their minds; they are darkened in their understanding, alienated from the life of God because of the ignorance that is in them, due to their hardness of heart. . . ." Though this indicates that by nature we are unable to use our minds responsibly and cannot be saved by following the dictates of reason, since Gentiles are plagued by "senseless minds" (Rom. 1:21) and Jews by "hardened minds" (2 Cor. 3:14), the *nous* is nevertheless involved in our renewal through Christ which results in a "new nature, which is being renewed in knowledge after the image of its creator" (Col. 3:10). To Paul that renewal of the mind (Rom. 12:2) is the basic renewal that initiates the ongoing metamorphosis, the process of being changed into the likeness of the Lord "from one degree of glory to another" (2 Cor. 3:18), a process which eventually allows the comment, "If anyone is in Christ he is a new creation; the old has passed away, behold, the new has come" (2 Cor. 5:17; cf. Gal. 6:15). Indeed, then "every thought [is] captive to obey Christ" (2 Cor. 10:5).

It is important to note, however, that this process is not initiated by the *nous;* it is rather the transformation through the power of the Spirit of God (1 Cor. 2:10ff.) of the "senseless" and "hardened" *nous* into an instrument enabling the Christian to think and to understand as one who is "in Christ," being equipped with the "hidden wisdom of God" (1 Cor. 2:7). For Paul and later for the Pastoral Epistles, "to know the truth" (2 Tim. 2:25) has pre-eminently

ethical significance.[32] When Paul prays for his congregations to be
"filled with the knowledge of [God's] will in all spiritual wisdom
and understanding" (Col. 1:9), it is a prayer for a life in conformity to Christ, "worthy of the Lord" (Col. 1:10, cf. Phil. 1:9-10).

Mind and reason are now in the service of the believer's discipleship to Christ. All people should, therefore, use their minds to the
best of their ability. Paul exhorts the Romans to "think with sober
judgement" in order to use their various gifts responsibly (Rom.
12:3ff.). He tells the Philippians to *think:* "Whatever is true, whatever is honorable, whatever is just, whatever is pure, whatever is
lovely, whatever is gracious, if there is any excellence, if there is
anything worthy of praise, think about these things" (Phil. 4:8).

For the New Testament, faith and the renewed reason are not
opposites. Rather, faith enables us to use our reason in the service
of God and the neighbor. God's gift does not destroy reason but
empowers it to guide us to serve God. Reason becomes an important
instrument for the ethical life. Indeed, "the whole law is fulfilled
in one word, 'You shall love your neighbor as yourself' " (Gal. 5:14).
But it is the mind and the application of reason which enables
Christians to articulate the meaning of this summary of the law in
the concrete situations in which they find themselves. Indeed, if
the Lord's servant is not quarrelsome but kindly to everyone, "an
apt teacher, forbearing, correcting his opponents with gentleness,"
God may very well grant that these very opponents may also
achieve the *epignosis aletheias,* i.e., come to know the truth (2 Tim.
2:24-25). Far from basing Christian ethics upon direct inspiration
that will guide the individual and the community every instant, it
is a renewed mind which helps the followers of Christ to live a life
for God and the neighbor.

The rapid success of Christianity in the Hellenistic world was par-
tially the result of the willingness of a majority of Christians to
accept from the prevailing cultural tradition whatever was true,
honorable, just, pure, gracious, etc.

It is a fact of major importance in the history of religion that the greatest of the apostles of Jesus Christ taught his followers to answer the
demands of the day and that he called them to fulfill the duties of the
day in a similar manner as the popular philosophy of the time. Thus the
young Christian religion was able to appropriate the heritage of the ethics

of antiquity. The treasure of maxims of popular philosophy as well as the wisdom of the rabbis was Christianized and it supplied the commentary to the brief paranesis of the apostles and missionaries.[33]

## 5. The Audience

The commonsense character of much of the specific ethical advice given in the New Testament, as well as the confidence in the mind as an organ of the Spirit enabling Christians to live in a style that appreciates everything true, honorable, just, pure, and lovely, would make it appear that the application if not the motivation of New Testament ethics did not deviate radically from the conventional ethical wisdom of the time. But the element in this ethics that seemed extremely peculiar to the cultured contemporaries of the early Christian movement, yet contributed most to the rapid spread and eventual victory of Christianity over the many competing religions in the Roman Empire, was the shocking openness to people of all races and classes, to women as well as slaves—its concern for the downtrodden, the outcasts, the sinners. Many stories in the New Testament reflect the annoyance of Jesus' fellow-citizens at his willingness to associate with tax-collectors and sinners (Matt. 11:19; cf. Luke 7:34). He states that his message is for the lost sheep of the house of Israel (Matt. 15:24), sends his disciples to the "lost sheep" (Matt. 10:6) and tells the chief priests and elders of the people that "the tax-collectors and the harlots go into the kingdom of God before you" (Matt. 21:31).

Such a message was bound to offend people who had invested much in the achievement of righteousness and who had always seen righteousness as the condition for God's blessing. They felt justified in praying:

The Lord rewarded me according to my righteousness; according to the cleanness of my hands he recompensed me. For I have kept the ways of the Lord, and have not wickedly departed from my God. For all his ordinances were before me, and his statutes I did not put away from me. I was blameless before him, and I kept myself from guilt. Therefore the Lord has recompensed me according to my righteousness, according to the cleanness of my hands in his sight (Ps. 18:20-24).

Even if the apocryphal Ezra sought mercy for everyone, since "no man alive is innocent of offence" because of the pervasiveness of sin (2 Esdras 8:34, NEB) the angel of the Lord answered him, "Never again rank yourself among the unjust, as you have so often done. . . . Ask no more questions, therefore, about the many who are lost. For they were given freedom and used it to despise the Most High, to treat his law with contempt and abandon his ways" (2 Esdras 8:47, 55-56, NEB). On God's behalf the angel declared, "Be sure that I shall not give any thought to sinners, to their creation, death, judgment, or damnation; but I shall take delight in the just, in their creation, in their departure from this world, their salvation, and their final reward" (2 Esdras 8:38-39, NEB). No wonder that Jesus' message to those who were lost created resentment among those who had so much invested in their righteousness and almost incredulous joy among those who knew that they were sinners.

When Christianity moved to the Gentile world its openness to all people was equally offensive and scandalous to the ears of the adherents of the moral philosophers and the devotees of the mystery cults. Origen quotes Celsus, the learned pagan opponent of the Christians, as describing their approach to the Gentile world in these words: "Let no one come to us who has been instructed or who is wise or prudent (for such qualifications are deemed evil by us); but if there be any ignorant, or unintelligent, or uninstructed, or foolish persons, let them come with confidence." And Celsus disdainfully continued, "By which words, acknowledging that such individuals are worthy of their God, they manifestly show that they desire and are able to gain over only the silly, and the mean, and the stupid, with women and children." [34]

Granted that Celsus put the most negative interpretation possible on the well-known attitudes of his Christian contemporaries, it is apparent that their open invitation to all kinds and conditions of people struck him as peculiar, mean and perverse. Origen in his defense frankly admits the charge that Christians seek unlikely prospects and says, "Such indeed does the Gospel invite, in order to make them better; but it invites also others who are very different from these, since Christ is the Saviour of all men, and especially of them that believe, whether they be intelligent or simple. . . ." [35] It is apparent that the learned Gentile opponents of Christianity did not consider its openness to all types of human beings an asset of this movement but a distinct liability.

The difference between Christianity and the mystery cults of the time that struck Celsus was that however obscurantist the cults were from the point of view of true philosophy, they seemed to choose their members according to far higher standards. Origen quotes Celsus as saying,

> That I bring no heavier charge than what the truth compels me, any one may see from the following remarks. Those who invite to participation in other mysteries, make the proclamation as follows: "Every one who has clean hands, and a prudent tongue"; others again thus: "He who is pure from all pollution, and whose soul is conscious of no evil, and who has lived well and justly." Such is the proclamation made by those who promise purification from sins. But let us hear what kind of person these Christians invite. Every one, they say, who is a sinner, who is devoid of understanding, who is a child, and, to speak generally, whoever is unfortunate, him will the kingdom of God receive.[36]

In his reply, Origen does not really deny the fact of the inclusiveness of the Christian proclamation, but rejects the hostile interpretation which Celsus has given to it.

> Now, in answer to such statements, we say that it is not the same thing to invite those who are *sick in soul* to be *cured*, and those who are *in health* to the *knowledge* and *study* of divine things. We, however, keeping both these things in view, at first invite all men to be healed, and exhort those who are sinners to come to the consideration of the doctrines which teach men not to sin, and those who are devoid of understanding to those which beget wisdom, and those who are children to rise in their thoughts to manhood, and those who are simply unfortunate to good fortune *(eudaimonia)*, or—which is the more appropriate term to use—blessedness *(makariotēta)*.[37]

The fact that the Christian movement enlisted people who would not be acceptable in Greek mysteries is incontrovertible. But while Celsus considered this a ridiculous weakness it proved to be its unique strength. Everybody without exception was a possible convert to the Christian life-style. When Celsus scoffed about the invitation of sinners, "What other persons would a robber summon to himself by proclamation?" Origen was prepared to reply, "A robber summons around him individuals of such a character, in order to make use of their villainy against the men whom they desire to slay and plunder. A Christian, on the other hand, *even though he invite those whom the robber invites* [my emphasis], invites them to a very different vocation, viz., to bind up these wounds by His word, and to apply to the soul, festering amid evils, the drugs obtained from the word. . . ." [38]

The power of New Testament ethics results from the fact that it addressed a much larger audience than the morally, ritually, or intellectually elitist ethical systems of the prevailing religious and philosophical movements in the Roman Empire. It addressed groups that other movements did not take seriously or openly rejected because they considered them racially, intellectually, sexually, or socially inferior. Jesus, the ultimate authority for all Christian proclamation, had always expressed his concern for these "outcasts." The Evangelists report him as saying that at the messianic banquet the poor, the maimed, the blind, and the lame would be the guests (Luke 14:16-24; cf. Matt. 22:1-10). He asserted that the first would be last and that he who humbled himself would be exalted. The most unlikely candidates, such as the "Good Samaritan," would inherit eternal life. His sermons reversed all conventional values. The kingdom of God was for those in need: the hungry shall be satisfied; those who weep shall now laugh; the hated, the outlaws, the despised are going to inherit heaven (cf. Luke 6:20-23). The signs of the kingdom are: "The blind receive their sight, the lame walk, lepers are cleansed, and the deaf hear, the dead are raised up, and the poor have good news preached to them" (Luke 7:22).

Writing as late as A.D. 180, Celsus clearly shows that an open invitation to the outcast and the rejected remained the hallmark of Christianity a century after the death of the early disciples. A decisive aspect of New Testament ethics is the audience for which it is intended. It seeks to reach the masses untouched by elitist philosophy and esoteric religion and to show them a new style of life brought into being through the encounter with the living Christ, which the Christians saw as a real possibility for all human beings: "For God sent the Son into the world, not to condemn the world, but that the world might be saved through him" (John 3:17).

# The Early Christian Fathers

**P**ERSONALITIES WHO ARE SELF-CONSCIOUSLY JEWS (e.g., Paul) or in close contact with and dependent on people who think as Jews (e.g., Luke) dominate the New Testament in spite of its outreach into the Gentile world. They argue with their Jewish brothers about the messianic claims of Jesus and about the proper understanding of the law, but this is essentially an argument within a common universe of discourse. Paul can say about his opponents in Corinth, "Are they Hebrews? So am I. Are they Israelites? So am I. Are they descendants of Abraham? So am I" (2 Cor. 11:22). And Luke sees Christ as "a light for revelation to the Gentiles, and for glory to [His] people Israel" (Luke 2:32).

The situation for the early Christian fathers of the second century was substantially different. They were mostly Gentiles living in a Gentile world, and they developed their ethics against the background of paganism. Even though there may have been an occasional document out of a Jewish-Christian tradition, the setting for the ethics of the early fathers was the pagan world of the Roman Empire. A staggering religious and philosophical syncretism dominated this world and threatened to absorb the youthful Christian movement. While Christian involvement with Gnosticism

**33**

appeared already in the New Testament canon, it became for the early Christian fathers a struggle for survival.

In this conflict the Christian movement developed three basic defenses of its integrity in an alien world: (1) the rule of faith, (2) the canon of Scripture, (3) the episcopal office.[1] These bulwarks against a strange and threatening environment were especially important because of the large number of relatively unlearned and simple adherents which the unique "open door policy" of the Christian missionaries had gathered, and because of the obvious attraction which various forms of Gnosticism exerted on them.

1. The *rule of faith* was to protect believers against false doctrine. It consisted of a short summary of the faith easily learned and remembered. Lietzmann has shown that short sloganlike confessions of faith in a divinity were current among the Gentiles, and the Acts of the Apostles report a dramatic incident in Ephesus where a large crowd shouted for two hours, "Great is Artemis of the Ephesians" (Acts 19:28-34), apparently a brief confessional statement of this kind.

Christians had developed similar statements, as for example, "Jesus is Lord." Paul writes a more elaborate version in contradiction to the popular formula current in the eastern cities of the Empire, "There is but one Zeus Serapis:" "There is one God, the Father, from whom are all things and for whom we exist, and one Lord, Jesus Christ, through whom are all things and through whom we exist" (1 Cor. 8:6). Even further developed summaries of the Christian faith appear in Romans 1:3-4 and Philippians 2:5-11. By the time of the early fathers this brief rule of faith had expanded to include statements concerning Mary and the Holy Spirit (Ign. *Eph.* 18:2), Jesus' birth, his true humanity (Ign. *Trall.* 9:1), his suffering under Pontius Pilate (Ign. *Trall.* 9:1), his preaching to the departed spirits and ascension (1 Peter 3:19, 22), and his return to judge the living and the dead (2 Tim. 4:1). Thus Lietzmann writes, "We see how all these parts of the teaching, so well known to us from the Apostles' Creed, appear already around the turn of the first century in churchly formulations and give these formulations fullness and strong definition." [2]

The importance of the developed rule of faith is so great that

Irenaeus saw it as a bulwark against heresy even for illiterate barbarians who

> diligently following the old tradition believe in one God, maker of heaven and earth and of all that is in them, through Christ Jesus the Son of God, who on account of his abundant love for his creation submitted to be born of a virgin, himself by himself uniting man to God, and having suffered under Pontius Pilate, and risen, and having been received up into splendor, is to come in glory as the Saviour of those who are saved, and the judge of those who are judged, and will send into eternal fire those who alter the truth, and despise his Father and his coming.

Irenaeus said that illiterate barbarians who cling to a memorized rule of faith like this in the absence of written documents may indeed be "barbarians" in the way in which they use language, but as far as doctrine, habit, and style of life *(conversatio)* are concerned, "they are, because of their faith, most wise, and are pleasing to God, living in all righteousness and purity and wisdom." [3]

The rule of faith guarantees the integrity of the doctrine of the Christians, then, but it also guarantees the integrity of their *conversatio,* their life-style. It is not only that the rule of faith protects them simultaneously against a perverse way of life. The rule has far more than intellectual or cognitive significance; it is the basis of the new life for Jews and Gentiles, for Greeks and barbarians. Indeed, by the time of Irenaeus it is more amazing to Christians that God has included Celtic and Teutonic barbarians among his people than that he once included Gentiles with Jews.

In the writings of the early fathers, rule of faith and life-style seem closely associated. Just as the awareness and acceptance of the saving deed of God, "that while we were yet sinners Christ died for us" (Rom. 5:8), leads for Paul to a detailed description of the new life in the body of Christ (Rom. 12-15), so the early Christian fathers see the continuity between the rule of faith and the new life very clearly.

Clement of Rome exalts faith when he writes to the Christians, "We, too, who by his will have been called in Christ Jesus, are justified not of ourselves nor through our own wisdom or understanding or piety, nor yet through the things we have accomplished in purity of heart, but through that faith through which almighty God has justified all men from the beginning . . ." (1 Clem. 32:4).[4] The immediate consequence is "What shall we do, brethren?" He answers this rhetorical question with a detailed description of the new life-style:

> So let our whole body be preserved in Christ Jesus, and let each put himself at the service of his neighbor as his particular spiritual gift dictates. Let the strong care for the weak, and let the weak respect the strong. Let the rich provide for the poor, and let the poor give thanks to God because he has given him one through whom his needs are met. Let the wise man show his wisdom not in words but in good deeds. Let the humble not draw attention to himself, but leave it to others to speak well of him. Let him who is continent not boast of it, but be mindful that it is another who bestows upon him his self-control.

Clement clinches his argument by reminding his readers: "Let us all bear in mind, brethren, of what sort of stuff we were made, who we are, and what kind of beings we came into this world, out of what grave and darkness our Creator and Master brought us into this world, having prepared his benefits for us before we were born. Since we have all these things from him, we ought to give thanks to him in everything . . ." (1 Clem. 38:1-4).[5] Again the basis for the new life is gratitude for the benefits prepared for us before we were born. Clement echoes Paul's words, "while we were yet sinners Christ died for us," and bases his entire call to a new way of life upon gratitude for the gifts received in God's prevenient grace.

For Ignatius of Antioch it is obvious that faith must be active in love. Of faith and love toward Jesus Christ he writes to the Ephesians, "These are the beginning and end of life, for the beginning is faith and the end is love. When the two exist in unity it is God, and everything else related to goodness is the result" (Ign. *Eph.* 14:1).[6]

The Shepherd of Hermas in his vision of the seven women proclaims that the first of these women is Faith, for "through her the elect of God are saved."[7] Continence is a daughter of Faith, and Simplicity, Knowledge, Innocence, Reverence, and Love are the daughters of one another. But it is clearly Faith which is the origin of them all.

2. But what about the *canon of Scripture,* the second of the supporting signposts guiding the early Christian movement? Christians

accepted the Scriptures of the Jewish people as authoritative. They spoke of "the books and the apostles" as their holy writings (2 Clem. 14:2).[8] If the number of these authoritative documents was at first not defined, it reflected the situation among their Jewish contemporaries at the time.[9]

The preface to Ecclesiasticus clearly states the Jewish attitude towards the Scriptures, including a summary of their content. "A legacy of great value has come to us through the law, the prophets, and the writers who followed in their steps," the author declares. And "for this Israel's traditions of discipline and wisdom deserve recognition. It is the duty of those who study the scriptures not only to become expert themselves, but also to use their scholarship for the benefit of the outside world through both the spoken and the written word" (NEB). For Jews the purpose of the Scriptures includes the life-style that can derive from their study and observance. The Scriptures are the major means to that end.

But while the Old Testament canon of the early Christian fathers was substantially identical with that of the Jewish community, the former read and interpreted these same writings in light of the advent of Jesus the Christ. It was the conviction of the Christians that the Bible of the Jewish people spoke prophetically about their Lord and Savior. This fact was the major reason for its authority among the Gentile Christians. Jesus' mission and message as the Christ of the Jews and Gentiles could not be explained without recourse to the Old Testament. But the life-style which the Old Testament fostered was not acceptable to the Gentile Christian movement. Circumcision, food laws, the observance of the Sabbath, much of what for any orthodox Jew characterized the Jewish conduct, seemed meaningless to the Gentile Christian community and fell by the wayside.

The shift was inevitable. Its cogent theological interpretation was one of the major achievements of first century Christianity. Von Campenhausen is correct in saying that "In this situation the decision was not made on merely pragmatic grounds, but that this new freedom received a systematic explanation was essentially the achievement of one person, Paul." [10] It was his theological interpretation of the Old Testament which made it authoritative for Gentile Christianity. Again in von Campenhausen's words: "For not the defense and preservation of the law but its dethronement made it finally possible for the church to accept the entire Old Testament as God's word, give it a Christian interpretation and preserve it as part of its own canonical Scriptures." [11]

It is the problem of the proper interpretation of the Old Testament in the Christian movement that occupies a prominent part in the early Christian fathers. The Lord's day has replaced the Sabbath (Ign. *Magn.* 9:1). What the Epistle of Barnabas calls "the new law of our Lord Jesus Christ, which is not tied to a yoke of necessity" has superseded sacrifices and fasting (*Barn.* 2:6).[12] But apparently to Barnabas the "new law of our Lord Jesus Christ" is not merely a more rigorous and more ethical form of legal religion, for he relates it to a new kind of offering, "its own offering which is not man-made" (*Barn.* 2:6).[13] The new life, the Christian life, as he explains later, begins "when we receive the forgiveness of sins and place our hope on the Name." Then "we become new, created again from the beginning." "God truly dwells in our 'dwelling place'—in us." When asked how this can take place, he attributes it to "the word of his faith, the invitation of his promise, the wisdom of his righteous ordinances, the commandments of his teaching; himself prophesying in us, himself dwelling in us . . . giving us repentance, he leads those who had been in bondage to death into the incorruptible Temple" (*Barn.* 16:8-9).[14]

The Old Testament remained the canon of the early Gentile Christians because they believed that the Lord himself guided them into an understanding of these writings which were in many respects apparently irrelevant. The Lord prophesies and dwells in individual Christians and enables them to read these Scriptures as books whose center is Christ and thereby helps them to a new life in Christ. The Epistle of Barnabas 19:1–21:9 describes this new life in detail, and includes such specific exhortations as "Love your neighbor *more than yourself* [and] do not murder a child by abortion, nor, again, destroy that which is born" (5b-5c), or "Share all things with your neighbor and do not claim that anything is exclusively yours; for if you are sharers in that which is imperishable, how much more so in what is perishable" (8a).[15] To these Gentile Christians, the entire Old Testament is primarily a book about Christ, and it becomes secondarily a resource for the new life in

Christ. For this purpose, they interpret it with the moral-allegorical exegesis which must seem to us fantastic or even absurd.

For those early Christian writers who are unwilling to go as far as the Epistle of Barnabas in the moral-allegorical exegesis of the Old Testament, the final argument against what they call "Judaizers," against people who demand a literal proof for the Christian claims from the Old Testament, is an appeal to Christ as the key to understanding. Ignatius writes to the Philadelphians,

> The priests are noble, but the High Priest, entrusted with the Holy of Holies, is nobler; he alone has been entrusted with the secrets of God; he himself is the door to the Father, through which enter Abraham and Isaac and Jacob, and the prophets and the apostles and the Church. All these are in the unity of God. But the gospel has something distinctive: the coming of the Savior, our Lord Jesus Christ, his passion and resurrection (Ign. *Phld.* 9:1-2).[16]

There were those who said to Ignatius that they did not find his message in the "original documents" or "charters," (which apparently meant the Old Testament), and so did not believe in the Gospel. They responded to his "It is written" by saying, "That is the question." To them he finally confessed, "For me the 'charters' are Jesus Christ; the inviolable charters are his cross and death and his resurrection and the faith which exists through him" (Ign. *Phld.* 8:2).[17] In spite of all justified complaints about the adequacy and orthodoxy of Ignatius' theological formulations, it is apparent that he grasped the central reality of the Christian proclamation: the original document is Jesus Christ. The victory of Christianity among the Gentiles was not the result of its clever allegorical interpretations of the Old Testament, its more imaginative utilization of the conventional wisdom of popular philosophy, or even its superior moral teaching, but the power of Jesus the Christ to conquer the hearts of Gentiles and give them a new birth and a new life.

3. Yet the institution most effective in containing the threats to the unity of the nascent Christian movement was the gradually evolving *office of the bishop*. Ethical guidance for people recently converted to Christianity and likely to bring a pervasive pagan attitude to this new life was offered at first by a polyform ministry of grace, reflected in the New Testament. But as time went by moral

authority was increasingly focused in an ordered ministry of bishops and deacons.

As early as the *First Letter of Clement* (ca. A.D. 96) a number of arguments for the importance of such a jurisdictional authority for Christian formation were offered. Some were based on nature, others on culture. Clement describes the majestic way in which the Father and Creator of the universe governs the world: "The heavens move at his direction and peacefully obey him. Day and night complete the course appointed by him nor interfere with one another. Sun and moon and the chorus of stars travel on their appointed courses according to his ordinance in harmony and with never a deviation." [18] He then concludes that, similarly, "Let us respect our rulers, honor our elders, train our youth in the discipline of the fear of God, guide our women toward what is good." [19]

The argument from culture suggested obedience to the leaders by comparing the Christian life to military service: "Let us consider those who serve under our military commanders, with what good discipline, subordination and obedience they carry out orders. Not all are prefects or tribunes or centurions or captains of fifty and so on, but each in his own rank carries out orders under the emperor and the commanding officer." [20] The thrust of the letter is clear: "Learn obedience, laying aside the arrogance and proud willfulness of your tongue. For it is better for you to find a small but creditable place in the flock of Christ than to appear eminent but be excluded from his hope." [21]

Nowhere in the Apostolic Fathers was the importance of the bishop for the disciplined Christian life more clearly stated than in the letters of Ignatius. "Pay attention to the bishop and the presbytery and deacons," [22] he writes to the Philadelphians. "Pay attention to the bishop so that God will pay attention to you." [23] "Let us be eager not to oppose the bishop, so that we may be subject to God." [24] Indeed, obedience to Christ is here equated with obedience to the bishop: "For when you subject yourselves to the bishop as to Jesus Christ, you appear to me to be living not in human fashion but like Jesus Christ. . . ." [25] Through the office of the bishop the shape of the Christian life is determined and the masses recently brought into the Christian movement are conformed to Christ. In such a disciplined community, rule of faith, canon of

Scripture, and the episcopal office were believed to enable even the most backward people to become useful members of the body of Christ.

When Christians encountered Celtic and Germanic tribes, they accepted these new Gentiles as openly as Paul had accepted the Gentiles he had met in the urban centers of the Hellenistic world. Irenaeus, a bright young man from Smyrna, became a bishop in Lyons and thereby, in his own words, "a resident among the Celts, and mostly accustomed to a barbarous language. . . ." [26] Yet this did not keep him from proudly asserting as early as A.D. 189 that Christ is the Savior of the barbarian Gentiles: "For the languages of the world are different, but the meaning of the [Christian] tradition is one and the same. Neither do the churches that have been established in Germany believe otherwise, or hand down any other tradition, nor those among the Iberians, nor those among the Celts, nor in Egypt, nor in Libya, nor those established in the middle parts of the world. . . . The preaching of the truth shines everywhere, and illumines all men who wish to come to the knowledge of the truth." [27] Indeed, "God has made the despaired-of Gentiles fellow heirs and of the same body and partners with the saints. . . ." [28]

In its outreach to the barbarians, the early church continued the same open attitude which characterized Paul's approach to the Gentiles: "to show the mighty acts of the Lord to all men" (Herm. *Sim.* 10.2.3). It was ultimately rooted in the belief that regardless of national background, political citizenship, culture or language, Christians possessed a common citizenship which made all other allegiances strangely irrelevant. As the Shepherd of Hermas puts it: "As one living in a foreign country, do not prepare for yourself more than is necessary to be self-sufficient, and be prepared so that whenever the ruler of this city wishes to cast you out for disobeying his law, you can leave his city and go to your own city and joyfully live according to your law" (Herm. *Sim.* 1.6). Christians lived "in the world," and cared very much for all the people in this world for whom their Christ had died.

This attitude produced a missionary outreach with astonishing results. "By the middle of the second century it could be said that there was not a single race of men on earth among whom converts to the Christian faith could not be found." [29] If this second-century claim seems somewhat premature in retrospect, it does not diminish the massive missionary achievement of the Christian movement. It rested on the openness of Christians to all kinds of people and on the offer of freedom from the anxiety of fate and death which clearly oppressed their fellow-citizens. Even as admittedly legalistic a Christian as the author of *The Shepherd of Hermas* was prepared to invite the same unlikely prospects into fellowship which Paul had approached almost a century earlier: "Be converted, you who walk in the commandments of the devil, which are bitter and cruel and foul, and do not fear the devil, for there is no power in him against you." [30]

It was this fearlessness which Christians were willing to demonstrate again and again in the second and third centuries that attracted ever new converts. Martyrs were witnesses, and not only old and wise pastors like Polycarp, but even simple prisoners of war whom Gothic warriors captured in Greece and Asia Minor. The historian Commodian reports that while captured pagan senators cursed their gods the Christian prisoners cared for the sick and suffering, and by their different approach to life and death they persuaded some of their new masters to adopt the new faith.[31]

Today when it is fashionable to speak of the post-Christian era, an anonymous letter from the second century may help us understand our current situation:

For Christians cannot be distinguished from the rest of the human race by their country or language or customs. They do not live in cities of their own; they do not use a peculiar form of speech; they do not follow an eccentric manner of life. This doctrine of theirs has not been discovered by the ingenuity or deep thought of inquisitive men, nor do they put forward a merely human teaching, as some people do. Yet, although they live in Greek and barbarian cities alike, as each man's lot has been cast, and follow the customs of the country in clothing and food and other matters of daily living, at the same time they give proof of the remarkable and admittedly extraordinary constitution of their own commonwealth. They live in their own countries, but only as aliens. They have a share in everything as citizens, and endure everything as foreigners. Every foreign land is their fatherland, and yet for them every fatherland is a foreign land. They marry, like everyone else, and they beget children, but they do not cast out their offspring. They share their board with each other, but not their marriage bed. It is true that they are "in the flesh," but they do not live "according to the flesh." They busy themselves on earth, but their citizenship is in heaven. They obey the established laws, but in their own lives they go far beyond what the laws require.

They love all men, and by all men are persecuted. They are unknown, and still they are condemned; they are put to death, and yet they are brought to life. They are poor, and yet they make many rich; they are completely destitute, and yet they enjoy complete abundance. They are dishonored, and in their very dishonor are glorified; they are defamed, and are vindicated. They are reviled, and yet they bless; when they are affronted, they still pay due respect. When they do good, they are punished as evildoers; undergoing punishment, they rejoice because they are brought to life. They are treated by the Jews as foreigners and enemies, and are hunted down by the Greeks; and all the time those who hate them find it impossible to justify their enmity. To put it simply: What the soul is in the body, that Christians are in the world. . . . It is to no less a post than this that God has ordered them, and they must not try to evade it.[32]

It was this faith that gave them the victory that overcame the world (1 John 5:4).

# III

# Tertullian

**T**HE OPEN INVITATION ITS MISSIONARIES EXTENDED to all human beings attracted many early converts to the new religion. It was this general appeal that produced a fellowship consisting at first of a high proportion of the disinherited, outcasts, and enslaved. Jesus had said, "Those who are well have no need of a physician, but those who are sick; I came not to call the righteous, but sinners" (Mark 2:17; cf. Luke 5:31). Small wonder that his followers were often those whom their contemporaries regarded as inferior. Paul was forced to observe about the Christians in Corinth, "Not many of you were wise according to worldly standards, not many were powerful, not many were of noble birth . . ." (1 Cor. 1:26f.). The death of Jesus on the cross, which his triumphant resurrection followed according to the faith of this fellowship, convinced many of his alienated and downtrodden partisans that suffering is God's way to victory. It gave meaning to their apparently meaningless lives. It was this radiant new meaning in life that attracted another type of person to the ranks of the movement—the well-educated person, who was also plagued by the emptiness and meaninglessness of life.

The *Passing of Peregrinus* illustrates how a well-educated and skeptical person of the second and third centuries would perceive the Christian movement and how Christianity exerted an attraction on sophisticated people. The author himself, Lucian of Samosata (ca. 120-180), was such a person. A rhetor schooled as a Sophist, Lucian abandoned his profession to travel as a free-lance writer across the Mediterranean world ridiculing the foibles of his age.

Lucian's story is an account of the life and death of Peregrinus, a Cynic philosopher who for a time in his early career joined the Christians and suffered imprisonment as a Christian. Eventually he abandoned Christianity and, in his later years, became so involved with Indian religious ideas that he cremated himself at the Olympic games of A.D. 165.[1]

Lucian tells us what happened when Peregrinus came in contact with the Christians. He says,

He learned the wondrous lore *(sophia)* of the Christians, by associating with their priests and scribes in Palestine. And—how else would it be?— in a trice he made them all look like children; for he was prophet, cult-leader, head of the synagogue, and everything, all by himself. He interpreted and explained some of their books and even composed many, and they revered him as a god, made use of him as a lawgiver, and set him down as a protector, next after that other, to be sure, whom they still worship, the man who was crucified in Palestine because he introduced this new cult into the world.[2]

As was likely to happen in the second century, the authorities arrested Peregrinus as a Christian and threw him into prison. Lucian continues,

Well, when he had been imprisoned, the Christians, regarding the incident as a calamity, left nothing undone in an effort to rescue him. Then, when rescue was impossible, every other form of attention was shown to him, not in any casual way but with assiduity; and from the very break of day aged widows and orphan children could be seen waiting near the prison, while their officials even slept inside with him after bribing the guards. Then elaborate meals were brought in, and sacred books of theirs were read aloud, and excellent Peregrinus—for he still went by that name —was called by them "the new Socrates."[3]

It is doubtful that Lucian's story is entirely accurate, for Christians would hardly call one of their heroes "the new Socrates," but it reflects the loyalty they showed to each other and the surprise that this attitude caused among their non-Christian neighbors.[4]

It also shows that they were eager to attach upper-class converts to their cause and place them in positions of leadership.

Lucian continues,

Indeed, people came even from the cities of Asia sent by the Christians at their common expense, to succour and defend and encourage the hero. They show incredible speed whenever any such public action is taken; for in no time they lavish their all.[5] So it was then in the case of Peregrinus; much money came to him from them by reason of his imprisonment, and he procured not a little revenue from it. The poor wretches have convinced themselves, first and foremost, that they are going to be immortal and live for all time, in consequence of which they despise death and even willingly give themselves into custody, most of them. Furthermore, their lawgiver persuaded them that they are all brothers of one another after they have transgressed once for all by denying the Greek gods and by worshiping that crucified sophist himself and living under his laws. Therefore they despise all things indiscriminately and consider them common property, receiving such doctrines traditionally without any definite evidence. So if any charlatan and trickster, able to profit by occasions, comes among them, he quickly acquires sudden wealth, by imposing upon simple folk.[6]

Lucian's story is the verification by a thoroughly skeptical observer of a most important Christian belief, the belief in eternal life. It was the Christians' confidence in eternal life which made them as a group so different from their non-Christian contemporaries, and in spite of their educational and social shortcomings and their obvious naiveté, objects of wonder and envy.

The place where the bored intellectuals of the Roman Empire were likely to encounter the distinctive faith of the Christians most powerfully displayed was in their amphitheater. Christians had been persecuted and thrown to wild animals as part of public spectacles as early as the reign of emperor Nero.[7]

The popularity of these shows and spectacles was almost universal and by no means limited to the city of Rome. Juvenal had ridiculed the *turba remi*, the mob of Remus, by saying, "The people that once bestowed commands, consulships, legions and all else, now meddles no more and longs eagerly for just two things—Bread and Games!" [8] And the African-born historian, Fronto, observed not much later, "The Roman people is absorbed by two things above all others, its food supplies and its shows." [9]

The scope of these spectacles is well-known. Suetonius reports

that 5,000 beasts were killed in one day at the *munera* with which
Titus inaugurated the coloseum in A.D. 80. But there were amphitheaters in every major city in the empire, and some, for example
the amphitheater in Thysdrus (El Djem) in the province of Africa
(Tunisia), were almost as large as the one in Rome.[10]

The spectacles in these amphitheaters were as cowardly as they
were cruel. Seneca's description should demonstrate this fact: "By
chance I attended a mid-day exhibition, expecting some fun, wit,
and relaxation,—an exhibition at which men's eyes have respite from
the slaughter of their fellow-men. But it was quite the reverse. The
previous combats were the essence of compassion; but now all the
trifling is put aside and it is pure murder. The men have no defensive armour. They are exposed to blows at all points, and no one
ever strikes in vain." Seneca continues, "Many persons prefer this
programme to the usual pairs and to the bouts 'by request.' Of
course they do; there is no helmet or shield to deflect the weapon.
What is the need of defensive armour, or of skill? All these mean
delaying death. In the morning they throw men to the lions and the
bears; at noon, they throw them to the spectators." [11]

By the second and third centuries many of the so-called criminals
butchered in this manner were Christians. "Criminals of both sexes
and all ages, who by reason of their villainy—real or supposed—and
their humble status had been condemned *ad bestias*, were dragged
at dawn into the arena to be mauled by the wild animals loosed
from the basement below." [12] It was in such a setting that martyrs
like Blandina died in the amphitheater in Lyons, Perpetua and
Felicita in Carthage and hundreds of Christians in the coliseum
in Rome.

It may have been in such a setting that Quintus Septimus Florens
Tertullianus, the first major Latin theologian and ethicist, was converted to Christianity. Tertullian was born about A.D. 160 in the
city of Carthage in the Roman province of Africa, the cradle of many
brilliant writers both Christian (e.g. Cyprian, Arnobius, Lactantius,
Minucius Felix and Augustine of Hippo) and pagan (e.g., Fronto,
the tutor of Marcus Aurelius, and the sparkling satirist Apuleius).
The son of a pagan centurion attached to the Roman provincial
government, he grew up outside of the church. He received a sound
upper-class education, including a study of the Greek language,

and eventually became a brilliant lawyer. After his conversion to Christianity he became famous as a spokesman for this movement and later for a rigorous deviant form, namely Montanism. His language utilized military and legal terms and introduced these words permanently into the theological vocabulary of the Christian church.[13] He died after A.D. 200, an old man, faithful to his vision of the Christian life, but now even at odds with the Montanists.[14]

Africa was prosperous in Tertullian's time. As W. H. C. Freund has observed: "The period 180-235 was in the main an era of internal well-being, perhaps more apparent to those who were enjoying it than to modern historians and economists probing into the causes of the economic collapse of the mid-third century." [15] Tertullian's writings affirmed the general prosperity of the empire. Arguing against the Pythagorean doctrine of the transmigration of souls and the implied stability of human population he says,

> Surely it is obvious enough, if one looks at the whole world, that it is becoming daily better cultivated and more fully peopled than anciently. All places are now accessible, all are well known, all open to commerce; most pleasant farms have obliterated all traces of what were once dreary and dangerous wastes; cultivated fields have subdued forests; flocks and herds have expelled wild beasts; sandy deserts are sown, rocks are planted; marshes are drained; and where once were hardly solitary cottages, there are now large cities. No longer are [savage] islands dreaded, nor their rocky shores feared; everywhere are houses, and inhabitants, and settled government, and civilized life. What most frequently meets our view [and occasions complaint], is our teeming population: our numbers are burdensome to the world, which can hardly supply us from its natural elements. . . .[16]

Tertullian wrote about the attraction of spectacles for himself and his African contemporaries in *De Spectaculis*. Apparently some defended the public shows:

> All things were created by God and given to man (as we Christians teach), and that they are really good, all being the work of a good Creator; and that among them we must reckon all the various things that go to make the public shows, the horse, for example, and the lion, and strength of body and charm of voice. It follows, they urge, that a thing cannot be counted foreign to God or hostile to Him that exists by His creation, nor must we suppose a thing hostile to God's worshippers, which is not hostile to God because it is not foreign to God." [17]

Tertullian continues, "How clever in argument human ignorance seems to itself! especially when it is afraid of losing something of this kind, some delight or enjoyment of the world!" He notes bitterly but acutely, "Why, you will find more men turned from our school *(secta)* by the danger to pleasure than by the danger to life! For even a fool does not dread death beyond a certain point—he feels it inevitable; but pleasure, a thing of such high value, even a sage does not despise; since neither fool nor sage has any delight in life apart from pleasure." [18]

He charged that all shows are idolatrous in origin and in present practice. As Christians try to keep their gullets and bellies free from defilement by eating food offered in sacrificial and funeral rites (here he quotes 1 Cor. 10:21: "You cannot drink the cup of the Lord and the cup of demons. You cannot partake of the Lord's table and the table of demons.") so they should also avoid defiling their nobler parts—their eyes and ears.[19]

Of course the fact that so many of the victims were Christians enters also into his discussion: "It is our duty," he says, "to hate these assemblies and gatherings of the heathen, were it only that there the name of God is blasphemed; that there every day, the shout is raised to set the lions upon us. . . ." [20] Or, as he says in *Apology* XL, "If the Tiber rises as high as the city walls, if the Nile does not send its waters up over the fields, if the heavens give no rain, if there is an earthquake, if there is famine or pestilence, straightway the cry is 'Away with the Christians to the lion!'" (It is typical of Tertullian that when quoting this cry *Christianos ad leonem,* he cannot help making his black humor observation, "What! shall you give such multitudes to a single beast?") [21]

No wonder he says to those who claim that these bloody spectacles serve to punish the guilty, "But who will pledge himself to me that it is always the guilty who are condemned to the beasts, or whatever the punishment, and that it is never inflicted on innocence too, through the vindictiveness of the judge it may be, the weakness of the advocate, the severity of torture?" And he concludes, "As for the Christian, God forbid *he* should need further teaching to hate the spectacle. No one, however, can fully set out the whole story here, unless he be still a spectator. I prefer to leave it incomplete than to remember." [22]

But remember he did. Apparently it was the Christian "obstinacy" in the amphitheater which one day changed his mind about these people and their faith. The conclusion to his *Apology* reflects this: "Nothing whatever is accomplished by your cruelties, each more exquisite than the last. It is the bait that wins men for our school. We multiply whenever we are mown down by you; the blood of Christians is seed. Many of you preach the endurance of pain and death. . . . And yet their words never find so many disciples as the Christians win, who teach by deeds." Remembering his own experience he continues,

That very "obstinacy" with which you taunt us, is your teacher. For who that beholds it is not stirred to inquire, what lies indeed within it? Who, on inquiry, does not join us, and joining us, does not wish to suffer, that he may purchase for himself the whole grace of God, that he may win full pardon from God by paying his own blood for it? For all sins are forgiven to a deed like this. That is why, on being sentenced by you, on the instant we render you thanks. There is a rivalry between God's ways and man's; we are condemned by you, we are acquitted by God.[23]

The same experience occurred to him again when he wrote to Scapula concerning the persuasive power of Christian martyrs: "For all who witness the noble patience of [these] martyrs, are struck with misgivings, are inflamed with desire to examine into the matter in question; and as soon as they come to know the truth, they straightway enroll themselves as its disciples." [24]

Persecution of Christians had come to the Roman province of Africa about A.D. 180 under the reign of Emperor Commodus when Vigellius Saturninus was proconsul (180/81). What appears to be a transcript of the trial, the so-called *Acts of the Scillitan Martyrs*,[25] has survived. The section which shows most clearly the conflict which so impressed Tertullian is at the beginning of the confrontation:

The proconsul Saturninus [26] said: "If you return to your senses, you can obtain the pardon of our Lord the emperor."
Speratus [the apparent spokesman for the Scillitans] said: "We have never done wrong; we have never lent ourselves to wickedness. Never have we uttered a curse; but when abused, we have given thanks, for we hold our own emperor in honour."
Saturninus the proconsul said: "We too are a religious people, and our

religion is a simple one: we swear by the genius of our Lord the emperor and we offer prayers for his health—as you also ought to do. . . ."

Speratus said: "I do not recognize the empire of this world. Rather, I serve that God whom no man has seen, nor can see, with these eyes. I have not stolen; and on any purchase I pay the tax, for I acknowledge my lord who is the emperor of kings and of all nations." [27]

It is clear that the claim of the Christians that they recognized only one lord and that he was not the Roman emperor was at the root of the conflict with the political authorities. Others may have been more offended by what they considered to be the Christian dissent against what we might call today the "civil religion" of the Roman Empire—dutiful conduct toward the gods, one's parents, relatives, benefactors, and country.

Caecilius, the pagan spokesman in the dialog *Octavius* by Minucius Felix, clearly stated this resentment: [28]

Seeing then that either chance is blind,[29] or nature uncertain, how much more reverent and better it is to accept the teaching of our elders as the priest of truth; to maintain the religions handed down to us; to adore the gods, whom from the cradle you were taught to fear rather than to know familiarly; not to dogmatize about divinities, but to believe our forefathers who, in an age still rude, in the world's nativity were privileged to regard gods as kindly or as kings! Hence it is that throughout wide empires, provinces and towns, we see each people having its own individual rites and worshipping its local gods. . . .

Hence the course of worship has continued without break, not impaired but strengthened by the lapse of time; for indeed antiquity is wont to attach to ceremonies and to temples a sanctity proportioned to the length of their continuance. . . .

Therefore, since all nations unhesitatingly agree as to the existence of the immortal gods, however uncertain may be our account of them or of their origin, it is intolerable that any man should be so puffed up with pride and impious conceit of wisdom, as to strive to abolish or undermine religion, so ancient, so useful, and so salutary. . . .

Is it not then deplorable that a gang—excuse my vehemence in using strong language for the cause I advocate—a gang, I say, of discredited and proscribed desperadoes band themselves against the gods? Fellows who gather together illiterates from the dregs of the populace and credulous women with the instability natural to their sex, and so organize a rabble of profane conspirators, leagued together by meetings at night and ritual fasts and unnatural repasts, not for any sacred service but for piacular rites, a secret tribe that shuns the light, silent in the open, but talkative in hid corners; they despise temples as if they were tombs; they spit upon the gods; they jeer at our sacred rites; pitiable themselves, they pity (save the mark) our priests; they despise titles and robes of honour, going themselves half-naked! What a pitch of folly! what wild impertinence! present tortures they despise, yet dread those of an uncertain future; death after death they fear, but death in the present they fear not: for them illusive hope charms away terror with assurances of life to come. . . .

And he concludes his impassioned plea by saying, as a typical citizen of a pluralistic world,

> To my mind things that are doubtful, as they are, should be left in doubt, and, where so many and such great minds differ, rash and hasty votes should not be cast on either side for fear of countenancing old wives' superstition, or of subverting all religion.

What brought the first Roman intellectuals into the church was the ability of the Christians to organize such disparate elements as "credulous women" and "illiterates from the dregs of the populace" into a powerful and effective community whose members could face death fearlessly and almost eagerly. As Tertullian himself had put it so colorfully, *Semen Est Sanguis Christianorum*, "The Blood of the Christians is seed!"

Christian ethics brought Tertullian himself into the church. In turn, he advanced the definition of Christian ethics, even if the church eventually discarded some of his own cherished positions.

The basis of Tertullian's ethics is the relationship God established with human beings in creation. Through this relationship, God has disclosed his goodness. Tertullian writes against Marcion: "The Creator's primary goodness is that by which it was God's will not to be eternally in hiding, that is, that there had to be something to which as God he might become known." [30] Indeed, "What good is so great as the knowledge and enjoyment of God?" [31] God created humanity because of his own goodness and humanity exists in order to reveal that goodness. God endowed the human being with his own image and likeness, with free choice and personal initiative.[32] And he gave his law to the human race "in the service of man's interest, so that through close attachment to God his liberty might not be mistaken for dereliction. Else he would have been put on a level with his own menials, the other animals, which God has left unfettered and free precisely because he cares less for them." [33] "God had brought the man into being not merely that he might live, but that he might live in uprightness, in deference, that is, to God and his law." [34]

Human sin and the Fall changed this situation and made God into a stern judge. For God meets all situations; he smites and heals, kills and makes alive, brings down and raises up.[35] The creature, turning against the good creator, made sin become the human condition,[36] and it passed from generation to generation.

But Tertullian insists also that "a portion of good in the soul, of that original, divine, and genuine good, which is its proper nature," remained.[37] "Thus some men are very bad, and some very good; but yet the souls of all form but one genus: even in the worst there is something good, and in the best there is something bad. . . . Just as no soul is without sin, so neither is any soul without seeds of good." [38] One's good can gain the ascendancy through faith, for "when the soul embraces the faith, being renewed in its second birth by water and the power from above, then the veil of its former corruption being taken away, it beholds the light in all its brightness." [39] In order to enable this better part to assert itself, God has allowed time for a contest enabling some human beings to defeat their enemy, the devil, by virtue of that same freedom of choice by which the devil had fallen from God even before humankind.[40]

Thus he proves "that the blame [for the Fall] was not God's but his own, and by gaining the victory humankind might honourably regain salvation." [41] In this new situation, with evil on the rampage, God's justice functions as a guide to humankind along the path of censure and correction.[42] God acts as protector of goodness by being a severe judge. Yet he continues to send rain upon good and evil and makes his sun rise on just and unjust, looks for the sinner's repentance rather than his death, and would rather have mercy than sacrifice.[43]

Tertullian is convinced that all human beings have access to this will of God, the law. For God is known through his creation: "The fact is that ever since things have existed their Creator has become known along with them: for they were brought into being with the intent that God might be made known." [44] "The great majority of the human race, though ignorant even of Moses' name, not to mention his written works, do nevertheless know Moses' God." [45]

"The knowledge inherent in the soul since the beginning is God's endowment, the same and no other whether in Egyptians or Syrians or men of Pontus. It is the God of the Jews whom men's souls call God. . . . God can never keep Himself hidden, can never be unattainable: he must at all times be understood, be heard, even be seen, in such manner as he will." [46]

The flowers, the shells on the seashore, the feathers of a bird, demonstrate this Creator God: "Can one little flower of the hedgerow—I say not the meadows—, one little shell from any sea you like —I say not the Red Sea—, one little moorcock's feather—I say nothing of the peacock—, permit you to judge the Creator a low-grade artificer?" [47] The result is that, "We first of all indeed know God himself by the teaching of Nature, calling Him God of gods, taking for granted that He is good, and invoking Him as Judge." [48] Creation points the human soul toward the Creator. "Nature is the teacher, the soul the disciple." [49] Since all human beings receive their souls from God, the soul even after the Fall retains a memory of its Author, his goodness, decrees, and its end. [50]

Thus the human soul remains an important witness on behalf of the Christian faith in spite of its own implication in sin. And this is a universal truth. In line with the openness of the Christian tradition to all human beings, Tertullian insists, "Not only the Latins and Greeks have received their souls from heaven. Among all people humanity is the same; the name differs, the soul is the same." [51] The fact that all human beings receive their souls from the one God makes cultural, ethnic, and racial distinctions ultimately irrelevant, and makes their souls witnesses to the truth of Christianity.

But this access to knowledge does little for the life of those outside the Christian fellowship. For "their teacher of truth is not God," and they interpret evil and good according to their own will and pleasure. [52]

On the other hand, Christians are taught to follow in Christ's steps. Tertullian quotes 1 Peter 2:20 [53] and in general calls for the imitation of Christ. [54] The result is a style of life eloquently described in Tertullian's *Apology:*

We are a body knit together as such by a common religious profession, by unity of discipline, and by the bond of a common hope. We meet together as an assembly and congregation, that, offering up prayer to

God as with united force, we may wrestle with Him in our supplications. This violence God delights in. We pray, too, for the emperors, for their ministers and for all in authority, for the welfare of the world, for the prevalence of peace, for the delay of the final consummation.

We assemble to read our sacred writings, if any peculiarity of the times makes either forewarning or reminiscence needful. However it be in that respect, with the sacred words we nourish our faith, we animate our hope, we make our confidence more steadfast; and no less by inculcations of God's precepts we confirm good habits. In the same place also exhortations are made, rebukes and sacred censures are administered. For with a great gravity is the work of judging carried on among us, as befits those who feel assured that they are in the sight of God; and you have the most notable example of judgement to come when any one has sinned so grievously as to require his severance from us in prayer, in the congregation and in all sacred intercourse. The tried men of our elders preside over us, obtaining that honour not by purchase, but by established character.

There is no buying and selling of any sort in the things of God. Though we have our treasure-chest, it is not made up of purchase-money, as of a religion that has its price. On the monthly day, if he likes, each puts in a small donation; but only if it be his pleasure, and only if he be able: for there is no compulsion; all is voluntary. These gifts are, as it were, piety's deposit fund. For they are not taken thence and spent on feasts, and drinking bouts, and eating-houses, but to support and bury poor people, to supply the wants of boys and girls destitute of means and parents, and of old persons confined now to the house; such, too, as have suffered shipwreck; and if there happen to be any in the mines, or banished to the islands, or shut up in the prisons, for nothing but their fidelity to the cause of God's Church, they become the nurslings of their confession.

But it is mainly the deeds of a love so noble that lead many to put a brand upon us. See, they say, how they love one another, for they themselves are animated by mutual hatred; how they are ready even to die for one another, for they themselves will sooner put to death. And they are wroth with us, too, because we call each other brethren; for no other reason, as I think, than because among themselves names of consanguinity are assumed in mere pretense of affection. But we are your brethren as well, by the law of our common mother nature, though you are hardly men, because brothers so unkind.

At the same time, how much more fittingly they are called and counted brothers who have been led to the knowledge of God as their common Father, who have drunk in one spirit of holiness, who from the same womb of a common ignorance have agonized into the same light of truth! But on this very account, perhaps, we are regarded as having less claim to be held true brothers, that no tragedy makes a noise about our brotherhood, or that the family possessions which generally destroy brotherhood among you, create fraternal bonds among us. One in mind and soul, we do not hesitate to share our earthly goods with one another. All things are common among us but our wives.[55]

For Tertullian, the Ten Commandments guide Christians in the quest for this life-style. But he is able to see sin relationally and as a result of the human estrangement from God, for he sees all commandments implied in the prohibition of idolatry, "the principal crime of the human race, the highest guilt charged upon the world, the whole procuring cause of judgment." [56] Indeed, he is prepared to equate idolatry with murder, adultery, fornication, fraud, arrogance, concupiscence, lasciviousness, drunkenness, unrighteousness, mendacity, an entire catalog of vices, and claims "in idolatry all crimes are detected, and in all crimes idolatry." [57]

It is remarkable how Tertullian manages to deduce his entire rigoristic ethics from the New Testament prohibition of idolatry. The Gentiles, he insists, are released from the bond of the Mosaic law in order that they might concentrate on this one law: the shunning of idolatry.[58] "This shall be our law," he says, "the more fully to be served because of its simplicity." [59] It must be seriously explained to those who want to become Christians and thoroughly instilled into converts.[60]

From this simple prohibition of idolatry Tertullian derives the Christian life-style. He speaks specifically concerning Christian employment and citizenship. Christians should avoid earning a living that involves them in idolatry. They should in no way support the idolatry of the pagan temples with their manual skills. Making idols is as blameworthy as worshiping them,[61] and it is no excuse to say that one has no other way to earn a living.[62] Instead of building or maintaining temples, Christian craftsmen can build houses, baths, and tenements. Even the specialist in the application of gold-leaf may practice shoe and slippergilding, for "luxury and ostentation have more votaries than all superstitions. Ostentation will require dishes and cups more easily than superstition." [63]

Along with crafts which support idolatry, Tertullian reprimands professions which do so. He mentions astrology as such a profession: "He cannot hope for the kingdom of the heavens, whose finger or wand abuses the heaven." [64] Businessmen must not swear and use the names of pagan gods in their transactions.[65] Particularly sensitive is the position of the schoolmasters and other professors of literature, because of the tendency their profession has to propagate idolatry.[66] As a learned man himself, Tertullian is aware that the propagation of the Christian faith depends to some degree on the learning of its representatives. He asks, "How could one be trained unto ordinary human intelligence, or unto any sense of action whatever, since literature is the means of training for all life? How do we repudiate secular studies, without which divine studies cannot be pursued?"[67] His answer is that since literary erudition cannot be avoided, Christians may be students of literature. But they may be no more; they may not be teachers. "Learning literature is allowable for believers, rather than teaching; for the principle of learning and teaching is different. If a believer teach literature, while he is teaching doubtless he commends, while he delivers he affirms, while he recalls he bears testimony to, the praises of idols interspersed therein."[68]

It is under the same heading of idolatry that Tertullian deals with the ethics of a Christian as a citizen. Specifically, he ponders the meaning of Jesus' saying, "Render therefore to Caesar the things that are Caesar's, and to God the things that are God's" (Matt. 22:21). "What things then, are Caesar's?" he asks, and replies, "Those, to wit, about which the consultation was then held, whether the poll-tax should be furnished to Caesar or no."[69] Tertullian insists that since the coin bore the likeness of Caesar it quite properly belongs to Caesar; since human beings are made in the image of God, they belong to him. "So . . . render to Caesar indeed money, to God yourself."[70] Christians must obey magistrates, princes, and powers, "but within the limits of discipline, so long as we keep ourselves separate from idolatry."[71]

Tertullian raises the question, "What shall believing servants or freemen do, officials likewise, when attending on their lords, or patrons, or superiors, when sacrificing?"[72] He insists on the strictest maintenance of the prohibition against idolatry even under these circumstances, according to the analogy of Joseph and Daniel in the Old Testament. Christians in such a position must not themselves offer sacrifices, authorize sacrifices by their presence, arrange for the delivery of sacrificial animals, assign to others the care of temples, or look after temple taxes. They must not arrange public spectacles or preside over them, address or even announce a pagan festival. Though Christians might make decisions concerning money, they must not make them concerning life, death, or personal honor, nor condemn, arrest, imprison, or torture. They must not even take an oath. If it is possible to refrain from this when in office—and Tertullian obviously doubts that it is—then a Christian may indeed hold office.[73]

In this context Tertullian addresses the question of Christian service in the military. His answer is eloquent and direct: "There is no agreement between the divine and the human sacrament,[74] the standard of Christ and the standard of the devil, the camp of light and the camp of darkness. One soul cannot belong to two lords—God and Caesar."[75] Noting that on the night of his betrayal Jesus admonished Peter not to defend him with a sword, Tertullian concludes, "The Lord . . . , in disarming Peter, unbelted every soldier."[76]

Tertullian's ethical advice is anything but permissive. He admits that it is difficult and dangerous to be a Christian, but that this is because it is difficult to abstain from idolatry.

Rigorous though it be, Tertullian's ethics does not consist of unrelated and arbitrary rules, but derives from a vision of total obedience to the Lord. Severe but not trivial, he proclaims a Lord whose demands are total and a stance of absolute opposition to a culture suffused with idolatry. He glories in the result:

> How is it that we alone are, contrary to the lessons of nature, branded as very evil because of our good? For what mark do we exhibit except the prime wisdom, which teaches us not to worship the frivolous works of the human hand; the temperance, by which we abstain from other men's goods, the chastity, which we pollute not even with a look; the compassion, which prompts us to help the needy; the truth itself, which makes us give offence; and liberty, for which we have even learned to die? Whoever wishes to understand who the Christians are, must needs employ these marks for their discovery.[77]

But if the general idolatry was the basis for Tertullian's rejection of the prevailing culture, did he leave a way open that would eventually permit Christians to support the Roman Empire should it cleanse itself from this basic and pervasive sin? It has been convincingly argued that the theologian so frequently associated with the Christ-against-culture pattern [78] may have been a pioneer in the advocacy of the Christian state.[79] Recognizing the inability of paganism to supply a plausibility structure for the Roman Empire, Tertullian claims that the Christians were in fact the only true and loyal subjects of the emperor. Substantiating this assertion he writes to the pagans: "Why dwell longer on the reverence and sacred respect of Christians to the emperor, whom we cannot but look up to as called by our Lord to his office? So that on valid grounds I might say Caesar is more ours than yours, for our God has appointed Him." [80]

Indeed, the emperors must be aware that their power derives from the only true God, the God whom the Christians worship, and not from the impotent demons worshiped by the pagans. Thus, the Christians alone are religiously significant for the empire, for they alone offer prayer for the safety of the emperors to the eternal, the true, and living God.[81] Since just and pious emperors were always aware of this fact, they had been friendly towards Christianity. Persecution began with Nero, whom everyone acknowledged as evil. Since that time, Tertullian asserts, good and competent emperors have generally been protectors of Christianity.[82] They realized that Christians are peaceful people who pray for the emperor and are useful to the empire.

It is significant that Tertullian does not polemicize against the empire as such but against the abuse of imperial power by lower magistrates and the excesses of unruly mobs against the Christians.[83] Describing the Christian attitude toward the empire he writes, "We offer prayer without ceasing, for all our emperors. We pray for life prolonged; for security to the empire; for protection to the imperial house; for brave armies, a faithful senate, a virtuous people, the world at rest, whatever, as man or Caesar, an emperor would wish." [84]

This is not the voice of a revolutionary or a rigid opponent of all culture. Here an advocate pleads that the emperors should recognize the Christians as their true friends in the interest of preserving the values of their culture. For it is an error to attribute the past success of Rome to its worship of pagan gods, its pagan reverence and respect.[85] On the contrary, with their consequent destruction of temples and holy places the victories of Rome exemplify *irreligiositas* and the utter powerlessness of the pagan gods. "The Romans, therefore, were not distinguished for their devotion to the gods before they attained to greatness; and so their greatness was not the result of their religion. Indeed, how could religion make a people great who have owed their greatness to their irreligion?" [86] "The sacrileges of the Romans are as numerous as their trophies." [87] Holding a view of history that contemplates the eventual triumph of Christ over all nations, Tertullian seems to suggest that once idolatry has been abandoned, the Roman Empire might flourish anew under emperors who will serve the one true God supported by their Christian subjects.

It appears that Tertullian was not the vaunted representative of a Christ-against-culture pattern but rather a proud Roman citizen who anticipated Christ above a culture cleansed from worthless and powerless idolatry. His view of history allows for revolutionary change. He does not advocate escape from the world but rather its transformation.

The shift from Tertullian to Canon III (A.D. 314) of the Council of Arles, that threatens excommunication to a Christian soldier who throws down his weapons even in times of peace, does not seem so extreme. The African convert seemed to anticipate a peaceful world ruled by a Christian emperor who himself would acknowledge the ultimate rule of the one true God.

# Clement
# of Alexandria

WHILE TERTULLIAN WAS THE LONELY INTELLEC-
tual, Clement of Alexandria was the director of an established
Christian school. At this school, which flourished in Alexandria
from the middle of the second century until the turn of the fifth,
Clement succeeded his brilliant teacher Pantaenus, and his own
student, the great theologian Origen, followed him in turn.[1]

We know almost nothing about Clement's life.[2] He was born
around 140 to 150 in Athens or perhaps in Alexandria. His parents
were pagans, so that he came to Christianity a convert like so many
contemporaries. He travelled widely and eventually settled in
Alexandria about 180.

Although Clement was apparently a prolific writer, only three
major works and one small treatise survive. The latter, *The Rich
Man's Salvation,* is the only complete work which can serve as an
illustration of Clement's teaching for the ordinary member of the
Christian movement. It deals with a new moral problem typical
for a metropolis like Alexandria, namely the chance of salvation
for a rich man who becomes a Christian. The solution is a charac-
teristic one for an Alexandrian; to spiritualize wealth. What
dooms us is not money but the love of money and all the human
passions connected with it which Jesus excoriates in Mark 10:17-

61

31. Indeed wealth is, in and of itself, the means that enables a Christian to feed the hungry and clothe the naked. Wealth can be an important tool in Christian service.[3]

But it is Clement's great trilogy that furnishes the first scholarly Christian ethics: *The Exhortation to the Greeks, The Instructor,* and *The Miscellanies.* Although there are apparent contradictions in these works, Ottmar Dittrich has suggested that one can reconcile them if one keeps in mind that *The Exhortation to the Greeks* addresses pagans, *The Instructor* simple believers, and only *The Miscellanies* the initiates whom Clement called "gnostics." [4]

*The Exhortation to the Greeks* is a fairly ordinary "Apology." Pointing out in great detail the absurdity and impiety of the heathen mysteries and fables, and decrying the cruelty of the sacrifices to the gods, Clement joins the philosophers in their conventional disapproval of popular religions. He finds in Plato the most perceptive of the philosophers, but attributes his superior insights to his dependence on the Hebrews.[5] Not only Plato, however, but other philosophers "declare the one only true God to be God, by His own inspiration, if so be they have laid hold of the truth." [6] He mentions as examples, Antisthenes, Xenophon, the Stoic Cleanthes, and the Pythagoreans. He also adds poets to his list of perceptive pagans, such as Aratus, Hesiod, Euripides and Sophocles.[7] It is obvious that Clement is pleased to use the resources of philosophy and poetry in his effort to invite the Greeks to salvation. If the Greeks desire to become "just and holy with understanding," [8] Clement wants to show them the way:

> Now we, I say, we are they whom God has adopted, and of us alone He is willing to be called Father, not of the disobedient. For indeed this is the position of us who are Christ's attendants: as are the counsels, so are the words; as are the words, so are the actions; and as are the deeds, such is the life. The entire life of men who have come to know Christ is good.[9]

Clement's second major treatise, *The Instructor,* clearly addresses the practical needs of ordinary men and women: "The Instructor being practical, not theoretical, his aim is thus to improve the soul, not to teach, and to train it up to a virtuous, not to an intellectual life." [10] As a human being and as God, Christ the Instructor gives us all good and all help. As God he forgives our sins and as a human being he trains us not to sin.[11] The virtue of man and woman is the same: "For if the God of both is one, the master of both is also one; one church, one temperance, one modesty; their food is common, marriage an equal yoke; respiration, sight, hearing, knowledge, hope, obedience, love all alike. . . . Common therefore, too, to men and women, the name of human being." [12]

For all Christians it should be obvious that "everything that is contrary to right reason is sin." [13] "Christian conduct is the operation of the rational soul in accordance with a correct judgment and aspiration after the truth. . . . Virtue is a will in conformity to God and Christ in life, rightly adjusted to life everlasting." [14] But here an important distinction appears between the reasonable conclusions of natural men and those of Christians. "The commandments issued with respect to natural life are published to the multitude; but those that are suited for living well, and from which eternal life springs, we have to consider, as in a sketch, as we read them out of the Scriptures." [15]

Clement undertakes a detailed analysis of the regulations which ought to govern the Christian life. About food, Clement asserts, "Some men, in truth, live that they may eat, as the irrational creatures. . . . But the Instructor enjoins us to eat that we may live." [16] This means that it is to be simple "ministering to life, not to luxury." [17] Only such is conducive to health and strength—which is the proper goal of eating. Indeed the Christian should heed Jesus' words, "When thou makest an entertainment, call the poor" (Luke 14:12-13), and Clement adds, "for whose sake chiefly a supper ought to be made."

Opposing any extreme asceticism, Clement states, "We are not, then, to abstain wholly from various kinds of food, but only are not to be taken up about them." [18] For "excess, which in all things is an evil, is very highly reprehensible in the matter of food." [19] But even decent table-manners are part of appropriate Christian behavior. He must not speak while eating, nor eat and drink simultaneously, and keep hand, couch and chin free of stains.

When discussing drinking, he asserts that "the natural, temperate, and necessary beverage . . . for the thirsty is water." [20] Wine should be considered as a strengthening tonic for a sickly body. It is totally inappropriate for boys and girls, "for it is not right to pour into the burning season of life the hottest of all liquids—wine—adding, as it were, fire." [21] For adults, on the other hand, Clement is willing to suggest that "toward evening, about suppertime, wine may be used." Here too moderation is in order, but "those who are already advanced in life may partake more hilariously of the draught, to warm by the harmless medicine of the vine the chill of age, which the decay of time has produced." [22]

Quoting a book *On Long Life* by a certain Artorius, Clement suggests two reasons for drinking wine—for the sake of health and for the purpose of relaxation and enjoyment: "For first wine makes the man who has drunk it more benignant than before, more agreeable to his boon companions, kinder to his domestics, and more pleasant to his friends. But when intoxicated, he becomes violent instead." [23] Again Clement insists on good manners. "We are to drink without contortions of the face, not greedily grasping the cup, . . . nor are we to besprinkle the chin, nor splash the garments while gulping down all the liquor at once. . . . " [24] It is Jesus' example of moderate drinking that should guide the Christian. He drank wine, but he did not teach under its influence. And the moderation advisable for men is imperative for women. Again quoting *Ecclesiasticus* (26:8), he says, " 'An intoxicated woman is a great wrath,' it is said, as if a drunken woman were the wrath of God." [25]

After discussing the way of eating and drinking appropriate for Christians, Clement turns to luxury in general. Apparently Alexandria had its share of conspicuous consumers who used silver urine vases and chamber-pots of crystal and gold.[26] Against people like this, he quotes with approval as divine scriptures the Book of Baruch 3:16-19: "Where are the rulers of the nations now? Where are those who have hunted wild beasts or the birds of the air for sport? Where are those who have hoarded the silver and gold men trust in, never satisfied with their gains? Where are the silversmiths with their patient skill and the secrets of their craft? They have all vanished and gone down to the grave. . . " (NEB). Clement points again to the example of the gospels as the model for the life of the Christian: "The Lord ate from a common bowl, and made the disciples recline on the grass on the ground, and washed their feet, girded with a linen towel—He, the lowly-minded God, and Lord of the universe." [27]

Clement also criticizes contemporary music. "Let the pipe be resigned to the shepherds," he exclaims, "and the flute to the superstitious who are engrossed in idolatry." [28] The obvious references to musical instruments in the Psalms (e.g. Psalm 150), Clement tends to allegorize as references to the human body as an instrument to praise God.[29] Even the hymns Christians sing to God as part of their worship should be "temperate," not "chromatic harmonies." [30]

In his counsel concerning laughter, he follows again the advice of *Ecclesiasticus* (21:20): "A fool laughs out loud; a clever man smiles quietly, if at all" (NEB), and he counsels moderation even in smiling.[31] Similarly he discourages needless talking, quoting with approval Ecclesiasticus 20:5; "One man is silent and is found to be wise; another is hated for his endless chatter" (NEB).[32] Indeed, no aspect of human behavior is too insignificant for Clement's comments; whistling for servants, spitting, frequent clearing of the throat and wiping one's nose in public—all meet with his disapproval, as do loud sneezing, hiccuping, cleaning one's teeth and digging in the ears. He summarizes all this advice by concluding, "In a word, the Christian is characterized by composure, tranquility, calmness, and peace." [33]

Clement's approach to human sexuality in Book II, Chapter 10, is a combination of insights from Plato and Moses with an occasional reference to Stoic authors. It is significant that he believes, as noted above, that Plato learned his valuable insights from studying Moses. While he does not completely condemn sex, he restricts it to marriage and even there exclusively to the purpose of reproduction.

Sexual intercourse is permissible because of the divine command, "Be fruitful and multiply" (Gen. 1:28), and for that purpose alone. For "in this role man demonstrates the image of God because he cooperates, in his human being." [34] Using the analogy of the farmer sowing his seed, he counsels that the seed should not be sown on rocky ground nor scattered everywhere, for it is the primary substance of generation and contains embedded in itself the principle of nature. Deviant sexual practices are as much an offense against nature [35] as against God. Clement asserts, "The clear conclusion that we must draw, then, is that we must condemn sodomy, all fruitless sowing of seed, any unnatural methods of having intercourse and the reversal of the sexual role in inter-course. We must rather follow the guidance of nature, which ob-viously disapproves of such practice from the very way she has fashioned the male organ, adapted not for receiving the seed, but for implanting it." [36]

This naturalistic approach leads him to discourage relations with a pregnant wife,[37] for "pleasure sought for its own sake, even with-in the marriage bonds, is a sin and contrary both to law and to reason." [38]

Indeed, Clement's attitude to sexual intercourse is essentially negative. He quotes with apparent approval the "sophist of Abdera" who called intercourse "a minor epilepsy" and considered it an incurable disease, and he graphically describes the severe loss of substance resulting from sexual intercourse. Marriage in itself merits esteem, "for the Lord wished men to 'be fruitful and multiply.'" [39] But even in marriage sexual pleasure should have severe restric-tions. Clement exclaims, "Why even unreasoning beasts know enough not to mate at certain times. To indulge in intercourse with-out intending children is to outrage nature, whom we should take as our instructor." [40] Again nature is for him as reliable a guide as the Lord himself, apparently also even in matters related to sex.

The remainder of Book II concerns proper clothing (preferably for Christians) and footwear. Clement insists that women should wear shoes and men go barefoot except during military service.[41] Furthermore, the Christian should not adorn himself with jewels or gold ornaments since a person who can afford such luxuries should rather give of his abundance to the poor. To say, "I have these things and am very rich, why should I not enjoy them," seems to Clement an expression inappropriate to a true human being and irresponsible to society.[42] Christians should know that "all things are . . . common, and not for the rich to appropriate an undue share." [43]

In Book III Clement turns to a discussion of true beauty. He writes, "The greatest of all lessons [is] to know oneself. For if one knows himself, he will know God and knowing God, he will be made like God, not by wearing gold or long robes, but by well-doing and by requiring as few things as possible." [44] Quoting the philosopher Heraclitus that "men are gods, and gods are men, for reason *(Logos)* is the same," [45] he asserts that "God is in man and man God. And the mediator executes the Father's will; for the Mediator is the reason *(Logos)*, which is common to both—the Son of God, the Saviour of human beings; His Servant, our Teacher." [46]

But there is still another beauty which characterizes human beings: love *(agape)*. This is the beauty which the Lord exhibited who, according to Isaiah 53:2-3, "had not form nor comeliness." [47] The outward appearance does not matter: goodness should ornament the soul. Clement inveighs against dyeing the hair or painting cheeks or eyes and quotes with approval the Greek comic poets who ridiculed such practices. But he is as hard on men as on women. He disapproves the practice of darkening gray hair and claims, "It is not possible for him to show the soul true who has a fraudulent head." [48] Men should not shave themselves, "For God wished women to be smooth, and rejoice in their locks alone growing spontaneously, as a horse in his mane; but has adorned man, like the lions, with a beard, and endowed him, as an attribute of manhood, with shaggy breasts,—a sign this of strength and rule." [49]

Again Clement emphasized the model of nature as significant for the moral life of human beings. But he continues, "The man, who would be beautiful, must adorn that which is the most beautiful thing in man, his mind, which every day he ought to exhibit in greater comeliness; and should pluck out not hairs, but lusts." [50] Full of admiration for the relatively simple life-style of the barbarians, he asserts, "Man may, though naked in body, address the Lord. But I approve the simplicity of the barbarians: loving an unencumbered life, the barbarians have abandoned luxury. Such the Lord calls us to be—naked of finery, naked of vanity, wrenched from our sins, bearing only the wood of life,[51] aiming only at salvation." [52] Again he alludes to the dangers of wealth. "Wealth seems to me to be like a serpent," he asserts, "which will twist round the hand and bite; unless one knows how to lay hold of it without danger by the point of the tail." [53]

To live the moral life, Christians must avoid associating with corrupt people and seek the company of the just.[54] They should treat slaves as they would treat themselves, for "they are human beings as we are." [55] He concludes the treatise with numerous quotations from Scripture, insisting that the church is the school of morality and the Bridegroom the only teacher.[56] Thus, he who says that he abides in Jesus ought to walk just as he walked.[57] He concludes his ethics for simple Christian believers with the exhortation to follow the example of the Instructor and to live as Christ himself had lived.

In the *Miscellanies,* Clement's most esoteric work, he addresses the Christian initiates, the gnostics. He admits that this book "will contain the truth mixed up in the dogmas of philosophy, or rather covered over and hidden, as the edible part of the nut in the shell." [58] But he considers such hidden communication sound procedure, "for, in my opinion, it is fitting that the seeds of truth be kept for the husbandmen of faith. . . ." [59] Aware that he will be criticized for his extensive use of Greek philosophy in this work, he answers his critics in advance by saying that "philosophy came into existence, not on its own account, but for the advantages reaped by us from knowledge. . . ." [60] For philosophy was necessary for the Greeks for righteousness before the advent of the Lord. "Now it becomes conducive to piety; being a kind of preparatory training to those who attain to faith through demonstration." [61]

As a result of his understanding of philosophy as the handmaid of Christian theology and ethics, Clement does not hesitate to use what he has learned from the Greek thinkers to explain his ethics in this his most technical work. In Chapter 9 of the second book of the *Miscellanies,* he offers a very philosophical definition of love *(agape).* "Love turns out to be consent in what pertains to reason, life, and manners, or in brief, fellowship in life, or it is the intensity of friendship and of affection, with right reason, in the enjoyment of associates." [62] From this it is obvious that learning and loving belong closely together and this definition of love illustrates his earlier assertion: "For it is not by nature, but by learning, that people become noble and good, as people also become physicians and pilots." [63]

It is this same philosophical approach that Clement uses to distinguish the various failures in human behavior. For example, he attempts to draw a precise line between sin *(hamartia),* mistake *(atucheme),* and crime *(adikema).* "It is sin, for example, to live luxuriously and licentiously; a mistake to wound one's friend in ignorance, taking him for an enemy; and crime to violate graves or commit sacrilege." [64]

But in spite of his considerable and admitted dependence on a multitude of Greek philosophers and poets, Clement is convinced that the Mosaic law is the ultimate source of all sound ethics and that the Greeks derived whatever is valid in their moral teaching from the Hebrews.[65] The valuable insight of Plato that man's chief good consists in the assimilation to God is in agreement with the Scriptures [66] and so is Xenocrates' definition of happiness as the possession of virtue.[67]

This leads eventually in Chapter 23 of Book II to a discussion of marriage from a Christian point of view. As in *The Instructor*, he insists here also that the purpose of marriage is the procreation of children.[68] Then he summarizes the opinions of the philosophers, from those like Plato who rank marriage among the good things in life, to Democritus and the Epicureans, who see it as a source of annoyances and distraction from more necessary things. He also mentions the Stoics, who consider it a matter of indifference. Clement grants that the Scriptures approve of marriage, but he immediately adds, "Though this is the case, yet it seems . . . shameful that man, created by God, should be more licentious than the irrational creatures. . . ." He uses the birds as a good example which shames many human beings. Again he uses nature as a model for human behavior.[69]

It is in the third book of the *Miscellanies* that Clement enters into a detailed discussion of sexual ethics in the context of the teaching of various gnostic sects. One of the serious challenges to his basic approach is the peculiar naturalism of the followers of Carpocrates and Epiphanes. One book attributed to Epiphanes, *Concerning Righteousness*, is so offensive to the eyes of nineteenth and twentieth century scholars that they have denied its existence [70] or depreciated it with statements like, "This work merely consists of the scribblings of an intelligent but nasty-minded adolescent of somewhat pornographic tendencies." [71] But Clement takes it seriously because it argues from the analogy of nature.

For Epiphanes, "the righteousness of God is a kind of universal fairness and equality." The sun and the stars are equally visible to all who have the power to see. "There is no distinction between rich and poor, people and governor, stupid and clever, female and male, free men and slaves." [72] From this generosity of God, animals profit as well as human beings. The sun causes food to grow for all. This was the will of the Creator and Father of all. "The laws, by presupposing the existence of private property, cut up and destroyed the universal equality decreed by the divine law." [73] For scriptural support, Epiphanes uses the saying of Paul in Romans 7:7; "Yet, if it had not been for the law, I should not have known sin." The idea of mine and thine came into existence through the laws so that the earth and money were no longer put to common use. "For God has made vines for all to use in common, since they are not protected against sparrows and a thief; and similarly corn and the other fruits." [74]

Epiphanes apparently identified the fall with the unnatural and legal establishment of private property, thus anticipating Karl Marx by some seventeen centuries. But Epiphanes extended this notion to the relationship of the sexes: "God made all things for the human being to be common property. He brought female to be with male and in the same way united all animals. He thus showed righteousness to be a universal fairness and equality. But those who have been born in this way have denied the universality which is the corollary of their birth and say, 'Let him who has taken one woman keep her,' whereas all alike can have her just as the other animals do." [75] He continues, "With a view to the permanence of the race, he has implanted in males a strong and ardent desire which neither law nor custom, nor any other restraint is able to destroy. For it is God's decree." [76]

Clement's reaction is interesting. In spite of his early appeals to the example of nature he does not argue that Epiphanes' teaching is contrary to natural law, but rather to the law and the gospel, quoting Exodus 20:13 and Matthew 5:28.[77] He calls the Old Testament "law" and the New Testament "gospel," but the distinction is really between an older and a newer law. When pushed in the direction of letting nature actually supply the standard for Christian behavior, he takes refuge in the Scriptures.[78] His concluding reaction to the gnostic heresies is: "We may divide all the heresies into two groups in making answer to them. Either they teach that one ought to live on the principle that it is a matter of indifference whether one does right or wrong, or they set a too ascetic tone and proclaim the necessity of continence on the ground of opinions which are godless and arise from hatred of what God has created." [79] He omits the position of Epiphanes, which he considers lawless according to an allegedly higher law of nature and of nature's God.

In discussing his own view of the ethical life, whose basis is the knowledge of God, Clement insists that we must be free from the control of passions. [80] "The task of the law is to deliver us from a dissolute life and all disorderly ways. Its purpose is to lead us from unrighteousness. . . ." [81] This is illustrated in Christian marriage, for Clement the paradigm of all ethical problems. It is certainly not the absolute evil some of the gnostics claim it to be. For Christians, it is possible to remain continent even in the married state. [82]

To the heretics' claim that Jesus did not marry and for this reason marriage is inappropriate for his followers, Clement responds, "In the first place he had his own bride, the Church; and in the next place he was no ordinary man that he should also be in need of some helpmeet after the flesh. Nor was it necessary for him to beget children since he abides eternally and was born the only Son of God." [83] Indeed, there is nothing meritorious about abstinence from marriage unless it arises from love to God, and true chastity is a gift of God's grace. [84] Continence applies not only to sex, but to all other human cravings. "It is continence to despise money, softness, property, to hold in small esteem outward appearance, to control one's tongue, to master evil thoughts." [85]

Since for Clement the gospel is the new law for the new man, he can speak of the "heightened perfection of the gospel ethic" [86] and claim that it "gains heavenly glory." But the commitment to sexual abstinence is not part of it: "All the epistles of the apostle [Paul] teach self-control and continence and contain numerous instructions about marriage, begetting children, and domestic life. But they nowhere rule out self-controlled marriage. Rather, they preserve the harmony of the law and the gospel and approve both the man who with thanks to God enters into marriage with sobriety and the man who in accordance with the Lord's will lives as a celibate, even as each individual is called, making his choice without blemish and in perfection." [87]

For Clement, the clue to Christian ethics is the eschatological dimension of the Christian life. He describes it in these words:

We ought to behave as strangers and pilgrims, if married as though we were not married, if possessing wealth as though we did not possess it, if procreating children as giving birth to mortals, as those who are ready to abandon their property, as men who would even live without a wife if need be, as people who are not passionately attached to the created world, but use it with all gratitude and with a sense of exaltation beyond it.[88]

In Book IV Clement discusses and extols martyrdom. However, he warns that those who do not avoid persecution when possible become accomplices in the crime of the persecutor.

Clement turns then to an examination of love. "This is love, to love God and our neighbor." He quotes Paul's observation that "Love is the fulfilling of the law" (Rom. 18:10), and insists that man and woman are equally able to share this perfection. Using Moses as an example, he immediately proceeds to list the accomplishments of Judith and Esther, Susanna and the sister of Moses. Then he lists a large number of Greek women known for their chastity, love and courage.[89]

The true gnostic, the perfect Christian, is a person who does good not from fear of punishment or hope of reward, but only "so as to pass life after the image and likeness of the Lord." [90] If he were asked "whether he would choose the knowledge of God or everlasting salvation; and if these, which are entirely identical, were separable, he would without the least hesitation choose the knowledge of God. . . ." [91] Such a person has achieved apathy and is waiting to put on the divine image. "For this is to be drawn by the Father, to become worthy to receive the power of grace from God. . . ." [92] This is the person who is always and in all things righteous: "Drawn by the love of Him who is the true object of love, and led to what is requisite [he], practices piety." [93] Even if God were to suspend all laws and allow such a person to do things counter to right reason, the true gnostic would not abandon the good.[94]

In view of this description of the true Christian, it is hard to classify Clement as a legalist. He often sounds like one because of his interest in details, in the ritual of morality, but underneath his concern with manners is always the realization that to love God is to fulfill the law and that this love is more a vision than mere training. Training is necessary, but it is not an end in itself. It must lead and does lead to a relationship with God in which obedience to the law and the gospel, as Clement uses these terms, becomes the expression of being "intimately joined with the Holy Spirit." [95] He can and does say, "Ye are made, so to speak by Him the Lord to be righteous as He is. . . ." [96]

This gives him a most impressive perspective of hope. "For we know not yet whether even he who is at present hostile may not hereafter believe. From which we clearly gather, if not that all are brethren, yet that to us they should seem such. And further, that all human beings are the work of the one God invested with one likeness—though in some that likeness may be more confused than in others—the recognition of this is reserved to the person of understanding, who through the creation adores the divine energy through which again he adores the divine will." [97]

Clement incorporated the cultural milieu of Hellenism and of the metropolis Alexandria so profoundly into his ethical system that it appears at first glance to be almost a branch of Greek philosophy, especially Stoicism or Neoplatonism. But there are significant differences. To be sure, for Clement sin is anything that goes counter to right reason. Any Stoic would have said that. But Clement also insists that sin is slavery resulting from the human obsession with pleasure. Here Clement's Christian vision and his understanding of the central significance of Jesus the Christ become apparent.

> The Lord purposed once again to loose him [the human being] from his bonds. Clothing Himself with bonds of flesh (which is a divine mystery), He subdued the serpent and enslaved the tyrant death; and, most wonderful of all, the very man who had erred through pleasure, and was bound by corruption, was shown to be free again, through His outstretched hands. O amazing mystery! The Lord has sunk down, but man rose up; and he who was driven from Paradise gains a greater prize, heaven, on becoming obedient.[98]

Clement connects the work of Christ *for* the Christian with the resulting style of life *of* the Christian perhaps most clearly in his little book *The Rich Man's Salvation*. Here he has the Savior say, "I gave you new birth, when by the world you were evilly born for death; I set you free, I healed you, I redeemed you." [99] A little later Christ continues, "I am your nurse, giving Myself for bread, which none who taste have any longer trial of death, and giving day by day drink of immortality." [100] And after this clear reference to the gift of Baptism and of the Eucharist, Clement follows with a description of Christ's work on behalf of the human race, having Him say, "On your behalf I wrestled with death and paid your penalty of death, which you owed for your former sins and your faithlessness toward God." [101]

While in some of the more philosophical works, especially the *Miscellanies,* this aspect of the Christian faith is not elaborated, it is always assumed. It is the work of Christ that frees human beings from their bondage to sin and the power of death and the devil. In the effort to live the life that Christ has made possible, Clement found Greek philosophy to be a helpful tool, but it never was a substitute for the work of Christ on behalf of the human race.[102]

In a manner that made him suspect to many of his Christian contemporaries, he used philosophy and tried with it to make Christianity attractive to those Greeks who had some philosophical education. By using philosophy, Clement believed he would be able to demonstrate to the cultured despisers of Christianity in his time the intellectual and moral superiority of the Christian worldview. For him, it was the total effect of the Christian faith on the life of its adherents which demonstrated its superiority. Clement asserted that philosophers spend their time seeking the probable, not the true. He also maintained, "For it is not that we may *seem* good that we believe in Christ, as it is not alone for the purpose of being seen, while in the sun, that we pass into the sun. But in the one case for the purpose of being warmed; and in the other, we are compelled to be Christians in order to *be* excellent and good." [103] It was the power of Christ to enable Christians to "keep warm" as well as "to see" that convinced Clement of the superiority of Christianity.

# Origen

**T**O EXAGGERATE THE IMPORTANCE of Origen for Christian thought is hardly possible." [1] With these words, Balthasar introduces his systematic development of Origen's world view based on quotations from his numerous writings, which Eusebius and Jerome report to have comprised two thousand books. Even those later Christian teachers who condemned Origen as a heretic borrowed his method of doing theology and copied his interpretation of Holy Scriptures. While Harnack and his disciples have emphasized Origen's dependence on Stoic and Platonic ethics [2] to the point where Anna Miura-Stange sees the similarities between Celsus, the eloquent opponent of Christianity, and Origen outweighing any differences,[3] more recent observers have asserted that Origen's ethical perspective is a radical turn from the concerns which dominate ancient philosophy. Hans Jonas has written, "Ultimately, 'good' and 'evil' are for Origen the only primary categories of mental action—a thoroughly different picture from that drawn by ancient philosophy with its main stress on the polarity of ignorance and knowledge. This means, moreover, in virtue of the absolute position of the spiritual agencies in the ontological scheme, that all movement in all of reality takes place solely in acts of moral decision and their answer by divine justice." [4]

75

Because of the devotion of his disciple the church historian Eusebius, we know more about Origen's life than of most early Christian theologians' lives. Much of Book VI of *The Ecclesiastical History* deals with his life and his work.[5] Born about A.D. 185 in Alexandria, Origen grew up in a Christian family as the son of a schoolteacher. At a very early age he became a student of Clement, whose thought influenced him profoundly. During the persecution of Christians under Emperor Septimus Severus, Origen's father Leonides was martyred. Origen himself, at the time seventeen years of age, desired to share his father's fate. As Eusebius tells it, only the fact that his mother hid all his clothes kept him from rushing to his death.[6] Since the state confiscated the property of "criminals," his father's death left him destitute, and he took up teaching to support his mother and six younger brothers.

At the same time, the persecution had left the catechetical school without teachers, for even Clement had departed, and Origen was asked to "preside over the school." [7] He was then eighteen years old.[8] In youthful enthusiasm, he began a life of strictest asceticism, fasting, abstaining from wine, going barefoot, never sleeping on a couch but on the floor, and eventually castrating himself, in accordance with Matthew 19:12. As even the devoted Eusebius came to admit, this was "proof of an immature and youthful mind." [9]

Aware that his education had been inadequate for the scholarly task he faced, Origen began about 210 to 212 a course of study under Ammonius Saccas, the most famous of the philosophers teaching at the time in Alexandria and perhaps the founder of Neoplatonism,[10] who later numbered among his students Plotinus, the first great systematician of the movement. Origen was then ready to articulate his own theological system. He traveled much and because of his growing fame was welcome in Christian circles everywhere. This apparently brought him into conflict with Bishop Demetrius of Alexandria, especially since he also preached occasionally without having been ordained a priest. When he was finally ordained around 230 in Caesarea, probably under the sponsorship of Bishop Alexander of Jerusalem, Demetrius insisted on his expulsion from Alexandria and Egypt and declared his ordination invalid because he was a eunuch [11] and probably also because of alleged heresies.

This action was not everywhere recognized, especially in Palestine, but it forced Origen to move to Caesarea where he continued to teach with great success. Arrested and tortured during the widespread and intensive persecution of Christians under Emperor Decius (249-250), he refused to recant. Eventually released, he died a few years later and was buried at Tyrus in 254.

In Origen, the Christian church finally produced a systematic thinker whom the non-Christian philosophers of his time took seriously. The grudging admiration of the Neoplatonist Porphyry reflects this. Commenting on the allegorical method as Christians applied it to the Old Testament, he writes, "But this kind of absurdity must be traced to a man whom I met when I was still quite young, who had a great reputation, and still holds it, because of the writings which he has left behind him, I mean Origen, whose fame has been widespread among the teachers of this kind of learning." [12] Unlike his teacher Ammonius Saccas, who had been raised within the church and left it after encountering philosophy, Origen, "a Greek educated in Greek learning, drove headlong toward barbarian recklessness; . . . and while his manner of life was Christian and contrary to the law, in his opinions about material things and the Deity he played the Greek, and introduced Greek ideas into foreign fables." [13] Indeed, Porphyry admitted that Origen was "always consorting with Plato" and was conversant with the writings of other philosophers. [14]

Thus the dialog of Christianity and philosophy begins in earnest. Through Origen, Christianity enters as a serious partner into conversation with the Hellenic world, not merely adapting Greek philosophy for its own purposes, but challenging it from a position of philosophical competence.

Origen summarizes his brilliant theological system in his book *The First Principles (Peri Archon* or *De Principiis)*, quoted usually by its Latin name since it has come to us only in a Latin translation. He probably wrote it in 225, but in any case before his final departure from Alexandria in 231. After Origen's death the Orthodox church suppressed the book because of its unconventional ideas, and its Latin translator Rufinus, an admirer of Origen's theology, bowdlerized it in the apparent belief that heretics had tampered with the original Greek. To study the work, one must rely on the text as reconstructed by Paul Koetschau [15] and made available in English by G. W. Butterworth.[16]

While *First Principles* is a key work in the development of Christian doctrine, it has also a number of important ethical implications. Origen begins with the assertion that Christians believe and are convinced that Jesus Christ is the truth and that the "knowledge which calls men to lead a good and blessed life" comes from the words and teaching of Christ.[17] The emphasis is from the outset on the importance of the "good and blessed" life. Origen insists that the words of Christ are not merely those he uttered during his earthly ministry, but include the entire Scriptures, for "Christ, the Word of God was in Moses and the prophets." [18]

Origen then turns to a discussion of the apostolic doctrine of God, Christ, and the Holy Spirit. This God is at work everywhere in the world, but Origen makes an interesting distinction between the work of the Father and the Son as over against the work of the Spirit.

> I am of the opinion, then, that the activity of the Father and the Son is to be seen both in saints and sinners, in rational men and in dumb animals, yes, and even in lifeless things and in absolutely everything that exists; but the activity of the Holy Spirit does not extend at all either to lifeless things, or to things that have life but are yet dumb, nor is it to be found in those who, though rational, still lie in wickedness and are not wholly converted to better things.[19]

The Holy Spirit is found only in those who "are already turning to better things and walking in the ways of Jesus Christ." [20] These are the people who are engaged in good deeds and who abide in God. The fact that Father and Son are active in both saints and sinners is obvious, since all human beings participate in reason, and thereby disclose some seeds of wisdom and righteousness.[21]

Indeed, all things "derive their share of being from him who truly exists," [22] including both righteous and sinners, rational and irrational creatures. Using Romans 10:6-8 as his proof text, Origen asserts that "Christ is 'in the heart' of all men, in virtue of his being the word or reason, by sharing in which men are rational." [23] All human beings have some communion with God since the kingdom of God is within them.[24] But God removes his spirit from sinners. This is how Origen explains Genesis 6:3, "My Spirit shall not abide in man forever, for he is flesh." While God the Father and God the Son are at work in all created beings, the saints alone share in God the Holy Spirit.

Origen attributes the difference between the good and the evil to free will. "It lies with us," he says, "and with our own actions whether we are to be blessed and holy, or whether through sloth and negligence we are to turn away from blessedness into wickedness and loss. . . ." [25] Only God is "essentially" stainless. In all creatures holiness is an "accidental" quality and what is accidental may be lost. Human beings, therefore, are not stainless by "essence" or by "nature." Nor are they polluted by nature: freedom is the key to their present situations as well as to ethics.

God created only what is good, but all rational creatures who are free to choose are capable of both good and evil. This includes even the devil.[26] The arrangement of the universe, which for Origen is far more complex than what is observable in the human world, accords with the choices the various rational creatures have made. These "principalities" in the universe hold their power and office not by chance or random assignment but "each has obtained his degree of dignity in proportion to his own merits. . . ." [27] This applies to angels as well as to devils who were not created as such but chose evil rather than good.[28] There is even a third order of rational creatures "who are judged fit by God to replenish the human race." [29] "Whole nations of souls are stored away somewhere in a realm of their own, with an existence comparable to our bodily life, but in consequence of the fineness and mobility of their nature, they are carried round with the whirl of the universe." [30] Those who show some inclination toward evil "come into bodies, first of men; then through their association with the irrational passions, after the allotted span of human life they are changed into beasts; from which they sink to the level of insensate nature." [31]

Origen teaches a system of divine justice that includes the transmigration of souls as part of the education of all creatures. It is ethically significant that human beings participate in this educational process and can move up or down on the scale of being. "On earth by means of virtue souls grow wings and soar aloft, but when in heaven their wings fall off through evil and they sink down and become earthbound and are mingled with the gross nature of matter." [32] Of course, Origen did not present these views as Christian dogma. They were speculations in an age in which the dogma of the church was still in flux. The influence of his Pythagorean teachers is profound and he is prepared to say, "These arguments must not, in our opinion, be taken as dogmas, but as inquiries and conjectures, intended to show that the problems have not been completely overlooked." [33]

The reality that makes the operation of progress and deterioration in the universe possible is the freedom of choice of all rational beings. "It is our own task to live a good life," and "God asks this of us not as his work nor as a thing which comes to us from somebody else, nor, as some think, from fate, but as our own task. . . ." [34] This means that one must interpret passages concerning Pharaoh's hardened heart and other similar statements in the Scriptures in such a way as to assign the responsibility for disobedience to human nature rather than to a divine decree.[35] No choices rational beings make are morally indifferent, for "the will's freedom always moves in the direction either of good or of evil, nor can the rational sense, that is, the mind or soul, ever exist without some movement either good or evil." [36] Human progress depends on these choices but it is not completed as a result of them. "Our perfection does not come to pass without our doing anything, and yet it is not completed as a result of our efforts, but God performs the greater part of it." [37]

Indeed, Origen compares the human situation to that of a navigator who is trying to bring a ship safely back to his harbor. While the skill of the navigator is important, it is a minor contributing factor when compared with the force of the winds, the state of the atmosphere and the visibility of the stars. He exclaims, "Why, even the sailors themselves from feelings of reverence do not often venture to claim that they have saved the ship but attribute it all to God; not that they have performed nothing, but that the efforts of God's providence are very much in excess of the effects of their art. So indeed with our salvation the effects of God's work are very much in excess of the effects of what we can do." [38]

But what is the divine contribution? It is that Christ has conquered death, the death to which fallen human beings are now prey. This is how Origen explains it:

But since it was to happen that some should fall away from life and bring death upon themselves by the very fact of their falling . . . , and yet it would certainly not have been logical that beings once created by God for the enjoyment of life should utterly perish, it was needful that before the existence of death there should exist a resurrection, the figure of which was shown in our Lord and Savior. . . . [39]

The Christ for us is the Christ who destroys the enemies of the human race, especially death, the last enemy. It is not that this destruction is that of a substance whose creator is always God, but "that the hostile purpose and will which proceeded not from God but from itself will come to an end. It will be destroyed, therefore, not in the sense of ceasing to exist, but of being no longer an enemy and no longer death." [40] While this quotation as it appears in Rufinus' version of the book tends to obscure the meaning, Origen teaches that God will restore eventually even the devil and all his minions, and thus be all in all.

Origen's concrete ethical advice appears against this background of a vast cosmic morality play in which the will of all rational beings is the decisive factor determining both the character of the play and the status of the individual player. As Jonas has pointed out, "The gnostic speculation that flourished before Origen had interpreted the fall and rise underlying the cosmic drama in terms of the loss and recovery of knowledge, in this respect staying closer to the classical tradition. In its place Origen puts corruption and correction of the will, and the responsibility of each subject for its place in the cosmic scale." [41] Furthermore, as Jonas correctly observes, even the rise in knowledge concomitant with reaching a higher order of being is the result of the morally correct exercise of the will. It is not knowledge that makes rational beings good, but goodness—the exercise of the will toward God—which results in greater knowledge.

Nowhere does Origen express his practical ethical teachings more clearly than in his book against Celsus. Forced to defend not only the Christian faith but also the Christian church against the specific attacks of an informed opponent, he stresses the ethical superiority of even the simple believer. Aware that many have chosen Christianity for the completely inadequate reasons of fearing punishment for sin and desiring reward for their good works, he nevertheless asserts, "Because it is useful to the many, the Gospel encourages those who are not yet able to choose that which ought to be chosen for its own sake, to select it as the greatest blessing. . . ." [42] It is better for them to "wash away the mire of wickedness in which they formerly wallowed" for ultimately inadequate reasons than to keep wallowing in the mire, that would only move them ever farther away from God.[43]

If people accept the Christian way of life initially for somewhat superficial reasons, the very process of following Christ will eventually change their motives. Christianity is for all and is able to help everybody. Granting differences in the commitments and talents of Christians who are seriously engaged in an effort to follow Christ, Origen wants them all in the church. For the church is also an educational institution that brings people who have entered for less than adequate reasons to greater insight.

It is Christ, the Word of God entering into those who seek God, who is "able to make known and to reveal the Father, who was not seen (by any one) before the appearance of the Word." [44] Christ is able to save and conduct the human soul to the God of all things.[45] God's love is so great that

> He gave to the more learned a theology capable of raising the soul far above all earthly things; while with no less consideration He comes down to the weaker capacities of ignorant men, of simple women, of slaves, and, in short, of all those who from Jesus alone could have received that help for the better regulation of their lives which is supplied by his instructions in regard to the Divine Being, adapted to their wants and capacities.[46]

To Celsus' taunting remarks that Jesus selected as his apostles "notoriously wicked men," Origen replies that Jesus manifested his power to heal souls precisely by selecting notorious and wicked men and raising them to such a degree of moral excellence "that they became a pattern of the purest virtue to all who were converted by their instrumentality to the Gospel of Christ." [47] Again he emphasizes the moral improvement Jesus' power effects: "For we assert that the whole habitable world contains evidence of the works of Jesus, in the existence of these Churches of God which have been founded through Him by those who have been converted from the practice of innumerable sins." [48] The result is a new life-style displaying a marvelous meekness of spirit, a complete change of character, a new humaneness, goodness and gentleness.[49]

Indeed, when called upon to define Christianity, Origen describes it as "a system of doctrine and opinions beneficial to human life, . . . which converts human beings from the practice of wickedness."[50] And he calls Jesus a living pattern to human beings, as to the manner in which they were to regulate their lives.[51] His pre-eminence among the members of the human race consists "in the preaching of salvation and in a pure morality."[52] When Celsus attacks Jesus' miracles and compares them to the tricks magicians use, Origen appeals to the totally different moral context in which Jesus' miracles occur. Granting a superficial resemblance, he asserts, "But now there is not a single magician who, by means of his proceedings, invites his spectators to reform their morals, or trains those to the fear of God who are amazed at what they see, nor who tries to persuade them to live as men who are to be justified by God."[53] Because of this total concentration on the eternal welfare of human beings, Jesus can save not only the wise but even "the most irrational of men, and those devoted to their passions, and who, by reason of their irrationality, change with greater difficulty. . . ."[54]

Those who are despised [by men like Celsus] for their ignorance, and set down as fools and abject slaves, no sooner commit themselves to God's guidance by accepting the teaching of Jesus, than, so far from defiling themselves by licentious indulgence or the gratification of shameless passion, they in many cases, like perfect priests, for whom such pleasures have no charm, keep themselves in act and in thought in a state of virgin purity.[55]

But this new moral power bestowed on the Christians does not exclude the wise, as Celsus has falsely alleged. "Truly it is no evil to have been educated, for education is the way to virtue. . . . Who would not admit that to have studied the best opinions is a blessing? But what shall we call the best, save those which are true, and which incite men to virtue?"[56] Wisdom is important, otherwise Paul would not have ranked "the word of wisdom" first in the catalog of charismata bestowed by God,[57] and Jesus' parables would not have an esoteric as well as an exoteric meaning.[58]

But when all is said and done, Celsus is correct on one issue; the Gospel does invite "foolish and low individuals, and persons devoid of perception, and slaves, and women, and children." [59] The reason is to make them better. The church is in a sense like a school for moral improvement, only far more effective than the philosophical schools that attempt the same. Christians instruct their converts in private before letting them officially enter their communities. Converts must evince a desire for a virtuous life. Indeed, the church appoints certain persons to make inquiries regarding the lives and behavior of potential members to prevent those who commit acts of infamy from coming into the public assembly. [60] Christians desire to instruct all human beings in the word of God and not only the likely prospects whom the philosophers select: they desire "to give to young men the exhortations appropriate to them, and to show to slaves how they may recover freedom of thought, and be ennobled by the word." [61]

Since all human beings "are inclined to sin by nature," [62] all are in need of this word of God as mediated by the churches of God. For unlike philosophical discourse, however distinguished by orderly arrangement and elegant expression, the word of God as preached by God "through their instrumentality transformed num- bers of persons who had been sinners both by nature and habit, whom no one could have reformed by punishment, but who were changed by the word, which moulded and transformed them according to its pleasure." [63] Against those who claim that it is useless to deal with certain kinds of people since the author of all things has created some human beings evil, Origen insists that evil is not the result of an act of the creator as some of the gnostics will have it, "but that many have *become* wicked through education, and perverse example, and surrounding influences, so that wickedness has been naturalized in some individuals. . . ." [64] But for the Word of God to change such a person "is not only not impossible, but is even a work of no very great difficulty. . . ." [65]

The secret is to entrust oneself to the God of all things and do everything with a view to please him. [66] Unaided human nature, however, cannot accomplish this. Only through the help of him whom it seeks can he be found. [67] "He makes Himself known to those who, after doing all that their powers will allow, confess that they need help from Him, who discovers Himself to those whom He approves, in so far as it is possible for man and the soul still dwelling in the body to know God." [68] Even the preaching of the ambassadors of Christ is not sufficient to reach the human heart, "unless a certain power be imparted to the speaker from God, and a grace appear upon his words; and it is only by the divine agency that this takes place in those who speak effectually."[69] And if the Christian teachers are in fact superior even to the wisest philosophers, even Plato, it is because they saw better "by means of the intelligence which they received by the grace of God." [70]

But granted the indispensability of grace, Origen's nondeterministic view of the world informs his ethics throughout. Good and evil are not predetermined as Celsus teaches. Things can get better or worse.[71]

Much in moral progress depends on human obedience to the law. Origen distinguishes two kinds of law, "the one being the law of nature, of which God would be the legislator, and the other being the written law of cities." [72] When the positive law does not contradict the natural law, i.e., the law of God, it is proper to obey the written law of cities.[73] But what happens "when the law of nature, that is the law of God, commands what is opposed to the written law?" [74] Reason will tell us "to bid a long farewell to the written code, and to the desire of its legislators, and to give ourselves up to the legislator God, and to choose a life agreeable to His word, although in doing so it may be necessary to encounter dangers, and countless labours, and even death and dishonour." [75]

For Origen, reason is the tool God has given to the human race to make these judgments. Not only Christians but all rational beings have access to the law of nature. "If the doctrine be sound, and the effect of it good, whether it was made known to the Greeks by Plato or any of the wise men of Greece, or whether it was delivered to the Jews by Moses or any of the prophets, or whether it was given to the Christians in the recorded teachings of Jesus Christ, or in the instructions of His apostles, that does not affect the value of the truth communicated." [76] The fact that God reveals his law to all human beings enables them to distinguish good and evil and makes them subject to punishment that falls on sinners if they disobey his law.[77]

Christians have a clear advantage because they have the laws of the Jews, superior to all other ever so reasonable laws available to human beings. "So far as can be accomplished among mortals, everything that was not of advantage to the human race was withheld from them [the Jews], and only those things which are useful bestowed." [78] As an example, Origen describes the reasonable way in which the Jewish law deals with slavery, namely, "that one of the same faith should not be allowed to continue in slavery more than six years." [79] Indeed, "the Jews . . . are possessed of a wisdom superior not only to that of the multitude, but also of those who have the appearance of philosophers; . . . the very lowest Jew directs his look to the Supreme God alone; and they do well, indeed, so far as their point is concerned, to pride themselves thereon, and to keep aloof from the society of others as accursed and impious." [80] Had they not slain the prophets and conspired against Jesus, they would have given the human race a pattern of a heavenly city superior to anything Plato has described.[81] "It was the fortune of that people in a remarkable degree to enjoy God's favour, and to be loved by Him in a way different from others. . . ." [82]

Of course, Origen interprets the law with the help of his allegorical method. Thus he attributes Celsus' attack against the Jewish law—that it contradicts the teachings of Christ—to a misunderstanding of the intention of Moses. Origen is not even momentarily embarrassed by Celsus' question of how God could command the Jews through Moses to gather wealth, to extend their dominion, to fill the earth, to put their enemies of every age to the sword, and tell them through Jesus that no one can come to the Father who loves power, or riches, or glory and that they should turn the other cheek.[83] Basing his answer on reason and common sense, he says,

Celsus, with all his boasts of universal knowledge, has here fallen into the most vulgar of errors, in supposing that in the law and the prophets there is not a meaning deeper than that afforded by a literal rendering of the words. He does not see how manifestly incredible it is that worldly riches should be promised to those who lead upright lives, when it is a matter of common observation that the best of men have lived in extreme poverty." [84]

The riches that the letter of the law promises the just refer to those riches that enlighten the eyes, "and which enrich a man 'in all utterance and in all knowledge.'" [85] The enemies to be slain are not other human beings, but "the flesh whose lusts are at enmity with God." [86]

Origen is willing to grant that sayings about war and punishment in the Old Testament may have had a literal meaning when the Jews had a land and government of their own. In line with his previously observed ethical rationalism, he states, "To take from them [the ancient Jews] the right of making war upon their enemies, of fighting for their country, of putting to death or otherwise punishing adulterers, murderers, or others who were guilty of similar crimes, would be to subject them to sudden and utter destruction whenever the enemy fell upon them. . . ." [87] Every rational person would grant a nation the right of self-defense. But this is merely the obvious and superficial meaning of the laws of the Old Testament. Christians are interested in their deeper sense. When this is taken into account, it becomes clear, "there is no discrepancy . . . between the God of the Gospel and the God of the law. . . ." [88]

Origen's stress on the rational character of God's law contrasts sharply with the conservative moral relativism of Celsus. For Celsus, it is obvious that laws are essentially a matter of arbitrary preference. He says, "If anyone were to make this proposal to all men, viz., to bid him select out of all existing laws the best, each would choose, after examination, those of his own country." [89] Using the writings of Herodotus as his source, he insists that all people consider their own laws the best even if the contents of those laws are diametrically opposed to each other.

With apparent glee, Celsus reports the story of the Persian King Darius, who allegedly confronted some Greeks and certain Indians called Callatians with the option to eat or to cremate their deceased fathers. While the Greeks were horrified by the idea of eating them they approved cremation. The Callatians, appalled by the idea of cremation, considered it their moral duty to eat them. [90] Celsus concludes that it is "an obligation incumbent on all men to live according to their country's customs, in which case they will escape censure. . . ." [91] By following Jesus, Christians became lawless people.

Origen attacks this ethical relativism as destructive of reason and philosophy. Celsus' attitude toward allegedly sacred animals is a case in point. In regard to sacred crocodiles, "it is a mark of exceeding stupidity to spare those animals which do not spare us, and to bestow care on those which make a prey of human beings." [92] It is reason rather than custom that enables people to distinguish between wise and foolish laws and to make intelligent ethical decisions.[93] He refers with obvious approval to the Lacedaemonian lawgiver Lycurgus who got into his power a man who had put his eye out: "But instead of taking revenge upon him, he ceased not to use all his arts of persuasion until he induced him to become a philosopher." [94] And Zeno, who when somebody said to him, "Let me perish rather than not have my revenge on thee," replied, "Rather let me perish if I do not make a friend of thee." [95]

In seeing no significant difference between animals and human beings and in claiming that even human cities, political institutions and forms of government are equaled by ants and bees, Celsus is not even true to the best in the Greek philosophic tradition.[96] Not only does he fail to understand that ants "do not act from reflection," [97] but merely according to irrational capacity with which divine nature has endowed them, but by reducing humanity to the insect level he tends to weaken the special sense of responsibility that characterizes human beings and "those principles of excellence which are common to Christianity and the rest of mankind." [98] In his assessment of humanity, God considers not so much human bodies alone, which may be similar to those of animals, but "the controlling reason which is called into action by reflection." [99]

> He who looks from heaven will see among irrational creatures, however large their bodies, no other principle than, so to speak, irrationality: while amongst rational beings he will discover reason, the common possession of men, and of divine and heavenly beings, and perhaps of the Supreme God Himself, on account of which man is said to have been created in the image of God, for the image of the Supreme God is his reason (*Logos*).[100]

The moral consequence of obscuring the difference between human beings and animals is the loss of social responsibility. Ignorant people will say, "Since, then, there is no difference between us and the ants, even when we help those who are weary with bearing heavy burdens, why should we continue to do so to no purpose?" [101] By denying what is uniquely human, Celsus destroys what is best in the wisdom of the human race. "For he does not perceive that, while he wishes to turn away from Christianity those who read his treatise, he turns away also the sympathy of those who are not Christians from those who bear the heaviest burdens [of life]." [102]

Far from supporting even the earthly welfare of human beings, an attack against Christianity tends to undermine it. For Origen, Christian ethics is the ethics of the future. It is the basis for obedience to the law for Greeks and barbarians,[103] and may very well bring universal peace: "But if all the Romans, according to the supposition of Celsus, embrace the Christian faith, they will, when they pray, overcome their enemies; or rather, they will not war at all, being guarded by that divine power which promised to save five entire cities for the sake of fifty just persons." [104] For this reason, Christians who refuse to bear arms render even more useful service to the rulers by their prayers than the "soldiers, who go forth to fight and slay as many of the enemy as they can." [105]

All Christians ought to be treated as priests who are customarily exempt from military service and allowed to keep their hands pure and wrestle in prayer with God on behalf of those who are fighting in a righteous cause and for the king who reigns righteously, that whatever is opposed to those who act righteously may be destroyed.[106]

Similarly, they ought to be excused from taking office in the government of the country since their service in the government of the church contributes even more significantly to the welfare of the commonwealth.[107]

And as we by our prayers vanquish all demons who stir up war, and lead to the violation of the oaths, and disturb the peace, we in this way are much more helpful to the kings than those who go into the field to fight for them. And we do take our part in public affairs, when along with righteous prayers we join self-denying exercises and meditations, which teach us to despise pleasures, and not to be led away by them. And none fight better for the king than we do. We do not indeed fight under him, although he require it; but we fight on his behalf, forming a special army—an army of piety—by offering our prayers to God.[108]

The ethics of Origen is deeply and logically embedded in his vision of God and the world. The cosmic drama occurs through practical ethics, the on-going process of decision making and choosing between good and evil. The ethical decisions of rational beings determine the various roles the players assume in the different acts of the drama. "Every rational nature can, in the process of passing from one order to another, travel through each order to all the rest, and from all to each, while undergoing the various movements of progress or the reverse in accordance with its own actions and endeavours and with the use of its power of free will." [109] Nobody is beyond help, nobody except God is safe from falling as the result of false ethical decisions.

What, then, is the advantage of being a Christian? During his ethical endeavors, the Christian has access to God in prayer and a powerful model and advocate in Christ who not only shows Christians what to do but also assists them in doing it.[110]

Origen not only talks about prayer but intersperses his writings with prayers. Through prayer the Christian is "made more capable of union with him who has 'filled' all 'the earth' and 'the heaven'. . . . " [111] He will participate in the prayer of the Word of God, Christ, who prays to the Father as his meditator.[112] The words of the prayer of the saints are thereby filled with power.[113]

But it is significant that for Origen the purpose of prayer is always the sanctification of the person praying. He understands the petition "thy kingdom come" in the Lord's prayer to mean that the kingdom of God, existing within us, should spring up, bear fruit, and be perfected in the person praying. "For every saint who takes God as his king and obeys the spiritual laws of God dwells in himself as in a well-ordered city, so to speak. Present with him are the Father and Christ who reigns with the Father in the soul that has been perfected. . . . " [114]

Even the petition "Give us this day our daily bread," has for Origen only a spiritual meaning.

"For the bread of God is that which cometh down out of heaven, and giveth life unto the world" John 6:33. Now "true bread" is that which nourishes the true man, who has been "made in the image of god," and he who is nourished with it also becomes "after the likeness" of the Creator. But what is more nourishing to the soul than the Word, and what is more precious to the mind of him who makes room for it than the Wisdom of God? And what is more appropriate to the rational soul than truth? [115]

If prayer makes the power of God available to Christians in the exercise of their ethical responsibility, it is Christ, the only begotten Word, who forms "every deed and word and thought of theirs." [116]

The saints, therefore, being "an image" of an image (that image being the Son), acquire an impression of sonship, becoming "conformed" not only "to the body of glory" of Christ, but also to him who is "in the body." They become conformed to him who is in "the body of the glory," as they are "transformed by the renewing of the mind." [117]

The model for the Christian life is Christ. The ethical task is to conform oneself to him. This includes asceticism, mystical experience, all in imitation of the life of Christ. In his *Exhortation to Martyrdom* Origen reminds his readers "that it is necessary to deny oneself and take up one's cross and follow Jesus. . . . " [118] Later he declares, "For us Jesus laid down his life. Let us therefore lay down ours, I will not say for his sake but for our own, and I think also for those who will be edified by our martyrdom." [119] We obtain eternal life with Christ's help. All depends on our decision. "God does not give it to us. He sets it before us. 'Behold, I have set life before thy face' Deut. 30:15. It is in our power to stretch out our hand, to do good works, and to lay hold on life and deposit it in our soul." [120] The life Christians lay hold on is Christ. They live in his shadow: "For the spirit before our face is Christ of whom we may say, 'In his shadow we shall live among the nations' (Lam. 4:20." [121]

For Origen, Christian ethics has an esoteric and an exoteric significance. It is the way to lay hold on life, "to be present with the Lord, that being present with him we may become one with God of the universe and his only begotten Son, being saved in all things and becoming blessed, in Jesus Christ, to whom be the glory and power forever and ever." [122] The exoteric significance of Christian ethics is that it supplies a bridge to the unbelievers, that it is a powerful missionary tool. Origen is aware that Christians live now among the "nations" and that this situation is likely to continue for the foreseeable future. It is their task to lead a Christian life also in order to invalidate the false accusations that are made against them by "persons who are prejudiced by the calumnies thrown out against Christians, and who, from a notion that Christians are an impious people, will not listen to any offer to instruct them in the principles of the divine word. . . . " [123]

In this task what Origen calls "the common principles of humanity" [124] prove useful. He observes that many things Christians teach "about a healthy moral life" are also taught by the enemies of their faith. "For you will find that they have not entirely lost the common notions of right and wrong, of good and evil." [125] In his dealings with them, he appeals to "the constant revolution of the unerring stars, the converse motion of the planets, the constitution of the atmosphere, and its adaptation to the necessities of the animals, and especially of man, with all the contrivances for the well-being of mankind. . . . " [126] If they grant this, the ethical implications are obvious: "Beware of doing aught which is displeasing to the Creator of this universe, of the soul and its intelligent principle. . . . " [127]

Origen has, indeed, a panethical view of the nature and destiny of the universe and all rational beings. The Christian faith is the way of salvation because Christ makes the ethical life not only desirable but possible.

# VI

# The Fourth Century

**I**T HAD BEEN ORIGEN'S CONVICTION that Christianity would eventually triumph and that the church would teach Greeks and barbarians obedience to the law and thus inaugurate an age of peace. But shortly after his death, the Roman Empire underwent a major crisis that threatened to destroy it. The Persians captured Emperor Valerian, a bitter enemy of Christianity, who had renewed bloody persecutions and caused the martyrdom of Xystus, Bishop of Rome, as well as of Cyprian, Bishop of Carthage. Though his son Gallienus was more tolerant, issuing the Edict of Toleration in 260, he was unable to maintain the imperial authority. Teutonic tribes invaded the empire at will. In order to find some minimal protection from the barbarians, the people elevated a number of local military leaders, the so-called 30 tyrants, to the position of "emperor" for their particular region. The empire threatened to disintegrate into its component parts.

But "at this point the incredible took place, and the miraculous happened. . . ."[1] The so-called Illyrian emperors, beginning with Claudius II (265), restored the power of the empire once more. In 268 Claudius defeated the Alemanic army near Lake Garda and in 269 overcame a huge Gothic army. When he died of the plague in 270, his successors managed to maintain the military momentum. Aurelian defeated the Scythians and Vandals and reconquered Egypt and Gaul. For his victories, he gave credit to *Sol Invictus,* the "unconquerable sun god," whose image he had stamped on his coins. "One God, one empire, one emperor—that was the goal which Aurelian sought." [2] Persecution of the Christians was nevertheless not part of his more urgent program, though he was contemplating such steps when he was murdered in 275 as the result of his secretary's conspiracy with some of his most prominent military leaders. Lactantius tells it in his bitter chronicles of the persecutors of the church, *Of the Manner in Which the Persecutors Died:*

> He was not, however, permitted to accomplish what he had devised; for just as he began to give loose to his rage, he was slain. His bloody edicts had not yet reached the more distant provinces, when he himself lay all bloody on the earth. . . . Examples of such a nature, and so numerous, ought to have deterred succeeding tyrants; nevertheless they were not only not dismayed, but, in their misdeeds against God, became more bold and presumptuous.[3]

Lactantius referred in the last sentence to the decisive and final battle against the Christians under emperor Diocletian (284-305). After more than forty years of peace, Diocletian began in 303 the last effort of the Roman Empire to destroy the Christian church. Eusebius, who lived through this persecution, describes in glowing detail the prosperity enjoyed by the church when this persecution began: "It is beyond our powers to describe in a worthy manner the measure and nature of that honour as well as freedom which was accorded by all men, to that word of piety toward the God of the universe which had been proclaimed through Christ to the world." [4] Christians held high office in the administration of the empire.[5] Apparently Diocletian's own wife and daughter were Christians. "The rulers in every church were honoured by all procurators and governors." [6]

The result of this general tolerance was, according to Eusebius, a lessening of discipline and a tendency to quarrel among clergy and laity. "Those accounted our pastors, casting aside the sanctions of the fear of God, were inflamed with mutual contentions, and did nothing else but add to the strifes and threats, the jealousy, enmity and hatred that they used one to another, claiming with all vehemence the objects of their ambition as if they were a despot's spoils. . . . " [7] Many Christians saw the persecutions suffered in the last years of Diocletian as God's punishment for their pride. From the perspective of the present it may have been the very discipline of the Christians combined with their increasing influence which made impossible any further toleration of what was in fact "a state within a state." Indeed it is this self-understanding of the Christians as God's own people,[8] that apparently both frightened the non-Christian world and strengthened the sense of identity and mission of the followers of Christ.

Long before Christianity received the official endorsement of the empire, large segments of the population were Christian, including some prominent citizens.[9] The movement had more followers in the Greek-speaking provinces of the empire than in the Latin-speaking areas. It was mainly an urban religion, although it became dominant in the rural areas of Roman Africa and Egypt.[10] In Mesopotamia, the city of Edessa was Christian in the third century. Even if there were few members of the senatorial aristocracy in the Christian movement, the military and political crisis of the empire in the middle of the third century overturned the established society.

The fourth century with its soldier emperors was an age of considerable social mobility. Service in the army and in the legal profession were ways by which talented and ambitious men of humble origin could rise to positions of influence and power. This was particularly true in the Eastern empire. The newly influential and powerful included some Christians, and even those who were not Christian were also outsiders to the hereditary aristocracy. Torn from their rural or tribal roots, whether from peasant stock or barbarians, they were ready for an institution which would supply a new life-style and plausibility structure. This Christianity was able to do.

In order to understand this, one may examine a third century document which gives some impression of the self-understanding and ethics of the Christian movement at that time, the so-called *Didascalia Apostolorum* or *The Teaching of the Apostles*.[11] The author describes the Christian movement as "God's planting and the holy vineyard," [12] as a group of people chosen by God who by their faith inherit His everlasting kingdom, who have received the power and fellowship of His Holy Spirit, and by Him are armed and made firm in the fear of Him, who are become partakers in the sprinkling of the pure and precious blood of the Great God, Jesus Christ, who have received boldness to call the Almighty God Father, as joint heirs and partakers with His Son and His beloved.[13]

The author lists the iniquities which the believer must eschew. Perhaps significant for the relative prosperity Christians had achieved by then, he mentions *avarice* first. "Flee therefore and depart from all avarice and evil dealing." [14] He quotes the commandment against covetousness and supports this Old Testament reference by an appeal to the Gospel (Matt. 5:27f.), which identifies evil desire with the evil act.[15]

The author then proceeds to summarize the law by saying: "But for men who obey God there is one law, simple and true and mild—without question, for Christians—this, that what thou hatest that it should be done to thee by another, thou do not to another." [16] The golden rule in this negative form is plausible and has much universal appeal even to those who have little previous philosophical or religious training, so that it can easily serve as a simple basis for ethics.

From this the author proceeds to some applications. Monogamy and the avoidance of sexual promiscuity and prostitution is mandatory.[17] Men should first avoid adornment and the beautification of their bodies to keep from leading women into temptation.[18]

The author follows these commandments with the advice to shun idleness, a vice accompanying prosperity. "Be thou always attending to thy craft and thy work, and be willing to do those things that are pleasing to God. . . ." [19] He clearly assumes the prosperity of some members of the church when he writes, "But if thou art rich and hast no need of a craft whereby to live, thou shalt not stray and go about vacantly. . . ." [20] Instead, the rich should use their time to study the Bible and avoid all books of the heathen. "For what hast thou to do with strange sayings or laws or lying prophecies, which also turn away from the faith them that are young?" [21]

Indeed, the Bible supplies all the varieties of literature needful; historical narrative, wise men and philosophers, songs and even a report concerning the beginning of the world.[22] When reading the Bible, however, one must be on guard not to accept what the author calls "the Second Legislation," namely, those laws which were given to the Jews after they had committed so many sins in the wilderness.[23] These laws are God's punishment, but "our Saviour came for no other cause but to fulfill the law, and to set us loose from the bonds of the Second Legislation." [24]

In line with the earlier advice to men, the third chapter counsels women to chastity.[25] Both chapters are full of references to the book of Proverbs, whose common sense approach would appeal to an unsophisticated audience.

Then the author discusses the qualifications of a "bishop," the man who leads a congregation. The type of person he advises for this office reveals the character of the fourth century Christian community. He should be at least fifty years old,[26] a man "who is now removed from the manners of youth and from the lusts of the Enemy." [27] Though it would be preferable if he had some education, the main qualification is that he knows the Bible and is advanced in years.[28] But when old men are not available in a small congregation, one may select a young man who "by meekness and quietness of conduct shows maturity." [29]

It is important that the bishop's wife be also a believer, that they have raised their children in the fear of God and obey him. "For if his household in the flesh withstand him and obey him not, how shall they that are without his house become his, and be subject to him?" [30] He must love orphans, widows, the poor and strangers. He must not be a respecter of persons, defer to the rich or neglect the poor. He himself should use food and drink sparingly.[31] As far as theology is concerned, the important knowledge is familiarity with the Scriptures, the interpretation of the Law in the light of the Gospel (which means the Old Testament in the light of the New) and awareness that the above mentioned "Second Legislation" does not apply to Christians.[32] The bishop must serve as an example for his people and he will be able to do that if he takes Christ for an example.[33]

The bishop should help to keep the Christian community pure. It was apparently a temptation for bishops even at that time to permit people of means to join the church or remain in it, in spite of public sins. For our author writes, "But if the bishop himself is not of a clean conscience, and accepts persons for the sake of filthy lucre, or for the sake of the presents which he receives, and spares one who impiously sins, and suffers him to remain in the Church: such a bishop has polluted his congregation with God. . . ." [34] It is the bishop's task to discipline the congregation: "Judge, therefore, O bishop, strictly as God Almighty; and those who repent receive with mercy as God Almighty. And rebuke and exhort and teach. . . ." [35]

The bishop is a physician who has the power to heal in imitation of Christ. He has "put on the person of Christ." [36] In obedience to Christ, the bishop has been made the physician of the church: "Do not therefore withhold the cure whereby thou mayest heal them that are sick with sins, but by all means cure and heal, and restore them sound to the Church." [37]

The bishop has a wider social responsibility.

As good stewards of God, therefore, dispense well, according to the command, those things that are given and accrue to the Church, to orphans and widows and to those who are in distress and to strangers, as knowing that you have God who will require an account at your hands, who delivered this stewardship unto you. Divide and give therefore to all who are in want. [38]

The laity should supply resources for such activities. "Set by part-offerings and tithes and first fruits to Christ. . . ." [39] They should present these offerings to the bishop directly or through the deacons. "And when he has received he will distribute them justly. For the bishop is well acquainted of those who are in distress, and dispenses and gives to each one as is fitting for him. . . ." [40]

Indeed, the author describes the bishop in the most glowing terms. He is "minister of the word and mediator," "your father, after God who begot you through the water," "your chief and your leader," "your mighty king." [41] He rules in the place of the Almighty: "But let him be honoured by you as God, for the bishop sits for you in the place of God Almighty." [42]

The author holds other offices in equally high esteem. "The deacon stands in the place of Christ. . . ." [43] The deaconess shall be honoured by you in the place of the Holy Spirit. . . ." [44] "The presbyters shall be to you in the likeness of the Apostles. . . ." [45]

The author calls the laity to work constantly and make the fruits of their labor available in order for their leaders to do their works of love. To them he says, "Now thus shall your righteousness abound more than their [Scribe's and Pharisee's] tithes and first-fruits and part-offerings, when you shall do as it is written: 'Sell all thou hast, and give to the poor.' " [46] This exhortation means that they are to give the gifts to the bishop. "For thou art commanded to give, but he to dispense. And thou shalt require no account of the bishop, nor observe him, how he dispenses and discharges his stewardship, or when he gives, or to whom, or where, or whether well or ill, or whether he gives fairly; for he has One who will require, even the Lord God. . . ." [47]

Of course, there are detailed instructions about the exercise of this immense power granted to the bishop. Bishops and deacons must be of one mind. They should judge the members fairly after having carefully heard both sides.[48] They must not be "hard, nor tyrannical, nor wrathful, and be not rough with the people of God." [49] The instructions go so far as to describe what the bishop should do if some man or woman who "has some worldly honor" enters the assembly while the meeting is in progress. Ignore them, says our author, and go on with the service. "And if there be no place, let one of the brethren who is full of charity and loves his brethren, and is one fitted to do an honour, rise and give them place, and himself stand up." [50] But if this turns out to be an older man or woman, the deacon should scan those who sit and make a younger person yield his place to the older person.

But if a poor man or woman should come, whether of the same district or of another congregation, and especially if they are stricken in years, and there be no place for such, do thou, O bishop, with all thy heart provide a place for them, even if thou have to sit upon the ground; that thou be not as one who respects the persons of men, but that thy ministry be acceptable with God.[51]

There are also detailed instructions for some of the other "orders" in the church. Of particular interest is the order of widows, whose main task was intercessory prayer. Apparently they were to pray "for those who give, and for the whole Church." [52] They were not supposed to give theological information, but refer inquiries to the "rulers." Some of them wanted to baptize new converts. This the

*Didascalia* disapproves with the somewhat far-fetched argument: "For if it were lawful to be baptized by a woman, our Lord and Teacher himself would have been baptized by Mary His mother, whereas He was baptized by John, like others of the people." [53]

Nevertheless, the position of deaconess was quite important because women were to minister to women as men were to minister to men. This especially applied to the practice of anointing those about to be baptized. If no woman was available for this assignment, the officiant, whether a bishop, presbyter, or deacon, might anoint the woman himself but on her head only.[54] After the baptism, the deaconess received the Christian and it was her task to

teach and instruct her how the seal of baptism ought to be (kept) unbroken in purity and holiness. For this cause we say that the ministry of a woman deacon is especially needful and important. For our Lord and Saviour also was ministered unto by women ministers, Mary Magdalene, and Mary the daughter of James and mother of Joseph, and the mother of the sons of Zebedee, with other women besides.[55]

Later the *Didascalia* discusses the raising of orphans, whom childless Christians should adopt. The bishop should see to it that these orphans marry within the community of faith and that every boy learn a trade so that he could eventually support himself. The *Didascalia* stresses that those members of the Christian community who have to depend for valid reasons on alms from the church should not feel in any way inferior. Indeed, receiving gifts under such circumstances is also a kind of service. "If a man has received on account of a fatherless childhood, or on account of indigence in old age, or on account of infirmity and sickness, or on account of the rearing of children, he shall even be praised: for he is esteemed as the altar of God, therefore shall he be honoured of God." [56]

Even the donors of gifts to the church are to meet certain standards. Not only should the bishop not give to the slothful or dishonest, but he should not accept gifts that would nourish orphans and widows from people whose manner of life is reprehensible. A list of the large group of evil-doers whose donations are unacceptable includes rich people who keep men shut up in prison; people who mistreat their slaves, oppress the poor, are lewd or abuse their body; forgers; dishonest advocates; false accusers; hypocritical lawyers; painters of pictures; makers of idols; workers in gold, silver or bronze; dishonest tax-collectors; spectators at shows; people who alter weights or measure deceitfully; innkeepers who mingle water with their wine; soldiers who act lawlessly; murderers; spies who procure condemnations; Roman officials defiled with war who have shed innocent blood without trial; perverters of judgment who deal unjustly and deceitfully with peasants; people who abuse the poor; idolators; the unclean; those who practice usury or extortion.

While this list seems somewhat confused, it is specific and goes beyond pious generalities. Apparently the Christian community maintained not only an internal discipline but high standards in its relationships with the outside world. Since intercessory prayer was the form of repaying gifts, the acceptance of gifts from flagrant offenders of the moral law would imply support of their offenses.[57] It is noteworthy that the list of offenses included not only obvious violations of the religious sensibilities of Christians, but offenses against social justice. The listing of dishonest advocates, hypocritical lawyers, lawless soldiers and soldiers who have shed innocent blood is of special significance in view of the importance of lawyers and soldiers at this particular period in the history of the empire.

If the *Didascalia* gives us an accurate picture of the discipline and the value system of the Christian movement at the beginning of the fourth century one can understand why its opponents would consider it dangerous and political leaders who could count on its support would consider it useful.

Another document from early fourth century Spain, the extreme western region of the empire, gives further insight into the specific rules governing some Christian communities. In the year 309, a number of bishops and presbyters met in a basilica in the town now called Granada, and proclaimed eighty-one decisions that reflected the moral climate and orientation of the western Christian church. Again, the random character of the prohibitions is striking. Even if the *Canons of Elvira* reflect profound tension within the movement, as one recent author has asserted,[58] they demonstrate the same concern for a disciplined Christian community that was apparent in the East.

Here, too, the position and power of the leadership is impressive. But it is again a position which implies special and rigorous obligations.

Even more strongly than in the East, the canons emphasize sexual restrictions. But it is apparent that even these restrictions are designed to enhance the discipline in the Christian community.[59] For example, they attempt to keep the family intact by prohibiting women from leaving their husbands,[60] men from committing adultery [61] and having sexual intercourse with boys.[62] Here belong also the restrictions on marriage outside the faith: "Heretics, if they are unwilling to change over to the Catholic church, are not to have Catholic girls given to them in marriage, nor shall they be given to Jews or heretics, since there can be no community for the faithful with the unfaithful. If parents act against this prohibition, they shall be kept out for five years." [63] And similarly: "No matter the large number of girls, Christian maidens are by no means to be given in matrimony to pagans lest youth, bursting forth in bloom, end in adultery of the soul." [64]

The clergy are to set an example of complete sexual discipline. "Bishops, presbyters, and deacons and all other clerics having a position in the ministry are ordered to abstain completely from their wives and not to have children. Whoever, in fact, does this, shall be expelled from the dignity of the clerical state." Further: "Bishops, presbyters, and deacons, if—once placed in the ministry— they are discovered to be sexual offenders, shall not receive communion, not even at the end, because of the scandal and the heinousness of the crime." [65]

There are other rules which demand regular church attendance,[66] the avoidance of idols in the home [67] and the appearance of being an idolater in public: "It is forbidden for any Christian to go up to the idol of the capitol, as a pagan does in order to sacrifice, and watch. If he does, he is guilty of the same crime." [68] And since idolatry is so closely associated with the holding of public office, Christians are not to attend church during the period they are holding such office: "A magistrate is ordered to keep away from the church during the one year of his term as *duumvir*." [69] But in spite of this stringent prohibition of idolatry and all contact with idols, there is no encouragement to destroy idols violently: "If someone has broken idols and on that account was put to death, inasmuch as this is not written in the Gospel nor is it found ever to have been done in the time of the apostles, he shall not be included in the ranks of the martyrs." [70]

There are rules concerning jobs that are unfit for Christians, e.g., a pantomime or charioteer must look for other employment if he wants to join the church.[71] Certain entertainment is also inappropriate: "If one of the faithful plays dice, that is, on a playing board, for money, he shall be kept away; if, having reformed, he stops, he may be reconciled to communion after a year." [72]

But even in this legalistic collection of rules and regulations the openness to sinners who want to change occasionally shines through. For example: "A prostitute who once lived as such and later married, if afterwards she has come to belief, shall be received without delay." [73] And the rigid waiting periods for full membership can be waived for sufficiently good reason: "Those who arrive at the first stage of faith, if their reputation has been good, shall be admitted to the grace of baptism in two years, unless under the pressure of illness reason compels help more rapidly for the one approaching death or at least the one begging for grace." [74]

Both the *Didascalia* and the *Canons of Elvira* suggest that at the beginning of the fourth century Christianity had become a disciplined community obedient to a powerful group of leaders. It designed regulations to order its life rather than its faith: purely theological concerns seemed to play a subordinate part in them.

This disciplined movement attracted all manner of people including magistrates and soldiers. Sometimes conflicts arose between church and state. Canon 56 shows the reluctance of the Christian establishment to recognize political officeholders as members in good standing in the church. Similarly, membership in the church interfered with advancement in the military. Eusebius tells of Marinus, a soldier of high rank who when forced to choose between further advancement in the military and faithfulness to Christ, chose the latter and was "beheaded for his testimony to Christ." [75]

But while such conflicts occurred, they were the exception rather than the rule, and the fourth century began with an official attitude of benevolent neglect toward the Christians. The more shocking were the intense and cruel persecutions which started in 303. In view of the importance of the Christian leadership so obvious in the above documents, this attack on the church focused on wiping out this leadership. Eusebius reports,

An imperial letter was everywhere promulgated, ordering the razing of the churches to the ground and the destruction by fire of the Scriptures, and proclaiming that those who held high positions would lose all civil rights, while those in households, if they persisted in their profession of Christianity, would be deprived of their liberty.[76]

Moreover, an order followed that "the presidents of the churches should all, in every place, be first committed to prison, and then afterwards compelled by every kind of device to sacrifice." [77]

Not all leaders, as Eusebius reports, were equal to this challenge but so many refused to yield that the empire ordered that even sterner measures be applied. The recalcitrants should be tortured and mutilated to force them to abandon their faith. Eusebius goes into considerable detail in describing the various tortures used to bring the Christians to renounce their faith. The result was that thousands were slaughtered, while additional thousands were awaiting the same fate in prison. As Eusebius described it: "In every place a countless number were shut up, and everywhere the prisons, that long ago had been prepared for murderers and grave-robbers, were then filled with bishops and presbyters, readers and exorcists, so that there was no longer any room left there for those condemned for wrongdoing." [78]

The role of Diocletian himself in these persecutions is not clear, and some scholars have placed most of the responsibility on Galerius.[79] Most scholars accept the fact that this last persecution under the aegis of the Roman Empire was the most dreadful of all. "All the cruelties of the earlier periods were multiplied, and were added to and exceeded by the new inventions due to the devilish imagination of the executioners." [80] But it must be stressed that the aim was to convert the Christians. "The purpose was to make the number of recanting clergy as large as possible, and thereby to create indifference among the rank and file of the churches." [81]

The persecution extended over a period of ten years though not with the same rigor in all sections of the empire. The beginning of the end came in 311 when the most violent persecutor, Galerius, became ill and apparently in exchange for intercession on his behalf granted the Christians toleration.[82] The edict of Galerius led to a similar statement by Maximin who wrote about the Christians, "The obstinacy and most unyielding determination of some [the Christians] was carried to such a length, that neither could they be turned back from their purpose by just reasoning embodied in the order, nor did they fear the punishment that threatened." As Emperor Maximin saw it, it was no use. "Since so long a passage of time has proved that they can in no wise be persuaded to abandon such obstinate conduct," [83] he said, the edicts ordering persecutions were revoked. Though later persecutions occurred sporadically and for short periods of time, the last great effort on the part of the Empire to wipe out the Christian faith had failed.

It was the "obstinacy" of the Christians, their "folly," which made any further persecution counter-productive in the eyes of the emperors. Instead of wiping out Christianity, the persecutions had produced sympathy for the Christians. It had removed those leaders who were not completely devoted and had welded the faithful remnant together into an organization that no amount of cruelty could destroy. As Tertullian had observed a century earlier, "the blood of the martyrs was seed."

At this point, a political figure arose who was able to use an alliance with this disciplined Christian community as an important element of his political program. Constantine had an inestimable importance for the history of Christian ethics. Christians had demonstrated their ability to be faithful to their Lord in the face of persecution, torture and death. Would they be able to follow him when the power of the government not only tolerated them but gave them every possible support? For the next fifteen centuries, the majority of Christians had to work out their ethics in the shadow of the Constantinian solution.[84]

Emperor Constantine and his spokesmen, both pagan and Christian, attributed his victory over Maxentius at the Mulvian bridge on October 28, 312, to the aid of the god of the Christians.[85] The Christians themselves described the event jubilantly: "Constantine, the superior of the Emperors in rank and dignity, was the first to take pity on those subjected to tyranny at Rome; and, calling in prayer upon God who is in heaven, and His Word, even Jesus Christ the Saviour of all, as his ally, he advanced in full force, seeking to secure for the Romans their ancestral liberty." [86] It may be significant that Eusebius considered the triumph of Constantine as much a victory for ancestral Roman liberty as for the freedom of religion of the Christians. For from the very beginning of this alliance, many saw the interests of the church and of the state to correspond.

Emperor Constantine himself poses many complex questions. Why did he align himself with the Christians? Did he know what Christianity really was? It is apparent that he was convinced that the religious policies of his predecessors had proven disastrous for the empire and the survival of this empire was his main objective.

Scholars have debated the sincerity of the emperor's conversion and some attribute it entirely to political calculation. The position which Jacob Burckhardt so colorfully expresses in *The Age of Constantine the Great* has become the conventional wisdom: "In a genius driven without surcease by ambition and lust for power there can be no question of Christianity and paganism, of conscious religiosity or irreligiosity; such a man is essentially unreligious, even if he pictures himself standing in the midst of a churchly community." [87] He called Constantine a "murderous egotist who possessed the great merit of having conceived of Christianity as a world power and of having acted accordingly." [88]

Constantine's first action after his victory over Maxentius was, however, a sharp break with tradition. During his triumphal entry into Rome and the march to the forum he was expected to proceed to the capitol in order to make the customary sacrifice in the temple of Jupiter. But, "the chariot suddenly turned aside and the emperor disappeared into the palace. The sacrifice was not offered." [89]

Moreover, half a year later Constantine and the eastern ruler Licinius issued the following joint proclamation:

When we, Constantine and Licinius, emperors, had an interview in Milan, and conferred together with respect to the good and security of the commonweal, it seemed to us that, amongst those things that are profitable to mankind in general, the reverence paid to the Divinity merited our first and chief attention, and that it was proper that the Christians and all others should have liberty to follow that mode of religion which to each of them appeared best; so that God, who is seated in heaven, might be benign and propitious to us, and to every one under our government.

And therefore we judged it a salutary measure, and one highly consonant to right reason, that no man should be denied leave of attaching himself to the rites of the Christians, or whatever other religion his mind directed him, that thus the supreme Divinity, to whose worship we freely devote ourselves, might continue to vouchsafe His favour and beneficence to us. And accordingly we give you to know that, without regard to any provisos in our former orders to you concerning the Christians, all who choose that religion are to be permitted, freely and absolutely, to remain in it, and not to be disturbed any ways, or molested. And we thought fit to be thus special in the things committed to your charge, that you might understand that the indulgence which we have granted in matters of religion to the Christians is ample and unconditional; and perceive at the same time that the open and free exercise of their respective religions is granted to all others, as well as to the Christians. For it befits the well-ordered state and the tranquillity of our times that each individual be allowed, according to his own choice, to worship the Divinity; and we mean not to derogate aught from the honour due to any religion or its votaries.

Moreover, with respect to the Christians, we formerly gave certain orders concerning the places appropriated for their religious assemblies; but now we will that all persons who have purchased such places, either from our exchequer or from any one else, do restore them to the Christians, without money demanded or price claimed, and that this be performed peremptorily and unambiguously; and we will also, that they who have obtained any right to such places by form of gift do forthwith restore them to the Christians: reserving always to such persons, who have either purchased for a price, or gratuitously acquired them, to make application to the judge of the district, if they look on themselves as entitled to any equivalent from our beneficence. — All those places are, by your intervention, to be immediately restored to the Christians. And because it appears that, besides the places appropriated to religious worship, the Christians did possess other places, which belonged not to individuals, but to their society in general, that is, to their churches, we comprehend all such within the regulation aforesaid, and we will that you cause them all to be restored to the society or churches, and *that* without hesitation or controversy: Provided always, that the persons making restitution without a price shall be at liberty to seek indemnification from our bounty.

In furthering all which things for the behoof of the Christians, you are to use your utmost diligence, to the end that our orders be speedily obeyed, and our gracious purpose in securing the public tranquillity promoted. So shall that divine favour which, in affairs of the mightiest importance, we have already experienced, continue to give success to us, and in our successes make the commonweal happy. And that the tenor of this our gracious ordinance may be made known unto all, we will that you cause it by your authority to be published everywhere." [90]

In fact, from the beginning Constantine was far more favorable toward Christianity than even the Constitution of 313 would lead one to believe. This first proclamation of religious freedom for the Roman Empire treated Christianity merely as one of the religions and singled Christians out for the restoration of their properties, because they alone had been the victims of previous persecutions. Yet Constantine had passed up the opportunity to show his "tolerance" by giving the customary respects to the ancient gods of the empire. Especially when the final conflict with Licinius came whose prize was world monarchy, Constantine identified himself very clearly with Christianity and its religious symbols, while Licinius put his trust in the ancient gods of Rome. When Constantine triumphed it was further evidence to him and his supporters of the power of the God he had embraced.

What Constantine and the Christian theologians of his time had in common was the conviction that God was the lord of history. This was the reason why in his opinion the emperors who had opposed Christianity had failed. If, indeed, the God of the Christians was the only true God, he would demonstrate this fact by giving Constantine victory over his enemies. As Dörries has put it:

These assumptions were a blending of the Roman understanding of religion, the Christian impact, and, not least, his own experiences in which, of course, both viewpoints had their part. The appeal to a heavenly champion was Roman. Thus Aurelian appealed to the sun god at Emesa before the battle which restored the unity of the empire at Palmyra. Roman, too, was the confidence in the power of magical signs. On the Christian side was the influence of the steadfastness of the martyrs, which pointed to a higher power. Above all was the Christian proclamation of the omnipotence of God. Constantine, the general, could not for a moment doubt that this Almighty God would disclose himself in the battle.

Finally, Constantine's personal experience led him to view the fates of the persecuting emperors as a demonstration that behind the sequence of events stood a higher power, intervening in their course and subjecting even the greatest rulers to its will. Everything depended on being in league with this power. He who showed himself to be the Lord of history was also the director of battles. With these assumptions the conclusion easily followed that military prowess did not suffice to win the battle. That Constantine should thus have called upon the Christian God to give the victory to his army is something new and special.[91]

Another proclamation of Constantine recorded by Eusebius bears this out further:

To all who entertain just and sound sentiments respecting the character of the Supreme Being, it has long been most clearly evident, and beyond the possibility of doubt, how vast a difference there has ever been between those who maintain a careful observance of the hallowed duties of the Christian religion, and those who treat this religion with hostility or contempt. But at this present time, we may see by still more manifest proofs, and still more decisive instances, both how unreasonable it were to question this truth, and how mighty is the power of the Supreme God: since it appears that they who faithfully observe His holy laws, and shrink from the transgression of His commandments, are rewarded with abundant blessings, and are endued with well-grounded hope as well as ample power for the accomplishment of their undertakings.

On the other hand, they who have cherished impious sentiments have experienced results corresponding to their evil choice. For how is it to be expected that any blessing would be obtained by one who neither desired to acknowledge nor duly to worship that God who is the source of all blessing? Indeed, facts themselves are a confirmation of what I say.[92]

For Constantine, then, the evidence is overwhelming that the worship of the true God results in "abundant blessings" and "power for the accomplishment of their undertaking." This may not be a sound and liberal Protestant reason for supporting Christianity that would befit Burckhardt's nineteenth century, but it made eminent sense to the superstitious and ambitious military genius whom Burckhardt described.

The rest of the so-called "Law of Constantine" recorded by Eusebius is almost a catechism of popular religiosity since time immemorial, and it explains why the majority of Romans were now willing to adopt Christianity.[93] Constantine claims that those who have made justice and probity the basis of their conduct have carried their undertakings to a successful issue. The persecutors have received "a recompense proportionate to their crimes." [94] "Many a time have their armies been slaughtered, many a time have they been put to flight; and their warlike preparations have ended in total ruin and defeat." [95]

On the other hand, Constantine insisted that he was God's chosen instrument for the accomplishment of the divine will:

Accordingly, beginning at the remote Britannic ocean, and the regions where, according to the law of nature, the sun sinks beneath the horizon, through the aid of divine power I banished and utterly removed from every form of evil which prevailed, in the hope that the human race, enlightened through my instrumentality, might be recalled to a due observance of the holy laws of God, and at the same time our most blessed faith might prosper under the guidance of his almighty hand.[96]

In this mission he wanted the help of his Christian subjects. He solicited their support in military service, while granting them the right to an honorable discharge.[97] The political leaders whom he selected for his administration were frequently Christians or, in the words of Eusebius, "such as were devoted to the saving faith." [98]

From a persecuted and suppressed minority the Christian church became "an established component of the empire." [99] Bishops ranked with the highest officials of the empire. The state exempted clergy from taxation. In return, the church became the welfare agency of the state. Under persecution it had developed the ability to care for the sick, the poor, orphans and widows. Eusebius describes how during the drought and the resulting famine and plague in the reign of Maximus Daza, the Christians cared in the midst of persecutions not only for their own but all their fellows:

> They alone in such an evil state of affairs gave practical evidence of their sympathy and humanity *(philanthropia)*: all day long some of them would diligently persevere in performing the last offices for the dying and burying them (for there were countless numbers, and no one to look after them); while others would gather together in a single assemblage the multitude of those who all throughout the city were wasted with the famine, and distribute bread to them all, so that their action was on all men's lips, and they glorified the God of the Christians, and, convinced by the deeds themselves, acknowledged that they alone were truly pious and God-fearing.[100]

Lactantius, a schoolteacher whom Constantine had selected to teach Latin to his son Crispus, describes in glowing colors the Christian humaneness which he hoped would undergird the new empire under Constantine.[101] In his *Divine Institutes,* which he wrote to influence the emperor, he uses and modifies concepts of Cicero and insists that we must preserve humaneness *(humanitas)* to be truly human beings [102] "What else is this preservation of humanity than the loving a man because he is a man, and the same as ourselves?" [103] Quoting Cicero's claim that a human being while obedient to nature cannot injure a human being, he concludes that it must be in accordance with human nature to help other people, especially those who cannot give you anything in return.[104] "Be bountiful to the blind, the feeble, the lame, the destitute, who must die unless you bestow your bounty upon them. They are useless to men, but they are serviceable to God, who retains to them the light." [105]

Arguing against the waste of money for spectacles so common in the empire, Lactantius reasoned that since "all pleasure is short and perishable, and especially that of the eyes and ears," [106] those who pay for such shows gain at best "empty favour and the talk of a few days." [107] As for public buildings which last longer than spectacles, Lactantius reminds his readers and the emperor that earthquake, fire, and war can destroy "or at any rate they decay and fall to pieces by mere length of time." [108] He concludes that "the only sure and true office of liberality is to support the needy and those considered useless." [109]

Perfect justice is that which protects human society, and "this is the chief and truest advantage of riches; not to use wealth for the particular pleasure of an individual, but for the welfare of many; not for one's own immediate enjoyment, but for justice, which alone does not perish." [110] Approving the praise of hospitality as a "principle virtue" by the philosophers, he nevertheless criticizes Cicero's assertion "that the houses of illustrious men should be open to illustrious guests." With obvious reference to Luke 14:12-14, he insists that the house of the just and wise ought not to be open to the illustrious but to the lonely and disheartened.[111] And he suggests that it is the proper work of those who seek justice "to support the poor and to ransom captives," "to protect and defend orphans and widows," to care for and assist the sick, and to bury strangers and the poor.[112]

To the question, "How can I possibly afford doing all this?" Lactantius replies, "That which you would have expended on superfluities, turn to better uses. Devote to the ransoming of captives that from which you purchase beasts; maintain the poor with that from which you feed wild beasts; bury the innocent dead with that from which you provide men for the sword [gladiators]." [113]

It is quite obvious that the persons whom Lactantius addresses are not the poor but the rich. As private tutor to the emperor's son,

Lactantius had access to Constantine and this gives this final version of the *Divine Institutes* special importance. This is evident from a direct address to the emperor in this text: "We now commence this work under the auspices of your name, O mighty Emperor Constantine, who were the first of the Roman princes to repudiate errors, and to acknowledge and honour the majesty of the one and only true God." [114] At the very end of the book Lactantius addresses the emperor again as the man whom "God raised . . . up for the restoration of the house of justice, and for the protection of the human race." [115]

Here one notes the first effort to influence the social and political position of the state by using the access of the church to a friendly emperor. Here also begins the glorification of the people in power which frequently was the price paid for such an opportunity. For Lactantius insists, "Thou, both by the innate sanctity of thy character, and by thy acknowledgement of the truth and of God in every action, dost fully perform the works of righteousness. It was therefore befitting that, in arranging the condition of the human race, the Deity should make use of thy authority and service." [116]

This imperial authority was used to change the law to be more in line with a Christian understanding of the nature and destiny of the human race. The legal historian Heinrich Geffcken has summarized these changes as follows:

The punishments of crucifixion and branding were abolished; the sexes were separated in the prisons; Sunday was declared to be a holy day, during which all public business, all lawsuits, and even the games of the circus were suspended. During Lent no penal sentence was passed, and criminals were no longer to be condemned to the gladiatorial shows. The conditions of slavery were largely mitigated, and were no longer allowed to entail the disruption of families; Jews, heathens, and heretics were forbidden to have Christian bondsmen. A heathen convert obtained his liberty, and a fugitive slave who had remained for three years in a monastery acquired his freedom, by taking the vow. Manumission was encouraged in every way; the ceremony itself was placed under the official patronage of the bishops, and took place on Sundays and festivals before the assembled congregation.

The laws of marriage were reformed in harmony with Christian principles. The *Lex Papia et Julia*, which denied to the unmarried the power of executing a will, was repealed. The ecclesiastical restrictions upon marriage gained an influence over legislation. Thus, with respect to prohibited degrees of kindred, all marriages between Christians and Jews were forbidden under pain of death, whilst alliances with heathens were less severely judged. because in such cases the danger of apostasy was less probable and the conversion of the heathen consort might be more confidently expected.

Adultery was treated as a capital crime. Those who compelled their daughters or female slaves to a life of public infamy were punished with confiscation and condemned to labour in the mines. Second marriages, though not absolutely forbidden, were regarded with disfavour, and excluded the contracting parties from office in the Church. The exposure and sale of children were interdicted; if the parents were unable to maintain them they were assisted from the public purse.[117]

Sometimes the argument given for the new law was illuminating. In prohibiting the branding of the face of criminals the law now stated, "that the face, which has been made in the likeness of celestial beauty, may not be disfigured."[118] And in 391 the emperors proclaimed, "All those persons whom the piteous fortune of their parents has consigned to slavery while their parents thereby were seeking sustenance shall be restored to their original status of free birth."[119]

But such authority here exerted in line with the claims of Christian ethics also meant control over the life of the church and the right to define true religion, as illustrated in an edict of September 1, 326: "The privileges that have been granted in consideration of religion must benefit only the adherents of the Catholic faith *(Catholica lex)*. It is our will, moreover, that heretics and schismatics shall not only be alien from these privileges but shall also be bound and subjected to various compulsory public services."[120]

The fourth century saw the great turning point. From a despised and persecuted status Christianity became the officially sanctioned ideology of the empire. As long as the new ideology established the legitimation and supplied the support for unity at home and victory abroad, the alliance of emperor and church seemed to work for the apparent benefit of both politicians and ideologues. But what if the empire faltered in spite of its new support? What if the support of the state jeopardized the integrity of the Christian movement? The vast new opportunities the fourth century opened up for Christian ethics were fraught with danger to its integrity and authenticity.

# VII

# Basil

CHRISTIANITY HAD WON THE WAR against the pagan Roman Empire but to win the peace proved more difficult. In spite of oppression and persecution, the courage of martyrs and confessors had achieved the Christian triumph. Now bishops and monks carried out the task of making Christian ethics a live option for the masses of people who joined the Christian movement.

A prime example of this group of new leaders was both a monk and a bishop, Basil the Great. He was born about 330 into a prominent Christian family in Caesarea, a city in Cappadocia. His maternal grandfather had died as a martyr and his parents were notable and devoted Christians. His younger brother, later known as Gregory of Nyssa, became an eloquent Christian teacher who played an important part in the development of the church's doctrine of Christ. His mother Emmelia, his grandmother Macrina, his sister Macrina, and another brother Peter, bishop of Sebaste, were all eventually venerated as saints.

After receiving an excellent education in Caesarea, in Constantinople, and finally in Athens, the philosophical center of the Greek-speaking world at the time, Basil returned to Caesarea about 356. For a short time he was a teacher of rhetoric, but under the influence of his sister Macrina he soon decided to leave the world and become a monk. He travelled over the entire eastern Mediterranean to study the unorganized monasticism existing at the time, which enabled him later to develop his own monastic rule.[1] He settled down in Pontus, near Annesi, to live a life of prayer and meditation.

In a moving letter to his friend Gregory of Nazianzen, Basil described his initial difficulties as a monk: "I have indeed left my life in the city, as giving rise to countless evils, but I have not yet been able to leave myself behind."[2] In order to achieve this goal he advocated total separation from the world, "the severance of the soul from sympathy with the body, and the giving up city, home, personal possessions, love of friends, property, means of subsistence, business, social relations, and knowledge derived from human teaching. . . . "[3]

To achieve this separation, Basil recommended study of "the divinely-inspired Scriptures. For in them are not only found the precepts of conduct, but also the lives of saintly men, recorded and handed down to us, lie before us like living images of God's government, for our imitation of their good works."[4] He also gave a detailed description of the dress, food, and behavior of the monk.[5]

Because of his background, ability and devotion, Basil became the recognized leader of monasticism in Cappadocia and Pontus. But about 364 the danger threatening the church from the Arian heresy brought him back to the world and his hometown. He was ordained to the priesthood in the same year, and after the death of Bishop Eusebius he was chosen bishop of Caesarea, in 370. He died nine years later after giving inspired leadership to the orthodox cause in the Arian controversy.

Basil's importance for the history of Christian ethics derives from the fact that he was not only a powerful defender of the orthodox faith but simultaneously concerned with its pastoral and ethical implications.[6] The remark attributed to him by the church historian Socrates Scholasticus is significant: "That pillar of truth, Basil of Cappadocia, used to say that 'the knowledge which men teach is perfected by constant study and exercise; but that which proceeds from the grace of God, by the practice of justice, patience and mercy.'"[7] His life as a monk had caused him to give attention to the discipline necessary to live a life of Christian discipleship.

What he had learned in this setting he later applied in his new responsibility as a bishop to the moral guidance of all Christians.

In 364 he wrote a letter which he meant apparently to guide the monks in Pontus whom he was leaving to assume his new responsibility in Caesarea. He insisted that the Christian life must be based upon the directions given in the "divinely inspired Scriptures."[8] And indeed, the letter consists of a collection of Scripture references which might guide the Christian. (Basil does not say "the monk," so that apparently he felt that such biblical rules could apply to all Christians.) The following section gives some indication of his method:[9]

The Christian ought to think thoughts worthy of his heavenly vocation (Heb. 3:1), and conduct himself worthily of the Gospel of Christ (Phil. 1:27). The Christian should not be frivolous (Luke 12:29) or easily drawn away by anything from the remembrance of God and from His will and judgments. The Christian, being in all things superior to the ordinances of the law, should neither swear nor lie (Matt. 5:20). He ought not to speak evil (Titus 3:2), to insult (1 Tim. 2:13), wrangle (2 Tim. 2:24), revenge himself (Rom. 12:19), render evil for evil (Rom. 12:17) or get angry (Matt. 5:22). He should be long suffering (James 5:8), should endure to suffer anything whatever, and should rebuke an offender in due season (Titus 2:15), not with a feeling for personal vengeance, but with a desire for his brother's correction (Matt. 15:18), according to the commandment of the Lord. The Christian should say nothing behind a brother's back with the purpose of slandering him, for it is slander in any case, even if what is said is true (2 Cor. 12:20 and 1 Peter 2:1). He ought to turn away from him who practices slander against a brother (James 4:11).[10]

Basil draws his scriptural references entirely from the New Testament, and he fails to quote either Proverbs or Ecclesiastes, so prominent in earlier Christian writings. When he mentions the Old Testament for ethical guidance, he uses the lives of the saints of the Old Testament as models. "The lover of chastity constantly peruses the story of Joseph, and from him learns what chaste conduct is . . . ," Basil writes.[11] "Fortitude he learns from Job. . . ."[12] From David and Moses the Christian learns how to be at the same time "meek and high-tempered, showing temper against sin, but meekness toward men."[13] Basil describes the manner in which to use these Old Testament models as follows: ". . . Just as painters in working from models constantly gaze at their exemplar and thus strive to transfer the expression of the original to their own artistry, so too he who is anxious to make himself perfect in all the kinds of virtue must gaze upon the lives of the saints as upon statues, so to speak, that move and act, and must make their excellence his own by imitation." [14] Christians should accompany this process with prayer, which helps them keep God ever before their eyes.

About the same time, Basil wrote a formal ethics *(Ta Ethika)*.[15] Here he used substantially the same approach as in the letter cited above by describing the rules that should govern the Christian life supported by scriptural evidence.[16] The basis of the Christian life is repentance for we live in the age of repentance and forgiveness, and "in the world to come there is the just judgment of recompense." [17] Although the chief commandments are love to God and the neighbor,[18] Basil gives a long list of commandments for the Christian substantiated by Scripture passages exclusively from the New Testament.

It is apparent that the gospel is to Basil a sharpening and deepening of the law. He writes, "As the law forbids bad deeds, so the gospel forbids the very hidden passions of the soul," and, "as the law makes a partial, so the gospel makes a complete demand as regards every good action." Further, "those cannot be counted worthy of the kingdom of heaven who do not show a righteousness of the gospel greater than that prescribed in the law." [19]

He gives detailed instructions for the formation of the Christian life. Christians should use any possessions beyond the basic necessities of life for the service of others, and everybody who is able to work should do so to be able to help those in need.[20] Christians should not get involved in lawsuits and should not go to court, not even to obtain "the clothes put on the body for necessary covering." [21]

After describing the spiritual duties of the leaders of the Christian church, he reiterated the rules concerning husbands and wives as found in the New Testament. Marriage should never be dissolved "unless one party be taken in adultery or be hindered as regards godliness." [22] Husbands must love their wives and wives should be subject to their husbands. Women should keep silence in church but inquire eagerly at home how to please God. Slavery is accepted and slaves ought to obey their masters "in all things in which the commandment of God is not broken." [23] In turn, "masters, remembering their true Master, whatever service they enjoy from their bond-servants should return the same to them according to their ability, in the fear of God and in kindness towards them, imitating the Lord." [24] Children should honor their parents and parents raise their children showing meekness and long-suffering and giving no excuse for anger and grief.[25] The new political situation is reflected in the counsel to soldiers not "to intimidate or make false accusations," [26] and rulers are to "be vindicators of God's ordinances." [27]

When summarizing his ethical teaching Basil insists again on Christ as the pattern to whom Christians are to be conformed.[28] He concludes by saying, "What is the distinguishing mark of a Christian? Faith working by love. What is the mark of faith? Unhesitating conviction of the truth of the inspired words, unshaken by any argument either based on the plea of physical necessity [29] or masquerading in the guise of piety." [30] A Christian is a person "born anew in baptism of water and Spirit," [31] and "cleansed from all pollution of flesh and spirit in the blood of Christ, to perfect holiness in the fear of God and love of Christ." [32] The mark of love toward God in the Christian is keeping God's commandment with a view to God's glory. The mark of love toward the neighbor is to seek not one's own good but the good of the loved one for the benefit of his soul and body.

On the surface Basil sounds extremely legalistic, yet it is the sacraments of Baptism and the Lord's Supper which for him are God's gifts making Christian ethics possible. To be a Christian means to put on Christ. To define the Christian life he quotes Romans 6:3-4, 6; Colossians 3:9-10; and Galatians 3:27 ("For as many of you as were baptized into Christ have put on Christ"),[33] which point to the power of baptism and of eating the body of Christ and drinking his blood to make the Christian life possible. This emphasis distinguishes Basil from those legalists who see the Christian life as a simple human possibility consisting of the painstaking obedience to a set of laws. The rules Basil offers are indeed detailed, but he knows that the power to obey them comes from God. "What is the mark of a Christian? To be born anew in baptism of water and Spirit." [34] The emphasis on new birth, on death and resurrection, and on renewal in the image of him who created humankind, makes God the source of the ethical life. And Basil insists that both flesh and spirit are to be cleansed.

Basil also avoids the notion which he might very well have taken over from his philosophical teachers, that the body and the flesh are the source of sin and that soul and spirit are not affected. He insists that both flesh and spirit are to be cleansed, and is prepared to say that "desire is a disease of the soul, whereas its health is continence." [35] And this "continence is a grace of God." [36]

Basil concludes his ethics by repeatedly asking the rhetorical question, "What is the mark of a Christian?" The answer he gives is "To love one another, even as Christ also loved us;" "To see the Lord always before him;" and "To watch each night and day and in the perfection of pleasing God by being ready, knowing that the Lord cometh at the hour he thinketh not." [37]

In the latter part of the fourth century when supporters of Christianity had largely taken over the government of the empire, the eschatological expectation of the Lord's coming was still a major ethical motive for those reborn through baptism and nourished by Christ's body and blood. But Basil's significance for the history of Christian ethics is most pronounced because he applied his ethical insights to his day to day work as a respected leader and bishop of the church. He not only wrote textbooks on ethics but used his ethics in the daily life of an important center of the Christian movement.

For an understanding of the resulting pastoral and episcopal practice, three sources are of particular significance: his homilies, his letters, and his *Address to Young Men on How They Might Derive Benefit from Greek Literature.*

Addressing working men [38] of Caesarea in a series of weekday Lenten sermons on the opening chapter of Genesis, he claimed that the Creator and the nature he created teach us basic moral laws: "We shall not be able to say in self-justification, that we have learnt useful knowledge in books, since the untaught law of nature makes us choose that which is advantageous to us." [39] And referring his listeners to the Golden Rule he continued, "Do you know what good you ought to do your neighbor? The good you expect from him yourself. Do you know what is evil? That which you would not wish another to do to you." [40] And as a disciple of Stoic moral philosophy he asserted, "Virtues exist in us also by nature, and the soul has affinity with them not by education but by nature herself. We do not need lessons to hate illness, but by ourselves we repel what afflicts us, the soul has no need of a master to teach us to avoid vice. Now all vice is a sickness of the soul as virtue is its health." [41] Basil claims that it is natural that temperance, justice, courage and prudence should be praised everywhere, for these "virtues concern the soul more than health concerns the body." [42] And quoting Ephesians, that "children love your parents," and "parents provoke not your children to wrath," he adds, "Does not nature say the same? Paul teaches us nothing new; he only tightens the links of nature." [43]

From this perspective which merges Stoic morality and Christian ethics, Basil addresses the issues of his age. One of the most serious ethical problems confronting him was the shocking difference between the very poor and the very rich. Poor people were still forced to sell their children into slavery in order to provide the barest necessities for the remainder of the family.[44] The rich, who were unwilling to prevent such tragedies, and indeed, made them possible, were severely castigated by Basil as thieves and robbers. "Are you not a thief," he said, "if you treat the possessions given to you to administer as if they were your property? A person who takes away the clothing of another is called a robber. Does somebody who refuses to clothe the naked although able to do so deserve another name?" [45] And he continued, "To the hungry belongs the bread which you keep from him, to the naked the clothing you preserve in your closet, to the barefoot the shoes which you let rot, to the needy the silver which you have buried." [46]

These and similar sermons [47] were credible and effective since Basil himself, who came from a wealthy family, had set a personal example. In obedience to Christ's advice that "if you will be perfect, go sell what thou hast, and give it to the poor," he sold his possessions and shared the proceeds with the poor.[48] Thenceforth his support came apparently from a foster-brother who had been given certain property, including slaves, by Basil's parents with the understanding that he would in turn provide adequately for his brother.[49] Basil himself owned nothing "but a cloak and a few books." [50] Thus he could withstand the threats of the powerful, including an Arian emperor, by insisting, "I dwell on the earth as a traveler." [51]

This very lack of personal wealth enabled Basil to castigate the rich and powerful of his age. He especially assailed usurers who preyed on the poor. Basing his position on Psalm 15:5, that he "who does not put out his money at interest, and does not take a bribe against the innocent" shall dwell on God's holy hill, Basil commented that the Christian is a person who hates usury. Quoting with approval the denunciation of taking interest from a brother as found in Ezekiel 22:12, Deuteronomy 23:19, and Jeremiah 9:6, he called the practice inhuman and told the loansharks of his time, "Are you seeking money and gain from the poor? . . . The poor man looked for help and found an enemy. He sought medicine and was offered poison. . . . You are like a physician who visits the sick and takes the remnant of their strength from them." [52] Repeatedly he warned the poor in his sermons against the treachery and deviousness of these money-lenders.

But he also saw wealth in itself as a mortal temptation to the Christian. Preaching on Matthew 19:16, he dealt with the problems created by riches. He described the conspicuous waste of the rich in the following words:

I am filled with amazement at the invention of superfluities. The vehicles are countless, some for conveying goods, others for carrying their owners; all covered with brass and with silver. There are a vast number of horses, whose pedigrees are kept like men's, and their descent from noble sires recorded. Some are for carrying their haughty owners about the town, some are hunters, some are hacks. Bits, girths, collars, are all of silver, all decked with gold. Scarlet clothes make the horses as gay as bridegrooms. . . . There must be some houses warm in winter, and others cool in summer. The pavement is of mosaic, the ceiling gilded. If any part of the wall escapes the slabs, it is embellished with painted flowers. . . ." [53]

If in spite of all this waste some wealth still remains, Basil observed that the rich will bury it or hide it away, saying "Who knows what the future will bring and what unforeseen needs we may have?" To them Basil replies, "It may be uncertain whether you will ever need your buried treasure but it is quite certain that you will receive punishment for your inhuman behavior." [54]

Rich people are prepared to fulfill all commandments except to give up their riches. And Basil claimed that he knew many who are prepared to fast, pray, implore God and do all the works of piety, as long as it does not cost them anything, but who refuse to give even a penny to a person in need. And he added, "What good is such virtue? The kingdom of heaven will not receive them." [55] "You who dress your walls, and let your fellow-creatures go bare, what will you answer to the Judge? You who harness your horses with splendor, and despise your brother when he is ill-dressed; who let your wheat rot, and will not feed the hungry; who hide your gold and despise the distressed." [56]

The moral eloquence of Basil's homilies and the concrete counsel offered to various correspondents in his letters are equally impressive. While Letter 22, referred to earlier, was not really a letter to a specific person but rather a summary of the ideal Christian life, other letters deal specifically with the ethical problems of individuals. To a monk who had become involved in adultery he wrote movingly, recalling his former way of life, "Remember all the saints whose lips you greeted with a kiss, all the holy persons that you embraced, all the people who fervently clasped your hands as undefiled, all the servants of God who, like hirelings, ran up and clung to your knees." [57] But even in such a case there is hope. "The tower of our strength has not fallen, brother; the remedies of amendment have not been locked; the city of refuge has not been closed. . . . The Lord knows how to raise up those who have been dashed down." [58]

And in a similar vein he wrote to a "fallen virgin": "The Lord wishes to purge you of the pain of the wound, and to show you the light after darkness. The good shepherd, who has left those which have not strayed, seeks you. If you give yourself over to Him, He will not delay, nor in His kindness will He disdain to carry you on His own shoulders, rejoicing that He has found his sheep which was lost." [59]

But not only monks and nuns were the object of his personal concern. When the slaves of a certain Eustochius had been insolent to a prominent citizen of Cappadocia by the name of Callisthenes, Basil interceded through a mutual friend by personal letter. He assured the offended nobleman that he was willing to reprimand the slaves personally in place of the severe punishment of the law.

He wrote to Callisthenes: ". . . Even if you have bound yourself by oath to give them over to the vengeance of the laws, a stern reprimand by us is no less effective in vindicating justice, nor is God's law held in slighter honour than the civil usages which play a part in the lives of men." [60] Actually, Basil hoped that if these offenders were turned over to him they might be converted to Christianity and thus the whole unpleasantness would redound to the glory of God.

No cause was too insignificant for his attention. He tackled the Byzantine bureaucracy and wrote to the governor of Cappadocia about an old man whose four-year-old grandson had been placed on the senatorial roll, which meant that the grandfather would have to serve in his stead despite an earlier imperial decree which had exempted him from this obligation because of his advanced years.[61] He interceded for a widow in financial trouble because of a conflict with the executor of her husband's estate.[62] He wrote letters of consolation to the bereaved [63] and fearlessly addressed the politically powerful.[64] And he used his letters also to give concrete advice on more complex ethical questions and on the finer points of an evolving canon law.

Especially letter 188 to Amphilochius, bishop of Iconium, is full of detailed rules in the area of moral theology based on the existing canons of the church. Some of his comments apply strictly to matters of church order but others are of broad ethical significance. "A woman who deliberately destroys a foetus is answerable for murder. And any fine distinction as to its being completely formed or unformed is not admissible amongst us." [65] The punishment he suggested was sincere repentance for ten years, a shorter penalty than that fixed by the Synod of Elvira. Moreover, he added: ". . . We should not determine the treatment according to time but according to the manner of repentance." [66]

In this same letter Basil presents a detailed discussion of the ethical significance of the distinction between voluntary and involuntary acts in which he follows the reasoning of Aristotle in Book III of the *Nicomachean Ethics*. But while he grants that there are clearly involuntary acts—if one, for example, throws a stone to ward off a dog and hits a person—the presence of anger and the desire does not take away from the voluntary character of the act and "passion" never constitutes a valid excuse for inherent evil deeds. As Basil states it: "He who in anger has used an axe against his wife is a murderer." [67] And he insisted that "entirely voluntary and admitting no doubt are, for instance, the acts of robbers and the attacks of soldiers." [68]

The juxtaposition of robbers and soldiers, not untypical for the age,[69] calls attention to Basil's ambivalence in regard to military service as expressed in his praise of a soldier of whom he is willing to say in one place: "We have come to know a man who proves that even in military life one may preserve the perfection of love for God, and that a Christian should be marked, not by the fashion of his clothing, but by the disposition of his soul." [70] But while he is ready to pray for people in the military service,[71] he also counsels another young man to serve as a civilian rather than a soldier.[72] Indeed, in a later commentary on the canons he wrote, "Those who march out to meet robbers, if they be laics, are debarred from the communion of the Good; but if they be clerics, they are deposed from orders. 'For all,' He says, 'that take the sword, shall perish with the sword.'"[73] So he held military service in low esteem, even for the legitimate cause of suppressing robbery.

But while Basil's comments condemn violence and usury, most of them deal with a variety of sexual offenses, from fornication and adultery to homosexuality, incest, and bestiality.[74] As in the decrees of Elvira, it is apparent that sexual discipline is a particular cause of concern for the bishop. As Samuel Laeuchli has noted, "In the turmoil of a decaying empire the Christian Church attempted to find its communal identity; in the crisis that had come about at the twilight of antiquity, the Christian elite sought to carve out a clerical image." [75] By establishing sexual codes, Christian leaders tried to define the specific and different character of Christian ethics. Basil's correspondence with the Christian leadership of this time promoted the same idea.[76]

It is apparent that the authority of bishops like Basil influenced Roman legislation, for some of these Christian standards were soon incorporated into Roman law. Celibacy which had been penalized was now permitted to men and women.[77] The Theodosian Code considered not only the rape but even the solicitation of maidens or widows consecrated to God a capital offense.[78] Marriages between close relatives became prohibited [79] as well as marriages between Christians and Jews.[80]

But in spite of Basil's serious, even punctilious, concern with obedience to the evolving canon law recorded in his letters, he was open to the ethical values of his cultural heritage. He hoped that Christian youths would take advantage of poetry and history and emulate the example of ancient wise men, even though these people had not been Christians. As Werner Jaeger has pointed out, "Basil insists on the direct reception into the Christian schools, which were still *in statu nascendi,* of ancient Greek poetry as a way of higher education." [81] Indeed in the vision of Basil and the other Cappadocian fathers, Christianity "emerges as the heir to everything in the Greek tradition that seemed worthy of survival." [82]

Basil's *Address to Young Men on How They Might Derive Benefit from Greek Literature* [83] has been called "the charter of all Christian higher education for centuries to come," [84] and makes Basil a pioneer for all later Christian humanism. With his devotion to the authority of the Scripture, he combined respect and love for those secular authors who help young people to live moral lives by praising virtue and rebuking vice. Basil quoted the words of one of his own teachers that the entire poetic work of Homer is a hymn to virtue.[85] Not only the classical literature but also the exemplary deeds of the ancients were for him ethically significant. Pericles, Euclid, Socrates, and many others were models for Christian young people.[86] Basil apparently saw no essential difference between the ethical teachings of Plato and those of Paul.[87] Indeed, though the Christian Scripture teaches virtue more perfectly and completely, the secular writers give us a very useful sketch of it. If read with discretion, they will aid young people to live a Christian life.

Such a positive evaluation of Greek culture enabled Basil to mediate between Christianity and its cultured despisers. He also made his ethical counsel persuasive not only to the poor and uneducated whose spokesman he always tried to be but also to the affluent leaders of his society, the class to which he himself belonged.

This ability to appeal to a broad spectrum of people may explain one of the great practical achievements of Basil's ethical concerns, that is, the establishment of vast charitable institutions later called *Basiliades* on the outskirts of Caesarea. The idea for such institu-

tional efforts to relieve poverty and disease came to him during a
severe famine which Gregory Nazianzen described as "the most
severe ever recorded." [88] The poor of Caesarea were at the mercy
of those who had hoarded supplies and used the opportunity to
drive up food prices. Relief to individual sufferers would not suffice
and Basil decided on more drastic measures.

> He gathered together the victims of the famine with some who were
> but slightly recovering from it, men and women, infants, old men, all
> who were in distress, and obtaining contributions of all sorts of food
> which can relieve famine, set before them basins of soup and such meat
> as was found preserved among us, on which the poor live. Then, imitat-
> ing the ministry of Christ, Who, girded with a towel, did not disdain to
> wash the disciples' feet, using for this purpose the aid of his own servants,
> and also of his fellow servants, he attended to the bodies and souls of
> those who needed it, combining personal respect with the supply of their
> necessity, and so giving them a double relief.[89]

This experience with massive institutional relief efforts led him to
develop a more collective approach to Christian social service. He
built hospitals for the sick as well as shelters for travelers and the
poor so extensive that they came to be called the "new city." [90]

The opportunity to launch this massive effort came unexpectedly
as a result of his conflict with the Arian emperor Valens. The courage and power demonstrated by Basil, the orthodox bishop, led the
emperor to give him "some fine lands for the poor under his care,
for they being in grievous bodily affliction were especially in need
of care and cure." [91] What actually happened is not easy to establish
since all sources seem somewhat overwhelmed by the miraculous
power of the holy bishop.[92] It is clear however that these reports
reflect the conviction prevalent in the church of the time that God
will support the orthodox cause and that even emperors are well
advised not to oppose a bishop. When the emperor's prefect expresses his amazement at Basil's open opposition saying, "No one
has ever yet spoken thus, and with such boldness, to me," Basil
replies:

> Why, perhaps you have not met with a bishop, or in his defence of
> such interests [the orthodox faith] he would have used precisely the
> same language. For we are modest in general, and submissive to every
> one, according to the precept of our law. We may not treat with haughti-
> ness even any ordinary person, to say nothing of so great a potentate.

But where the interests of God are at stake, we care for nothing else, and make these our sole object. Fire and sword and wild beasts, and rakes which tear the flesh, we revel in, and fear them not. You may further insult and threaten us, and do whatever you will, to the full extent of your power. The emperor himself may hear this—that neither by violence nor persuasion will you bring us to make common cause with impiety, not even though your threats become still more terrible." [93]

The net result of the confrontation was an increase of Basil's influence. He used it to develop his social service institutions. They are glowingly described by Gregory Nazianzen in his *Panegyric on S. Basil:*

A noble thing is philanthropy, and the support of the poor, and the assistance of human weakness. Go forth a little way from the city, and behold the new city, the storehouse of piety, the common treasury of the wealthy, in which the superfluities of their wealth, aye, and even their necessities, are stored, in consequence of his exhortations, freed from the power of the moth, no longer gladdening the eyes of the thief, and escaping both the emulation of envy and the corruption of time: where disease is regarded in a religious light, and disaster is thought a blessing, and sympathy is put to the test. . . .

There is no longer before our eyes that terrible and piteous spectacle of men who are living corpses, the greater part of whose limbs have mortified, driven away from their cities and homes and public places and fountains, aye, and from their own dearest ones, recognizable by their names rather than by their features: they are no longer brought before us at our gatherings and meetings, in our common intercourse and union, no longer the objects of hatred, instead of pity on account of their disease; . . .

He [Basil] however it was, who took the lead in pressing upon those who were men, that they ought not to despise their fellowmen, nor to dishonour Christ, the one Head of all, by their inhuman treatment of them; but to use the misfortunes of others as an opportunity of firmly establishing their own lot, and to lend to God that mercy of which they stand in need at His hands. He did not therefore disdain to honour with his lips this disease, noble and of noble ancestry and brilliant reputation though he was, but saluted them as brethren, not, as some might suppose, from vainglory (for who was so far removed from this feeling?), but taking the lead in approaching to tend them, as a consequence of his philosophy, and so giving not only a speaking, but also a silent, instruction.

The effect produced is to be seen not only in the city, but in the country and beyond, and even the leaders of society have vied with one another in their philanthropy and magnanimity towards them. Others have had their cooks, and splendid tables, and the devices and dainties of 'confectioners, and exquisite carriages, and soft, flowing robes; Basil's care was for the sick, and the relief of their wounds, and the imitation of Christ, by cleansing leprosy, not by a word, but in deed.[94]

While not the first such effort to institutionalize Christian charity, the extent of Basil's efforts was impressive, even if we make allowance for the hyperbole of a panegyric. In a very matter-of-fact letter of 372 to Elias, governor of Cappadocia, the extent and scope of his charitable institutions is quite apparent. Defending himself against the calumnies of his detractors, he wrote: "Whom do we wrong when we build hospices for strangers, for those who visit us while on a journey, for those who require some care because of sickness, and when we extend to the latter the necessary comforts, such as nurses, physicians, beasts for travelling and attendants?" [95] Letters Basil wrote in the following year (373) to tax assessors requesting immunity from tax assessment for poorhouses under his jurisdiction give further evidence of the extent of the charitable institutions he established.[96]

Thus Basil was not only eloquent in counseling deeds of love to the men and women under his care, but he also complemented this advice by the establishment of institutions of Christian social service. Under the leadership of monks and bishops like Basil of Caesarea the Christian faith generated a complex understanding of Christian service as philanthropy.[97] A key to this development may have been Basil's unique combination of theology and ethics, of pastoral and social concern, and of faith and love.

# VIII

# John Chrysostom

**B**ASIL'S CAREER AS A BISHOP and influential leader
of the Christian church had been confined to Caesarea, a relatively insignificant town in the mountain regions of the extreme east
of the empire. John of Constantinople, later called Chrysostom
(golden mouthed), was born in 354 [1] in Antioch, a major center of
civilization, and served eventually as the eminent and controversial
bishop of Constantinople, the capital of the eastern empire. Antioch, John's birthplace, was prominent for Christian art. Eight
great temples to the ancient gods were located there as well as an
abundance of smaller temples and shrines.[2] It had an old Christian
tradition, indeed the name "Christian" had first been used to describe the followers of Jesus in this city (Acts 11:26). Cicero had
called Antioch the "Queen of the East" because of its educational
advantages.[3]

Here John was born as the son of a high-ranking military officer
named Secundus and his wife Anthusa. Secundus died shortly after
his son's birth and the child was raised together with his older sister
by his mother. Though his father may have been of Latin parentage
(as his name suggests) his mother spoke only Greek and John never
understood any other language. Despite the loss of the father at
such an early age the family remained prosperous. The twenty-

year-old widow—who, obeying the highest standards of Christian conduct of the time, never remarried—was able to secure for her son the best education Antioch had to offer. What her decision meant, Chrysostom described in one of his books by attributing the following words to her:

No words are adequate to describe the tempest-tossed condition of a young woman who, having but lately left her parental home, and being inexperienced in business, is suddenly racked by an overwhelming sorrow, and compelled to support a load of care too great for her age and sex. For she has to correct the laziness of servants, and to be on the watch for their rogueries, to repel the designs of relations, to bear bravely the threats of those who collect the public taxes, and harshness in the imposition of rates. And if the departed one should have left a child, even if it be a girl, great anxiety will be caused to the mother, although free from much expense and fear: but a boy fills her with ten thousand alarms and many anxieties every day, to say nothing of the great expense which one is compelled to incur if she wishes to bring him up in a liberal way. None of these things, however, induced me to enter into a second marriage, or introduce a second husband into thy father's house: but I held on as I was, in the midst of the storm and uproar, and did not shun the iron furnace of widowhood.[4]

Even if this speech was a rhetorically embellished recollection of Chrysostom, it reveals the social milieu of his youth. It explains his instruction in rhetoric by Libanius, a confirmed disciple of the old gods of paganism, but then the most famous teacher in Antioch. Other bright young Christian students from prosperous families had studied under Libanius. Basil of Caesarea and Gregory of Nazianzen had frequented his school.[5] And among John's fellow students were Theodore (later bishop of Mopsuestia) and Maximus (later bishop of Seleucia).[6]

John described Libanius as a person who "exceeded all men in his reverence for the gods."[7] Yet his nostalgia for the ancient gods did not keep him from concern for the earthly welfare of humanity. It was this critical concern with social ethical issues like forced labor, slavery, wealth and poverty, city administration, etc., which he, however, addressed relatively late in his life[8] which furnishes a bridge between him and the ethical position of John Chrysostom. Thus Christian students, while rejecting Libanius' theology, shared with him their interest in "philanthropy" in the special sense that this word had come to assume in the hellenistic world. Origen had claimed that "Christ had to die for us *dia philanthropia*" [9] and the importance of philanthropy as a key to Christian ethics had been noted earlier in connection with Basil of Caesarea. In Antioch in the fourth century *philanthropia* had come to describe an attitude toward the human race in which Christians and reform-minded pagans like Libanius tried to compete with each other.

Even the emperor at the time, a fierce defender of the old pagan religion, Julian—whom the Christians called "the Apostate" since he had been raised a Christian—supported this consensus of the educated class. The more or less compulsory reading of Christian literature in his youth had not only given him ample ammunition for his attack against the Christians,[10] which he always called Galileans and tried to exclude from Greek civilization, it had also made it obvious to him that pagan religion would have to adopt some of the ethical practices of these very same people in order to establish credibility in the eyes of the people. In a letter to a pagan priest whom he addressed as the Supreme Pontiff of the restored cult—a position he had assumed when he became emperor— he wrote about the criteria for the selection of priests:

The most upright men in every city, by preference those who show most love for the gods, and next those who show most love for their fellow men, must be appointed, whether they be poor or rich. And in this matter let there be no distinction whatever whether they are unknown or well known. For the man who by reason of his gentleness has not won notice ought not to be barred by reason of his want of fame. Even though he be poor and a man of the people, if he possess within himself these two things, love for God and love for his fellow men, let him be appointed priest. And a proof of his love for God is his inducing his own people to show reverence to the gods; a proof of his love for his fellows in his sharing cheerfully, even from a small store, with those in need, and his giving willingly thereof, and trying to do good to as many men as he is able.[11]

The reason he gave for this order is most interesting:

For when it came about that the poor were neglected and overlooked by the priests, then I think the impious Galileans observed this fact and devoted themselves to philanthropy. And they have gained ascendancy in the worst of their deeds through the credit they win for such practices. For just as those who entice children with a cake, and by throwing it to them two or three times induce them to follow them, and then, when they are far away from their friends cast them on board a ship and sell them as slaves, and that which for the moment seemed sweet, proves to be bitter for all the rest of their lives—by the same method, I say, the Galileans also begin with their so-called lovefeasts, or hospitality, or service of tables . . . and the result is that they have led many into atheism. [Julian considered Christianity a form of atheism.] [12]

The summary of Julian's understanding of "philanthropy" which he shared with Libanius was not so alien from the approach of John Chrysostom:

You must above all exercise philanthropy, for from it result many other blessings, and moreover that choicest and greatest blessing of all, the good will of the gods. For just as those who are in agreement with their masters about their friendships and ambitions and loves are more kindly treated than their fellow slaves, so we must suppose that God, who naturally loves human beings, has more kindness for those men who love their fellows. Now philanthropy has many divisions and is of many kinds. For instance it is shown when men are punished with moderation with a view to the betterment of those punished, as schoolmasters punish children; and again in ministering to men's needs, even as the gods minister to our own.[13]

Thus, in spite of profound theological differences between pagans and Christians there was a noteworthy ethical consensus among the philosophically trained which expressed itself in later years in Libanius' frequent appeals to Christian emperors and their "philanthropy." [14]

It was this consensus which was not without influence on John Chrysostom. It is apparent that Chrysostom's general philosophical and moral context is very similar to that of his teacher Libanius and the would-be reformer of Greek paganism, emperor Julian.

But Julian's early death in June of 363 while on a military campaign against the Persians brought his hope to revive the ancient Greek religion to an end. Thus during John Chrysostom's youth the danger to the orthodox faith came less from pagan rulers than from emperors like Valens who sympathized with Arianism. Antioch, an intellectual center in the east, was also the center of religious controversy among the Christians and for awhile there were "no fewer than *four bishops* of Antioch: an Arian, two Nicaean Catholics, and an Apollinarist." [15] But young John found the religious controversies in his hometown further stimulation in his desire to dedicate himself to "the blessed life of monks and the true philosophy." [16]

After a very brief entanglement in what he called later "the lusts of this world" [17] he became a catechumen and soon afterwards was baptized at the age of eighteen (372). He immediately began his theological education under Diodorus of Tarsus, a learned ascetic whom Emperor Julian had described as "a sharp-witted sophist of that religion of the peasants [Christianity]," [18] but whom Harnack has called one of the Antiochian theologians, "distinguished by methodical study of Scripture, sober thinking in imitation of Aristotle, and the strictest asceticism." [19] John probably studied with him between 372 and 375.[20] Because of Diodorus' failure to state a clear position on the subject of the two natures and one person of Christ, he was seen by later generations as a forerunner of Nestorianism and more than 100 years after his death he was condemned by a synod in Constantinople. As a result of this posthumous association with Nestorianism few of his writings survived and his influence on Chrysostom is difficult to assess. Other sources for Chrysostom's theology were Basil, Gregory of Nazianzen, and particularly Eusebius, Bishop of Emesa.[21] Soon after his theological studies John decided to become a monk. In his letter to Theodore, a fellow-monk and somewhat younger man who had temporarily withdrawn from the monastic life incurring John's displeasure and deep concern, he summarized his attitude towards monasticism which had a profound significance for his ethical approach.

For there is no man free, save only he who lives for Christ. He stands superior to all troubles, and if he does not choose to injure himself no one else will be able to do this, but he is impregnable; he is not stung by the loss of wealth; for he has learned that we "brought nothing into this world, neither can we carry anything out"; he is not caught by the longings of ambition or glory; for he has learned that our citizenship is in heaven; no one annoys him by abuse, or provokes him by blows; there is only one calamity for a Christian which is, disobedience to God; but all other things, such as loss of property, exile, peril of life, he does not even reckon to be a grievance at all. And that which all dread, departure hence to the other world,—this is to him sweeter than life itself.

For as when one has climbed to the top of a cliff and gazes on the sea and those who are sailing upon it, he sees some being washed by the waves, others running upon hidden rocks, some hurrying in one direction, others being driven in another, like prisoners, by the force of the gale, many actually in the water, some of them using their hands only in the place of a boat and a rudder, and many drifting along upon a single plank, or some fragment of the vessel, others floating dead, a scene of manifold and various disaster; even so he who is engaged in the service of Christ drawing himself out of the turmoil and stormy billows of life takes his seat upon secure and lofty ground. For what position can be loftier or more secure than that in which a man has only one anxiety, How he ought to please God? [22]

It was this basic question, "How do I please God?" which preoccupied Chrysostom's life. It had drawn him to the monastery against his mother's expressed wishes,[23] and eventually involved him against his deepest inclinations in the major religious and political controversies of his age. After living for awhile as a monk in the mountains near Antioch he returned to the city in the winter of 380/381 and was made a deacon. He was ordained a priest in 386. In 397 Nectarius the eleventh Bishop and first "Patriarch" of Constantinople died. Because of the political importance of the position located at the capital of the eastern part of the Roman Empire, it attracted all kinds of candidates. The incumbent, if he were the right person, would exert considerable influence on the emperor and his court. He was invited to all court ceremonies, performed the marriage for the imperial family and baptized the children of the emperor.

Palladius in his *Life of Chrysostom* described the scramble for the position in the following words: "Immediately a crowd of people who were not called for, rushed forward to secure the supreme position—men who were not men, presbyters by office, yet unworthy of the priesthood; some battering at the doors of the officials, others offering bribes, others again going on their knees to the populace." [24] And Fr. Baur has observed: "The fourth century was accustomed to much in this respect." [25] And he lists state officials like Nectarius, Chrysostom's predecessor, and Ambrose of Milan who might have been unbaptized pagans or catechumens when selected to lead the church. Emperor Constantius in 356 appointed one of the officers of his guard to become a bishop and emperor Valens selected a sergeant named Marathon who was the paymaster of the pretorians to be Bishop of Nicomedia.[26]

It is against this background that the selection of Chrysostom, a brilliant preacher and a renowned ascetic, seems surprising. He was the choice of Eutropius, guardian of the youthful emperor Arcadius. In 395 Eutropius had successfully arranged the marriage of the emperor to Aelia Eudoxia, the daughter of a Teutonic nobleman who had served under Valentinian II. He found it equally easy to manage the appointment of a new patriarch. While the choice of Eudoxia is relatively easy to explain—she had been raised by a family loyal to him and was likely to strengthen his influence with the emperor—the selection of John Chrysostom is bewildering. Perhaps his reputation as an ascetic led Eutropius to the conclusion that he would not interfere in politics. In any case after practically being kidnapped from Antioch to avoid the protest of the population who might not want to lose such a popular preacher, he was taken by imperial coach to Contantinople and consecrated its bishop December 15, 397.[27]

But any illusions concerning Chrysostom's harmlessness were short-lived. His immediate attempts to reform the clergy created tensions in the ecclesiastical institutions. His efforts to assert the church's right to grant asylum to fugitives brought him into conflict with the empire. Banished from Constantinople in 403 he was briefly recalled, then exiled again. He died in 407 while being moved from one place of banishment to another, since wherever he resided a congregation of Christians would assemble around him.

Chrysostom's ethics reflected his life. He began his career as a spokesman for orthodox Christianity by writing treatises in defense of monasticism. At that stage in his development he considered the monastic life a special opportunity for disciplined discipleship and he encouraged friends to choose this style of life since he was convinced that God's justice expresses itself in judging human beings according to their deeds. Thus he took great pains to describe both the punishment in hell for evildoers as well as the rewards in heaven for those who do well.[28] From the same perspective he addressed a young widow advising her to avoid a second marriage and to give up her wealth to heaven by giving it to the poor and to live for the eventual reunion with her departed husband "for infinite and endless ages." [29]

But even in his earliest writings his concern for all humanity, his *philanthropia,* is apparent. Not only monks and widows are exhorted to live a life of moral discipline. He tells catechumens, people preparing for baptism, that not only the spiritual elite but anybody who has received baptism will be freed from all evil: "If any man be effeminate, or a fornicator, or an idolator, or a doer of whatever ill you please, or if he be full of all the wickedness there is among men: should he fall into this pool of waters [baptism], he comes up again from the divine fountain purer than the sun's rays." [30] Indeed, in spite of Chrysostom's emphasis on the importance of human effort he is willing to assert in the context of baptism: "Without toil, and exertion, and good works, righteousness is produced. For such is the lovingkindness of the Divine gift that it makes men just without this exertion." [31] It is not merely a "laver of remission of sins" or a "laver of cleansing" but a "laver of regeneration." And he continues, "This nature of ours, rusted with the rust of sin, and having gathered much smoke from our faults, and having lost its beauty which He had from the beginning bestowed upon it from himself, God has taken and cast anew." [32] But the result must be a disciplined life. Chrysostom warns against sinning after baptism, "For the laver is able to remit former sins, but there is no little fear, and no ordinary danger lest we return to them, and our remedy become a wound." [33] Sinning after baptism is dangerous indeed: "For by how much greater the grace is, by so much is the punishment more for those who sin after these things." [34]

Chrysostom is convinced that it is possible and imperative for all Christians to live lives of disciplined obedience to God. Evil comes from sloth, virtue from discipline.[35] He describes the human ethical condition as follows: God dispenses all things, he provides for all. Human beings are free agents. Some things God works, others he merely permits. He wills nothing evil to be done; all things are not done by his will, but some by ours also. All evil things are done by our will alone, all good things by our will conjointly with his influence; nothing happens without his knowledge. Thus he works all things and even what he merely permits is to us part of his design. Human beings knowing this should be able to figure out what is morally good, what is morally evil and what is indifferent. Virtue is good, vice is evil; riches and poverty, life and death are indifferent. If one understands this purpose of God one will also understand that the righteous are afflicted that they may be crowned, the wicked that they may receive the punishment of their sins. But, Chrysostom warns, all sinners are not punished in this life lest the masses should disbelieve the resurrection. Similarly, not all the righteous are afflicted, lest human beings should come to the conclusion that vice and not virtue is approved by God.[36]

In view of the open situation in which the human race finds itself, he considers it the task of the preacher to encourage men and women to use their power as free moral agents to choose righteousness. For this reason he added a moral application at the end of his sermons.[37]

Again and again he emphasized the importance of works validating faith: "Though a man believe rightly on the Father, the Son and the Holy Ghost, yet if he lead not a right life, his faith will avail nothing towards his salvation." [38] Or, "Faith is not sufficient to bring men to the Kingdom, nay, it even hath power in this way most to condemn those who exhibit an ill life." [39] While he praises "right faith," he is convinced "unless we add also a life suitable to our faith we shall suffer the extremest punishment." [40] Or in commenting on Ephesians 1:4, "That you may not then, when you hear that 'He hath chosen us,' imagine that faith alone is sufficient, he [Paul] proceeds to add life and conduct. To this end, saith he, hath He chosen us, and on this condition, 'that we should be holy and without blemish.' And so formerly he chose the Jews . . . Now if men in their choices choose what is best much more doth God. And indeed the fact of their being chosen is at once a token of the lovingkindness of God, and of their moral goodness." [41] There can be little doubt that Chrysostom advocates a position which is later called "Semi-Pelagian," and his student John Cassian, the founder of Semi-Pelagianism, could with good reason appeal to his teacher in support of his views.[42]

It is true that Chrysostom will frequently describe himself as a "sinner," but this has to be taken largely as a rhetorical device, for he has observed, "For if, being sinners, when we account ourselves to be what we are, we become righteous, as indeed the Publican did; how much more, when being righteous we account ourselves to be sinners." [43]

True Christians consider themselves sinners because they are so virtuous that humility enables them to avoid any claims to virtue.

"Let us beware therefore of saying anything about ourselves, for this renders us both odious with men and abominable to God. For this reason, the greater the good works we do, the less let us say about ourselves; this being the way to reap the greatest glory both with men and with God." [44] Indeed, nothing makes our accomplishments so worthless as the effort to remember the good deeds we have done. It produces two evil results, "it both renders us remiss, and raises us to haughtiness." [45]

We should forget our moral accomplishments not because they are worthless but because their contemplation makes us insensible to the task still ahead of us. And using Paul as an example, he suggests, "We, too, should reckon up, not how far we have advanced in virtue, but how much remains for us." [46]

But while Chrysostom writes as a monk who is frequently eloquent in his defense of monasticism and who reflects certain monastic attitudes in all his writings, his ethics is designed for all Christians and he does not consider the monastic life everyone's vocation and the condition for the "Christian life." Only in the matter of marriage does he see a difference between the monk and the persons who follow Christ in the world. While the latter may live with a spouse, otherwise it is their duty to do all things just like the monk.[47] He states explicitly: "Christ's Beatitudes were not addressed to solitaries [monks] only: since in that case the whole world would have perished, and we should be accusing God of cruelty." [48]

In spite of his exalted view of virginity, marriage is not seen by him as a serious barrier to the life of Christian obedience.[49] "If any persons have been hindered by the marriage state, let them know that marriage is not the hindrance but their purpose which made an ill use of the marriage. Since it is not the wine which makes drunkenness, but the evil purpose, and the using it beyond due measure. Use marriage with moderation, and thou shalt be first in the kingdom." [50]

Otherwise Christ has made no difference between the monk and the person who lives in the world. "Listen to what Paul says concerning love *(agape)*, the chief of all that is good. He says of it that the same love is demanded of people who live in the world as Christ demands of his disciples. . . . And if he had said only this, it would be proof enough that the same demands are laid on monks and the people in the world." [51] He praises marriage highly. "Indeed, he who condemns marriage does damage to true virginity." [52] Virginity, on the other hand, is a counsel for the few: "You hear this word virginity, a notion implying much labor and effort; do not worry, this does not deal with a precept nor does it have the force of a commandment, it concerns only those who freely and of their own free will choose it in expectation of reward." [53]

By contrast he considers almsgiving essential for salvation, "For without virginity indeed it is possible to see the kingdom, but without almsgiving it cannot be. For this is among the things that are essential and hold all together. Not unnaturally then have we called it the heart of virtue." [54]

Here it becomes clear that Chrysostom's ethics has a profound social dimension. While still in Antioch he had not only concerned himself with personal morality but also had begun to construct a wide-reaching social ethics. In his *Homilies Concerning the Statues* he had explained to his listeners that all human beings have access to moral law.[55] "When God formed man he implanted within him from the beginning a natural law. And what then was this natural law? He gave utterance to conscience within us; and made knowledge of good things, and of those which are the contrary, to be self-taught." [56] To Chrysostom it is self-evident that fornication is evil and chastity good, or that murder is wicked and stealing wrong. Because he was convinced that conscience had taught this to everyone, the prohibition of murder and adultery in the Ten Commandments is given without any further explanation.

In the case of the commandments which are not self-evident, Chrysostom observed that God gave the people a reason why they should obey them. "When, for instance, He gave the commandment respecting the Sabbath, 'On the seventh day thou shalt do no work,' He subjoined also the reason for this cessation. What was this? 'Because on the seventh day God rested from all His works which He had begun to make' (Exod. 20:6). And again: 'Because thou wert a servant in the land of Egypt'" (Deut. 21:18).[57] The explanation was necessary because this commandment was not one accurately defined in our conscience (and for that matter "a kind of partial and temporary one").[58]

The commandments which are necessary and support all human

life are: "Thou shalt not kill; Thou shalt not commit adultery; Thou shalt not steal." [59] Through conscience and with the aid of reason, human beings are able to choose virtue and to avoid vice quite apart from the revealed law. "For the conscience and reason doth suffice in the law's stead. By this he [Paul] showed first, that God made man independent so as to be able to choose virtue and to avoid vice." [60] Nevertheless, humanity abuses its freedom through sin, which has its origin in Paradise. Chrysostom attributes not only all suffering, disease, death and decay to sin, but also the subordination of humans to each other. Thus the subordination of woman to man is the result of sin. God says "almost apologetically" to the woman: I have created you initially as having equal honor with the man and intended that you should participate in the same dignity—but now as a result of sin I subject you to the man.[61]

But the events described in Genesis 3 demonstrate also that even after the fall humanity has access to the knowledge of virtue. For Chrysostom it is significant that immediately after committing the first sin Adam hid himself. "But if he had not known he had been doing something wrong, why did he hide himself? For then there were neither letters, nor law nor Moses. Why then does he recognize sin and hide himself?" [62] According to Chrysostom humanity attained a certain freedom even after the fall so that Adam would hide himself and could confess his sins—even though in the process he tried to shift much of the blame to "the woman." Mortal humanity after the fall remains for Chrysostom morally responsible. It has conscience, access to an unwritten law, a certain freedom and reason enabling the human race to adjust to changing circumstances.

Thus the universally observed human predicament is not only or even primarily the result of the fall of Adam and Eve, but rather constantly reinforced and reappropriated by their descendants. He says:

Yesterday we accused women, but really not women but Eve that she introduced servitude through sin. Women might say, why should we be condemned because that one woman sinned? Why does failure of that one woman mean the guilt of the entire sex? Slaves could say the same. Only Canaan [63] acted insolently toward his father. Why does this punishment affect the whole race? And people who fear the political authorities might raise the objection why should they bear the yoke of subjection since others lived lives of crime.[64]

To these questions Chrysostom replies that the answer applies equally to every one of them: People in the past have sinned and brought about slavery by their disobedience to God, but once this slavery had been introduced, later generations reconfirmed this new evil situation through their own sin. If these succeeding generations would have been able to claim that they had kept themselves free from sin, their objection to their present enslavement might seem valid, but since they ratified the sins of their ancestors through their own sin, their pretended innocence is merely an excuse.[65] And he continues: "I never said that sin does not produce slavery and I blamed the nature of sin not the variety of sins. All incurable diseases of the body cause death, yet they are not all the same. Thus all sins result in slavery yet not all sins are of the same kind." [66]

It is significant that Chrysostom sees the subordination of woman to man, slave to master, and subject to ruler as analogous and equally the result of human sin both original and actual.

And while Chrysostom insists that human beings are endowed with conscience and reason and have access to natural law, he says they are unable to live up to their possibilities. Human nature is not able to remain within the limits God ordained for the race. The fact that human beings always want more is the main reason for the ruin of humankind.[67]

Thus, in spite of considerable human freedom acknowledged by Chrysostom, Christian ethics cannot be based on conscience, reason, and law so positively regarded by him, but depends ultimately on God's grace. Commenting on Romans 5:17, "For if by the wrongdoing of that one man, Adam, death established its reign, through a single sinner, much more shall those who receive in far greater measure God's grace, and his gift of righteousness, live and reign through the one man, Jesus Christ," Chrysostom observes:

What he says amounts to this nearly. What armed death against the world? The one man's eating from the tree only. If then death attained so great power from one offence, when it is found that certain received a grace and righteousness out of all proportion to that sin, how shall they still be liable to death? And for this cause, he does not here say "grace," but "superabundance of grace." For it was not as much that we must have to do away with the sin only, that we received of His grace, but even far more. For we were at once freed from punishment, and put off all iniquity, and were also born again from above (John iii, 3) and rose again with the old man buried, and were redeemed, justified, led up to adoption, sanctified, made brothers of the Only-begotten, and joint heirs and of one Body with Him, and counted for His flesh, and even as a Body with the Head, so were we united unto Him![68]

The result is the possibility of a completely new manner of life. Repeatedly Chrysostom describes this new life-style. For example, when explaining the significance of the fact that Christians are instructed by their Lord to pray to God as "Father," he comments:

For he who calls God Father, by him both remission of sins, and taking away of punishment, and righteousness, and sanctification, and redemption, and adoption, and inheritance, and brotherhood with the Only-begotten, and the supply of the Spirit, are acknowledged in this single title. For one cannot call God Father without having attained to all those blessings. Doubly, therefore, doth He awaken their spirit, both by the dignity of Him who is called on, and by the greatness of the benefits which they have enjoyed.[69]

This very same prayer also teaches the reality of the fellowship of all Christians.

He [Jesus] teaches, moreover, to make our prayer common, in behalf of our brethren also. For He saith not, "my Father, which art in Heaven," but, "our Father," offering up his supplications for the body in common, and nowhere looking to his own, but everywhere to his neighbor's good. And by this He at once takes away hatred, and quells pride, and casts out envy, and brings in the mother of all good things, even charity, and exterminates the inequality of human things, and shows how far the equality reaches between the king and the poor man, if at least in those things which are greatest and most indispensable, we are all of us fellows. For what harm comes of our kindred below, when in that which is on high *we are all of us knit together, and no one hath aught more than another; neither the rich more than the poor, nor the master than the servant, neither the ruler than the subject, nor the king than the common soldier, nor the philosopher than the barbarian, nor the skillful than the unlearned?* For to all hath He given one nobility, having vouchsafed to be called the Father of all alike.[70]

Here Chrysostom is insisting on the unity and equality of the body of Christ, in which and through which the Christian's life is lived. And though human beings should long for heaven and the things in heaven,

He hath bidden us make the earth a heaven and do and say all things, even while we are continuing in it, as having our conversation there;

insomuch that these too should be objects of our prayer to the Lord. For there is nothing to hinder our reaching the perfection of the powers above, because we inhabit the earth; but it is possible even while abiding here, to do all, as though already placed on high.[71]

And he insists that each one who offers this prayer assumes responsibility for the whole world:

For He did not at all say, "Thy will be done" *in me,* or *in us,* but everywhere on the earth; so that error may be destroyed, and truth implanted, and all wickedness cast out, and virtue return, and no difference in this respect be henceforth between heaven and earth.[72]

Indeed, Chrysostom entertains the hope that if Christians live in obedience to God's will, "there will be no difference between things below and above, separated as they are by nature; the earth exhibiting to us another set of angels." [73]

But in spite of this amazing optimism concerning the possibilities open to the human race thanks to the work of Christ in its behalf, Chrysostom is aware of the differences between angels and humans, as his explanation of the next petition indicates. Unlike most of the Fathers who interpret the petition "Give us this day our daily bread" spiritually or mystically, he emphasized that Jesus was addressing human beings "encompassed with flesh and subject to the necessities of nature, and incapable of the same impassibility with the angels." [74] We are to obey God's commands just like the angels but God condescends to the infirmity of our nature:

Thus, "perfection of conduct" saith He, "I require as great, not however freedom from passions; no, for the tyranny of nature permits it not: for it requires necessary food." But mark, I pray thee, how even in things that are bodily, that which is spiritual abounds. For it is neither for riches, nor for delicate living, nor for costly raiment, nor for any other such thing, but for bread only, that He hath commanded us to make our prayer. And for "daily bread," so as not to "take thought for the morrow." Because of this He added, *"daily* bread," that is, bread for one day. And not even with this expression is He satisfied, but adds another too afterwards, saying, "Give us *this day;"* so that we may not, beyond this, wear ourselves out with the care of the following day.[75]

Yet, Chrysostom's moral optimism does not lead him to deny sin as ongoing reality in the Christian life. He writes:

Then forasmuch as it comes to pass that we sin even after the washing of regeneration, He, showing His love to man to be great even in this case, commands us for the remission of our sins to come unto God who loves man, and thus to say, "Forgive us our debts, as we also forgive our debtors." Seest thou surpassing mercy? After taking away so great evils, and after the unspeakable greatness of His gift, if men sin again, He counts them such as may be forgiven. For that this prayer belongs to believers is taught us both by the laws of the church, and by the beginning of the prayer. For the uninitiated could not call God Father. If then the prayer belongs to believers, and they pray, entreating that sins may be forgiven them, it is clear that not even after the laver is the profit of repentance taken away. Since, had He not meant to signify this, He would not have made a law that we should so pray. Now He who both brings sins to remembrance, and bids us ask forgiveness, and teaches how we may obtain remission, and so makes the way easy; it is perfectly clear that He introduced this rule of supplication, as knowing, and signifying, that it is possible even after the font to wash ourselves from our offenses; by reminding us of our sins, persuading us to be modest; by the command to forgive others, setting us free from all revengeful passion; while by promising in return for this to pardon us also, He holds out good hopes, and instructs us to have high views concerning the unspeakable mercy of God toward man.[76]

Thus sin is real but forgiveness is even more real. "Therefore manifold as thy weakness may be, thou mayest of right be confident, having such a one to reign over thee, who is able fully to accomplish all, and that with ease *even by thee*" (Italics added).[77]

Christians as forgiven sinners are called to be agents of God in the world, for he is willing to exercise his reign through such feeble instruments. Chrysostom insists that Christian ethics, in contradistinction to the contradictory and obscure teachings of pagan philosophers and gnostics, is basically simple and easy to comprehend: "For if it had not been so, how could the publican, and the fisherman, and the unlearned, have attained to such philosophy."[78] Consistent with the tradition of openness to all kinds of human beings, the learned Chrysostom—himself a student of the greatest pagan teachers—stresses the basic simplicity of the Christian faith. "Christ hath taught us what is just, and what is seemly, and what is expedient, and all virtue in general, comprising it in few and plain words: at one time saying that, 'on two commandments hang the Law and the prophets'; that is to say, on the love of God and on the love of our neighbor: at another time, 'Whatsoever ye would that men should do to you, do ye also to them; for this is the Law and the prophets.'"[79]

The anti-elitist thrust of this observation is clearly spelled out: "These things even to a laborer, and to a servant, and to a widow woman, and to a very child, and to him who appeareth to be exceedingly slow of understanding, are all plain to comprehend and easy to learn." [80] The teachers of Christian ethics "are publicans, and fishermen, and tentmakers, not such as have lived for a short time, but such as are now living forever." [81]

Against this background it is relatively easy to understand that Chrysostom, who saw himself as the successor of such "fishermen and tentmakers," was unimpressed by the absolute claims of the Byzantine emperor and had to come in conflict with a corrupt church and an arrogant empire. His ethical views were the basis for the confrontation. The conflict with the ecclesiastical institution came first. While still in Antioch he had written against young women living as housekeepers with priests.[82] As bishop of Constantinople he tried to enforce the decision of the Council of Nicaea, which had stated that no bishop, priest or any other cleric was allowed to keep such a housekeeper unless she was his mother, sister or aunt.[83]

He also attempted to cut back the expenditures of his own office. He stopped the completion of a new marble palace begun by his predecessor and sold the marble pillars [84] that had been purchased for that purpose and built hospitals instead "so that strangers coming to that city, and there falling ill, could obtain medical care." [85] While always encouraging almsgiving he tried to make sure that the generosity of the people would not be abused by the clergy. He said, "If any ruler of the church lives in abundance and wants nothing, though he be a saint, give not [to him], but prefer to him one that is in want, though he be not so admirable." [86] Such advice seemed to some as if he were subverting contributions to the ecclesiastical institution.

But his sharpest rebukes were directed against the rich. In an early series of sermons on Lazarus, he took the position that the rich and avaricious are a certain kind of robber. "They lie in wait and plunder the passersby and collect in their homes like in caves and hiding places the possessions of others." [87] But, he added, while they might escape earthly justice, the story of Lazarus and Dives demonstrates that they will not escape God's judgment.

He suggested instead that people safeguard their riches by giving them to the poor. In a sermon preached in Constantinople he said:

> Wealth is like a fugitive slave. To-day he is here, to-morrow there. It is a fugitive who not only is himself in flight but makes others into fugitives, especially those who try to be its guardians. How can you capture this fugitive? The only means are utterly different from those applied to other fugitives. If you try to keep this fugitive he will escape, if you send him away to the right or the left you will keep him. This may sound strange. But look what the farmers do. If they keep their wheat locked up and in a pile vermin and rats will come and everything is lost. But if they spread it to the right and to the left in the fields they not only keep their wheat but multiply it. It is the same with wealth. Keep it in boxes and locked up or bury it in the ground and it easily escapes. But if you, like the farmer his wheat, throw your wealth to the starving, it will not escape but bring fruit.[88]

The best way to maintain your wealth, he suggested, was to turn it over to widows, orphans, the sick, and prisoners. "If so many hands hold it, your wealth cannot escape. In such a place it is safe and brings fruit." [89]

Attacking the selfishness of the rich, he asserted:

> Don't be less reasonable than wild animals. Among them everything is held in common, the earth, springs, pastures, mountain woods, and no one has more than the other—but you, who are human beings, the mildest of all living things, act wilder than wild animals. You keep locked up that which could support the life of thousands of the poor and often you keep in one house the livelihood for many thousand poor people. And yet we humans not only have nature in common but many other things, the heavens, the sun and the moon, the multitude of stars, air and ocean, fire and water, the earth, life and death, youth and old age, disease and health, the need for food and clothing. And we have also in common the spiritual gifts, the Holy Supper, the body of the Lord, the precious blood, the promise of the kingdom, the bath of rebirth, the unspeakable gifts which "eye has not seen nor ear heard," neither have entered the heart of man (1 Cor. 2:9).[90]

In view of these physical and spiritual ties between all human beings it is absurd to be so obsessed by riches as to be unable to preserve our equality,[91] especially since riches are of so little practical importance. Indeed, Chrysostom observed, the rich need the poor far more than the poor need the rich:

> And that thou mayest see it more clearly, let us suppose, if it seem good, two cities, the one of rich only, but the other of poor; and neither

in that of the rich let there be any poor man, nor in that of the poor any rich; but let us purge out both thoroughly, and see which will be more able to support itself. For if we find that of the poor able, it is evident that the rich will more stand in need of them.

Now then, in that city of the affluent there will be no manufacturer, no builder, no carpenter, no shoe-maker, no baker, no husbandman, no brazier, no rope-maker, nor any such trade. For who among the rich would ever choose to follow these crafts, seeing that the very men who take them in hand, when they become rich, endure no longer the discomfort caused by these works? How then shall this our city stand? "The rich," it is replied, "giving money, will buy these things of the poor." Well then, they will not be sufficient for themselves, their needing the others proves that. But how will they build houses? Will they purchase this too? But the nature of things cannot admit this. Therefore they must needs invite the artificers thither, and destroy the law, which we made at first when we were founding the city. For you remember, that we said, "let there be no poor man within it." But, lo, necessity, even against our will, hath invited and brought them in. Whence it is evident that it is impossible without poor for a city to subsist: since if the city were to continue refusing to admit any of these, it will be no longer a city but will perish. Plainly then it will not support itself, unless it shall collect the poor as a kind of preservers, to be within itself.[92]

And then turning the argument around, he continued:

But let us look also upon the city of the poor, whether this too will be in a like needy condition, on being deprived of the rich. And first let us in our discourse thoroughly clear the nature of riches, and point them out plainly. What then may riches be? Gold, and silver, and precious stones, and garments silken, purple, and embroidered with gold. Now then that we have seen what riches are, let us drive them away from our city of the poor: and if we are to make it purely a city of poor persons, let not any gold appear there, no not in a dream, nor garments of such quality; and if you will, neither silver, nor vessels of silver. What then? Because of this will that city and its concerns live in want, tell me? Not at all.

For suppose first there should be need to build; one does not want gold and silver and pearls, but skill, and hands, and hands not of any kind, but such as are become callous, and fingers hardened, and great strength, and wood and stones: suppose again one would weave a garment, neither here have we need of gold and silver, but, as before, of hands and skill, and women to work. And what if one require husbandry, and digging the ground? Is it rich men who are wanted, or poor? It is evident to every one, poor. And when iron too is to be wrought, or any such thing to be done, this is the race of men whereof we most stand in need.

What respect then remains wherein we may stand in need of the rich? except the thing required be, to pull down this city. For should that sort of people make an entrance, and these philosophers (for I call them philosophers, who seek after nothing superfluous) should fall to desiring gold and jewels, giving themselves up to idleness and luxury; they will ruin everything from that day forward.[93]

As a matter of fact, the poor do not need the rich at all. In view of this analysis Robert von Pöhlmann seems justified in saying that "The criticism of the ruling class as found, e.g., in Lactantius, Basil, John Chrysostom, Ambrose, and Salvian and many others is in its severity and reckless boldness every bit as sharp as any Socialist critique." [94] Recalling the fellowship of the Jerusalem congregation, Chrysostom wrote:

> The fellowship was not only in prayers, nor in doctrine alone, but also in social relations. . . . This was an angelic commonwealth, not to call anything of theirs their own. Forthwith the root of all evils was cut out. . . . No talk of "mine" and "thine" then. Hence gladness waited at their table; no one seemed to eat of his own, or of another's . . . neither did they consider their brethren's property foreign to themselves; it was the property of a Master; nor again deemed they aught their own, all was the brethren's.[95]

Chrysostom was convinced that all private wealth is the result of wrongdoing. "So destructive a passion is avarice, that to grow rich without injustice is impossible." [96] He claimed that Jesus himself had suggested this by saying, "Make yourselves friends of the mammon of unrighteousness" (Luke 16:9).[97] And even should one obtain wealth by inheritance, one receives only what had originally been gathered by injustice. The reason he gives is the original equality of all human beings:

> Tell me, then, whence art thou rich? From whom didst thou receive it, and from whom he who transmitted it to thee? From his father and his grandfather. But canst thou, ascending through many generations, show the acquisition just? It can not be. *The root and origin of it must have been injustice. Why? Because God in the beginning made not one man rich, and another poor.* Nor did He afterwards take and show to one treasures of gold, and deny to the other the right of searching for it: but *he left the earth free to all alike.* Why then, if it is common, have you so many acres of land, while your neighbor has not a portion of it? It was transmitted to me by my father. And by whom to him? By his forefathers. But you must go back and find the original owner.[98] (Italics added).

To Chrysostom the desire for private property, if not *the* root of all evil, is certainly *a* root of all evil. God in his wisdom has given the human race many things to be held in common. He again mentions here the elements and the heavenly bodies "whose benefits are dispensed equally to all as brethren." [99] And he adds, "We are all formed with the same eyes, the same body, the same soul, the same structures in all respects." [100] We are all creatures of the earth, descendants of one ancestor living in the same world. But this does not seem to teach us the obvious lesson. Neither does the fact, observed by Chrysostom, that those things that we use in common as "baths, cities, marketplaces, walks" do not cause contention but are used peaceably.

But when one attempts to possess himself of anything, to make it his own, then contention is introduced, as if nature herself were indignant, that when God brings us together in every way, we are eager to divide and separate ourselves by appropriating things, and by using those cold words "mine and thine." Then there is contention and uneasiness. But where this is not, no strife or contention is bred. This state therefore is rather our inheritance, and agreeable to nature. Why is it, that there is never a dispute about a market-place? Is it not because it is common to all? But about a house, and about property, men are always disputing. Things necessary are set before us in common; but even in the least things we do not observe a community. Yet those greater things He hath opened freely to all, that we might thence be instructed to have these inferior things in common. Yet for all this, we are not instructed.[101]

His hope is that through the Christian proclamation the obsession with private possessions might cease. If people would distribute their wealth to the poor the original equality would be restored. As he had observed in regard to the communal life of the Christian fellowship in Jerusalem, "When riches were done away with, wickedness also disappeared." [102]

Thus he looks to the future with some optimism. "For by grace of God much forbearance, much virtue has been planted everywhere." [103] Great strides have been taken. Some people have voluntarily renounced their wealth. "For did not Paul leave here his tools, Peter his rod and hook, and Matthew his seat of custom? And was not the whole world opened to them more than to kings? Were not all things laid at their feet?" [104]

And he observed, "Do we not see many similar occurrences even now? Many men of poor and humble means, who did but handle the spade, and had hardly a sufficiency of necessary food, having but the character of monks have been celebrated above all men, and honored of kings." [105] "If thou wouldst be truly rich, become poor. For such are the paradoxes of God." [106]

Some have voluntarily chosen virginity. "Perceive how great is the power of Christ's coming? How He dissolved the curse [placed on woman, because of Eve]? For indeed there are more virgins than before among women, there is more modesty in those virgins, and there are more widows [women who remain single after their husband's death to serve through the church]." [107]

In spite of all obstacles Chrysostom's ethics is basically optimistic:

Let us show forth then a new kind of life. Let us make earth, heaven; let us hereby show the Greeks [pagans] of how great blessings they are deprived. For when they behold in us good conversation, they will look upon the very face of the kingdom of Heaven. Yea, when they see us as gentle, pure from wrath, from evil desire, from envy, from covetousness, rightly fulfilling all our other duties, they will say, "If the Christians are become angels here, what will they be after their departure hence? If where they are strangers they shine so bright, how great will they become when they shall have won their native land?" Thus they too will be re-formed, and the word of godliness "will have free course," not less than in the apostles' times.[108]

And again harking back to the apostolic church he continued:

For if they, being twelve, converted entire cities and countries; were we all to become teachers by our careful conduct, imagine how high our cause will be exalted. For not even a dead man raised so powerfully attracts the Greek, as a person practising self-denial. At that indeed he will be amazed, but by this he will be profited. That is done, and is passed away; but this abides, and is constant culture to his soul.[109]

Chrysostom did not consider this new life particularly difficult. It was a real option for everybody. And it should be demonstrated in the world and not by the pious escaping into the wilderness.

I say nothing burdensome. I say not, do not marry. I say not, forsake cities, and withdraw thyself from public affairs; but being engaged in them, show virtue. Yea, and such as are busy in the midst of cities, I would fain have more approved than such as having occupied the mountains. Wherefore? Because great is the profit thence arising. "For no man lighteth a candle, and setteth it under the bushel." Therefore I would that all the candles were set upon the candlestick, that the wax might wax great.

Let us kindle then His fire; let us cause them that are sitting in the darkness to be delivered from their error. And tell me not, "I have a wife, and children, belonging to me, and am master of a household, and cannot duly practise all this." For though thou hadst none of these, yet if thou be careless, all is lost; though thou art encompassed with all these, yet if thou be earnest, thou shalt attain unto virtue. For there is but one thing that is wanted, the preparation of a generous mind; and neither age, nor poverty, nor wealth, nor reverse of fortune, nor anything else, will be able to impede thee.

Since in fact both old and young, and men having wives, and bringing up children, and working at crafts, and serving as soldiers, have duly performed all that is enjoined. For so Daniel was young, and Joseph a slave, and Aquila wrought at a craft, and the woman who sold purple was over a workshop, and another a centurion, as Cornelius; and another in ill health, as Timothy; and another a runaway, as to any of these, but all were approved, both men and women, both young and old, both slaves and free, both soldiers and people.[110]

Far from preaching an elitist ethics for the few, Chrysostom's ethics was designed for all Christians and was to be practiced in the world by everybody in order to change the world according to God's purpose.

In the realization of this vision of Christian responsibility in the world, Chrysostom came into sharp conflict with the society as he found it and with its rulers in Constantinople. While he held fast to Paul's exhortation in Romans 13:1, "Let every soul be subject unto the higher powers," and commented, "It was not for the subversion of the commonwealth that Christ introduced His laws, but for the better ordering of it," he did not see this an endorsement of every individual ruler.[111] He observed: "He [Paul] does not say, 'For there is no ruler but of God,' but it is the thing he speaks of, and says, 'there is no power but of God.'" Thus, Paul's statement is an endorsement of order and opposes anarchy wherever it may appear.[112] Chrysostom is convinced that if you were to remove the "authority," all things would go to ruin, and "neither city, nor country, nor private nor public buildings, nor anything else would stand . . . while the more powerful devour the weaker."[113]

Government exists for our benefit. "It was for this that from of old all men came to an agreement that governors should be maintained by us, because to the neglect of their own affairs, they take charge of the public and on this they spend their whole leisure, whereby our goods are kept safe." [114] "For it is in no small degree that they contribute to the settled state of the present life, by keeping guard, beating of enemies, hindering those who are for sedition in the cities, putting an end to differences among any." [115]

In view of his "social contract" notion of government as expressed in the phrase, "from of old all men came to an agreement that governors should be maintained," it is easy to understand why Chrysostom clashed with the arbitrary rule of the powerful like the imperial chamberlain Eutropius who had been instrumental in his election, and later with the emperor himself. For him the ultimate ruler was God.

Chrysostom has been described as a fanatic ascetic, whose rigorous ethics did not contribute to the welfare of the church or the empire.[116] This evaluation needs correction. Far from advocating some extreme rigorism he understood and practiced a Christian life which, with the help of God, might change the world. His ethics was based on the notion of human freedom, retained by the race even after the fall. Aided by God's grace, human beings could and should use their freedom to obey God's law, for faith without works was a dangerous illusion. The law itself was accessible to all people by means of conscience and reason. It was "natural law," plausible even to those who disobeyed it, since it obviously supported human life and community. Thus the consensus among educated pagans and Christians was not surprising. But Christ had reduced the bewildering complexity and contradictions of pagan moral teachers to few and plain words. It was now possible for everybody to live the moral life. In fact, since wealth was seen as a main barrier to Christian obedience, the poor and those who had voluntarily divested themselves of their possessions were more likely to follow Christ.

Such discipleship is achievable and may indeed transform the world. In order to accomplish this goal all Christians must be enlisted in the task. The priest is more important than the monk because he carries on amid the crowd and is compelled to tolerate the errors and sins of the multitude. But in such a position he may contribute to the transformation of the world according to God's purpose. Chrysostom became a bishop because he believed that this would place him in a better position to enlist the multitudes, "men and women, young and old, slaves and free, soldiers and people" in this task. He was certain that Christians were not called to escape the world; they were challenged to change it. Even though the ultimate hope for the human race was heaven, Chrysostom was convinced that the transformation of this earth into the vestibule of heaven was the task of Christian ethics. For this goal church and empire, priests, monks and laity were called by God to cooperate.

# Augustine

**1. *Ethics and Experience***

UGUSTINE [1] WAS BORN ON NOVEMBER 13, 354, the same year as John Chrysostom, not in a major cultural center like Antioch but in Thagaste, a rural town in Numidia (the modern Souk Ahras in Algeria). About 78 kilometers from the port of Hippo and the Mediterranean the town was located in a hilly area inhabited mostly by small landlords and peasants.[2] While Chrysostom came from a well-to-do family and had been taught by Libanius, a man who earlier had instructed a future Roman emperor, Augustine's parents were people of modest means belonging to a "dour and petty gentry"[3] who had to make considerable personal sacrifices in order to finance their son's education.[4] He had to interrupt it temporarily when the funds available to the family gave out.[5] Augustine himself observed that the education he had received, "was more a matter of my father's ambition than of his means, for he was only a poor citizen of Thagaste."[6]

While his father, whose name was Patricius, was a pagan and became a Christian only at the very end of his life,[7] Augustine's mother Monica, certainly the most influential person in his life, was a convinced and persuasive Christian. She saw to it that the boy was inscribed as a catechumen in his youth[8] and was brought up a Christian.[9] After attending the school in Thagaste where he claimed to have been an indifferent student who hated (and by the way never mastered) Greek but loved Latin literature,[10] he was sent to Madaura, a small university town. Here his teachers were pagans who cherished the classics and he received a sound education, or as he later described it: "Here words may be learned; here you can attain the eloquence which is so necessary to persuade people to your way of thinking; so helpful in unfolding your opinion." [11]

At 17 years of age he went on to Carthage, the major cultural center in Roman North Africa, indeed "the second city in the Western Empire " [12] where he continued his studies, attended the theater and became a "master in the school of rhetoric." [13] Here he also underwent his first conversion experience. It happened as he read the now lost essay of Cicero called *Hortensius.* While this was a pre-Christian book Augustine claimed later that its reading had changed his life and led him for the first time to a serious study of the Bible.[14] But this confrontation with the Bible proved of dubious benefit for the young scholar. Steeped in the classics he was initially repelled by the biblical writings, which seemed inferior in style and content to the literature he loved. Indeed, this first "conversion" brought about no great change in his way of life. He remained an ambitious young teacher dedicated to a successful career.

At this time also he started living with a woman whom he never intended to marry, since she did not fit into his career plans and whose name he never mentioned. We know practically nothing about her except that Augustine lived with her for the next 15 years. To this "unblessed" union, quite common at the time among people of his class a son was born who was named Adeodatus ("given by God"),[15] who stayed with his father even after Augustine's relationship with his mother was terminated.[16] Adeodatus, apparently a brilliant youth, died at an early age after he and his father had returned to Africa.

But while still in Africa Augustine taught rhetoric, first in Thagaste and later at Carthage, and came under the influence of Manichaeism. It was the above-mentioned first conversion which made him ask the philosophical questions to which he found at that time no satisfactory answers in the Scriptures. As he later remembered it, he joined the Manichaeans "because they used to say, that, apart from all terror of authority, by pure and simple reason, they would lead within to God, and set free from all error those who were willing to be their hearers." [17] And he added, "For what else constrained me, during nearly nine years, spurning the religion which had been set in me from a child by my parents, to be a follower and diligent hearer of those men, save that they said that we are alarmed by superstition, and are commanded to have faith before reason. But they urge no one to have faith, without having first discussed and made clear the truth." [18]

The legalism and dogmatism of African Christianity exemplified by Donatism, the dominant church in Numidia in Augustine's time, would make the apparent open-mindedness of the Manichaeans seem particularly attractive to a young student of philosophy. This stubbornness of the prevailing Donatist version of Christianity in North Africa Augustine remembered later when he quoted them as insisting "As I lived yesterday, so shall I live to-day, what my parents were before me that I am also." [19] Such abject loyalty to "the old-time religion" repelled him and against this background Augustine's infatuation with Manichaeism becomes understandable. As he later observed: "Who would not be enticed by such promises, especially the mind of a young man desirous of the truth . . . disdainful . . . of old wives' fables, and desirous to grasp and drink in, what they promised, the open and pure truth?" [20]

While he never became a full-fledged member of the Manichaeans, but remained what they termed a "hearer," it was the association with this particular illegal and secret religious society that shaped his life for the next nine years. Eventually disillusioned with Manichaeism he decided in 383 to go to Rome for richer fees, higher dignity, better students, and without his mother, Monica.[21]

By then he had developed his own eclectic philosophical stance utilizing Stoicism, Pythagoreanism and Ciceronian skepticism. When Rome proved to be a disappointment he did not hesitate to use his Manichaean connection to obtain an appointment as professor of rhetoric in Milan, at the time the seat of the rulers of the Western Empire. It is likely that Augustine received his position not only because of his rhetorical skill but also because he was perceived by Symmachus, a pagan, a senator, and at the time the prefect of the city of Rome, as an ally against Catholic orthodoxy because of his Manichaean leanings.[22]

In Milan he met Ambrose, who was instrumental in his final conversion to Christianity. In him he found the model his biological father had never been. As he observed later:

> To him [Ambrose] I was led by Thee without my knowledge, that by him I might be led to Thee in full knowledge. That man of God received me as a father would and welcomed my coming as a good bishop should. And I began to love him, of course, not at first as a teacher of the truth, for I had entirely despaired of finding that in Thy Church—but as a friendly man.[23]

He admired Ambrose's eloquence and listened to him regularly in order to learn the secrets of his rhetorical effectiveness.

But while at first concerned only with the form of Ambrose's presentation he gradually became fascinated by the content as well.[24] It was particularly the brilliant use of the allegorical method in regard to the Old Testament, something new in the West at that time,[25] that enabled Augustine to take this part of the Bible seriously. He decided to abandon Manichaeism and became again a catechumen in the Catholic church. He was helped in this decision by his growing confidence that the Ciceronic skepticism of the so-called "New Academy" undercut the absolute claims of the Manichaeans. Thus it was a combination of the influence of the intellectual respectability of Ambrose and the equally intellectual respectability of the "New Academy" and its relativizing attack against Manichaean claims to absolute certainty that dethroned the authority of the Manichaeans for Augustine.[26]

But something else occurred in those years which, while not equally well documented in the *Confessions,* seems to have been of great importance for Augustine's later ethical position and his attitude toward church and empire. He became witness to a major conflict between Ambrose and the emperor, i.e. church and state, that occurred during his years in Milan. When Augustine arrived in Milan in 384, the emperor was 13 years old and Ambrose was a leading personality in the privy council of the Milan court. Indeed he almost seemed to play the role of a chancellor or clerical minister of state.[27]

When at this seemingly propitious moment the representatives of the old pagan religion led by Symmachus asked for the restoration of the privileges they had lost under Emperor Gratian, the older brother of Valentinian II, Ambrose led the opposition to this appeal.[28]

Symmachus had requested "the restoration of that condition of religious affairs which was so long advantageous to the state."[29] And he insisted that Rome could say: "This worship [the old Roman religion] subdued the world to my laws, these sacred rites repelled Hannibal from the walls and the Senones from the Capitol."[30]

Again the claim was made that the military success of the Roman legions in the past was attributable to the faithfulness of Rome to the rites of the old religion, and that Christianity was undermining the glory that was Rome. The way in which Ambrose replied was to develop a most interesting and unconventional philosophy of history. Discussing the claim that worship of pagan gods had given victory to Rome over Hannibal, Ambrose made the personified Rome assert: "Hannibal also worshipped the same gods," and then proceeded as follows: "Trophies of victory depend not on the entrails of the flocks [the pagan sacrifices], but on the strength of those who fight."[31] And giving here a most pragmatic explanation of the great Roman victories, Ambrose quoted Rome as saying, "I subdued the world by a different discipline than pagan religion. Camillus was my soldier who slew those who had taken the Tarpeian rock, and brought back the standards taken from the Capitol; valour laid those low whom religion had not driven off."[32] Ambrose rejected the claim that the adoption of Christianity had decreased the military fortunes of the Roman Empire and set the recent military reverses of the Roman legions into perspective by observing: "It is perchance a new thing for the barbarians to cross their boundaries?"[33]

Under pagan às well as Christian rulers some military conflicts had been won, others lost. Such successes or failures cannot supply the basis for making decisions about ultimate questions: "Come and learn on earth the heavenly warfare; we live here, but our warfare is there."[34]

Unlike the conventional Christian apologetics, which attributed the prosperity and the victories of recent emperors to their positive attitude toward orthodox Christianity, Ambrose suggested a different approach.[35] He attributed military victory to stronger legions and to the valour of soldiers rather than to right religion or worship, a point of view radically different from the earlier position symbolized by Emperor Constantine and his Christian apologists who had always associated military success with the acceptance of the true God.[36] The presentation of this new interpretation of history by Ambrose occurred while Augustine was in Milan and could not fail to influence the latter. For in those years Augustine had become increasingly fascinated by Ambrose.

Monica was now allowed to join him again and finally succeeded in getting her son to dismiss his mistress, who returned to Africa. He kept Adeodatus in Milan. With the support of his mother he "wooed" and was engaged to a girl "as yet some two years too young to marry," [37] which promptly caused him to take another mistress.[38] Thus it was a time of great turmoil affecting not only his personal life but his professional life as well. He tells us, "How wretched I was at that time," explaining that once when preparing to recite a panegyric of the emperor in which "I was to deliver many a lie, and the lying was to be applauded by those who knew I was lying. My heart was agitated with this sense of guilt and it seethed with the fever of my uneasiness." [39] He then decided to take a walk and while walking along one of the streets of Milan, "I saw a poor beggar—with what I believe was a full belly—joking and hilarious." [40]

At this moment Augustine realized that this beggar was obviously happier than the famous professor of rhetoric, "for what he had obtained through a few coins, got by his begging, I was still scheming for by many a wretched and tortuous turning—namely the joy of a passing felicity." [41] While in such inner turmoil he came under the influence of "certain books of the platonists" in Latin translation, (actually treatises of Plotinus, the Neoplatonist) which affected him profoundly—and he became a Christian Neoplatonist, a matter of considerable importance for his later articulation of Christian ethics.

This philosophical "pre-conversion" to Neoplatonism prepared the way for his subsequent conversion to Christianity. While it did not change his life, it changed his mind and removed some of the intellectual obstacles that had stood in his way. A little later he experienced his famous conversion to the Christian faith which occurred with the help of a verse from St. Paul's Letter to the Romans. Soon afterwards he resigned his professorship and, following a period of preparation, was baptized in 387 together with his son Adeodatus and his longtime friend Alypius.[42]

Shortly thereafter Augustine returned to North Africa—but without Monica who had died on the homeward journey—and in 388 arrived in Thagaste. He sold his property, gave the money to the poor and began to live with his son (who died shortly afterward) and other friends as a monk. A few years later, while visiting nearby Hippo, he was ordained a priest (391) and, against his expressed wishes, was ordered to move to Hippo. In 395 the old bishop who had recently ordained him obtained special permission from the metropolitan in Carthage to consecrate Augustine as his associate bishop, a position which after the subsequent death of the older man he filled alone for about 35 years. He never again left Africa although he travelled widely, frequently, and for extended periods of time.

He served his diocese as a pastor of pastors and the church at large through his voluminous writings in which he upheld the catholic faith against the great heresies of the day, Manichaeism, Donatism, Pelagianism, and in the last years of his life, Arianism. This predominantly Eastern heresy arrived in Africa in 427 with Gothic soldiers who brought along their own bishop. Augustine died in 430 at the age of 76 while the Vandals were besieging Hippo. His long life had been lived at the political and cultural centers of the Western Empire. He had met and engaged the major political and intellectual movements of his age.

## 2. The Influence of Ambrose and the Philosophical Tradition

"Ever since Tertullian's era, it was the African church which had, more than any other, concerned itself with the practical problems of the day: Church discipline, church unity and the variety of the sacraments were discussed, fought over and finally settled."[43] Small wonder that Augustine, the most important African, if not Christian, theologian made profound and lasting contributions to Christian ethics.

As indicated earlier in this chapter, one of the most significant theological influences on Augustine had come from Ambrose, who had articulated his ethics in numerous sermons and dogmatic treatises, especially in *On the Duties of the Clergy*.[44] In this treatise the profound influence of Stoic philosophy and the emphasis on the cardinal virtues mediated through Cicero,[45] is apparent, although Ambrose makes the conventional claim that the Stoics had derived much of their valid insights from the sacred writings of the Christians.[46]

Ambrose placed a great deal of emphasis on the importance of good works, especially virginity (on which he wrote profusely), justice towards enemies, depreciation of property and wealth, and the condemnation of usury. He insisted also that some of the ethical questions raised by the philosophers simply did not apply to Christians. Cicero had popularized the ethical tradition of the Greek philosophers and summarized their value system by submitting his version of the hoary "lifeboat" ethics: "Suppose there were two to be rescued from a sinking ship—both of them wise men—and only one small plank, should both seize it to save themselves? Or should one give place to the other?" He had answered, "Why, of course, one should give place to the other, but the other must be one whose life is more valuable either for his own sake or for that of his country." [47]

The influence of the New Testament is apparent in Ambrose's comment on Cicero's ethics:

> Some ask whether a wise man ought in case of a shipwreck to take away a plank from an ignorant sailor? Although it seems better for the common good that a wise man rather than a fool should escape from shipwreck, yet I do not think that a Christian, a just and a wise man, ought to save his own life by the death of another; just as when he meets with an armed robber he cannot return his blows, lest in defending his life he should stain his love toward his neighbor. The verdict on this is plain and clear in the books of the Gospel. "Put up thy sword, for every one that taketh the sword shall perish with the sword." What robber is more hateful than the persecutor who came to kill Christ? But Christ

would not be defended from the wounds of the persecutor, for He willed to heal all by His wounds.[48]

This combination of Christian ideas drawn from the New Testament as well as from the prudential and natural-law ethics of the philosophers, that characterized so much of the Christian ethics of the time, was clearly expressed in the following observation of Ambrose:

> Why dost thou consider thyself greater than another, when a Christian man ought to put others before himself, to claim nothing for himself, usurp no honours, claim no reward for his merits? Why, next, art thou not wont to bear thy own troubles rather than to destroy another's advantage? For what is so contrary to nature as not to be content with what one has or to seek what is another's, and to try to get it in shameful ways. For if a virtuous life is in accordance with nature—for God made all things very good—then shameful living must be opposed to it. A virtuous and a shameful life cannot go together, since they are absolutely severed by the law of nature.[49]

It was a Christianized version of Ciceronian ethics that furnished the basis for Augustine's ethics. The emphasis on God's grace, so dominant in Augustine's teaching, was present already in Ambrose: "I dare say," he wrote, "that a human being cannot walk upright if he does not have God as his precursor." [50] "That person is most perfect who understood that it is impossible to walk without God." [51]

And, though an advocate of the importance of free will,[52] his emphasis was on the work of Christ: "I shall not glory because I am just but because I am saved, not because I am free from sins but because my sins are forgiven." [53]

## 3. *Ethics and Free Will*

When Augustine began to develop his own ethical system he could follow the direction in which his teacher Ambrose had pointed him.[54] Indeed, at first his emphasis on free will was if anything even more pronounced than Ambrose's. He himself remembered in his *Retractions* I, 9, that while on his way back to Africa and delayed in Rome he had begun to write three volumes *On Free Will*.[55] At that time he was still arguing primarily with Manichaeans— who had taught "an evil nature, unchangeable and co-eternal with

God." [56] As a result he stressed that the origin of evil is found in the free will of the rational creation, and

No one is compelled to sin either by his own nature or by another, it remains that he sins by his own will. If you want to attribute his sin to the Creator you will make the sinner guiltless because he has simply obeyed the laws of the Creator. If the sinner can be rightly defended he is not a sinner, and there is no sin to attribute to the Creator. Let us then praise the Creator whether or not the sinner can be defended. If he is justly defended he is no sinner and we can therefore praise the Creator. If he cannot be defended, he is a sinner so far as he turns away from the Creator. Therefore praise the Creator. I find, therefore, no way at all, and I assert that there is none to be found, by which our sins can be ascribed to the Creator, our God. I find that he is to be praised even for sins, not only because he punishes them, but also because sin arises only when a man departs from his truth. [57]

In writing, "No one commits sin in doing what there was no means of avoiding," [58] he had taken a position which Pelagius later was able to quote against him. Yet in his Anti-Pelagian writings he argued in a manner which left no doubt as to the centrality of grace in his ethics. In the law God shows us what evil we should shun and what good we should do. But he insisted that this is "all that the letter of the law is able to effect." [59] Actually to shun evil and to do good is impossible "without the Spirit of grace." He plainly stated, "If this be wanting, the law comes in merely to make us guilty and to slay us." [60] The law teaches us the difference between evil and good—but grace alone enables us to shun evil and to do good. And the very process of turning toward grace is itself the work of grace. "To desire the help of grace is the beginning of grace." [61] He continued: "It is to be confessed, therefore, that we have free choice to do both evil and good; but in doing evil everyone is free from righteousness and a servant of sin, while in doing good no one can be free, unless he has been made free by Him who said, 'If the Son shall make you free, then you shall be free indeed.'" [62]

Only through the grace of God are human beings delivered from evil. Without it they do absolutely no good thing, whether in thought or will and affection or action. [63] To the obvious question of why anybody preaches that we should turn away from evil and do good, since it is not our doing at all but God who works in us, Augustine replied that such moral exhortation is ethically useful because by this means God may make "out of evil people who are rebuked, good people who may be praised." [64] He did not for a moment stray from the position that even the improvement resulting from moral preaching and rebuke is the work of the gracious God.

The present predicament of the human race is radically different from the original situation of Adam. Adam was created that he might first of all show what free will was capable of, and then what the kindness of God's grace and the judgment of God's righteousness could accomplish. [65] Augustine made the following distinctions between the moral potential of Adam and of all his descendants: "The first man was able not to sin, was able not to die, was able not to forsake good. . . . Therefore the first liberty of the will was to be able not to sin." [66] Through the fall, the human situation has fundamentally changed. Human beings after the fall who are not regenerate "are most righteously judged according to their deservings. For either they lie under the sin which they have inherited by original generation, and depart hence with that inherent debt which is not put away by regeneration, or by their free will have added other sins besides; their will, I say, *free* but not *freed*—free from righteousness but enslaved to sin." [67]

On the other hand those who are elected and predestined by God are in a far better position than Adam ever was. Unlike Adam they are not able to sin. And, he continued, while "the first immortality was to be able not to die, the last will be much greater, not to be able to die." [68] The problem of ethics, as Augustine saw it, was that human beings have a "free" but not a "freed" will. "There is always within us a free will,—but it is not always good; for it is either free from righteousness when it serves sin,—and then it is evil, —or else it is free from sin when it serves righteousness—and then it is good. But the grace of God is always good; and *by it* it comes to pass that a man is of a good will, though he was before an evil one." [69]

Thus for Augustine the ethical question was ultimately reduced to a theological question. "Whosoever, then, are made to differ from that original condemnation by such bounty of divine grace, there is no doubt but that for such it is provided that they should hear the gospel, and when they hear they believe, and in the faith which worketh by love they persevere unto the end." [70] The possibility of Christian ethics is the gift of God. For the faith which makes love possible, and which is active in love, "is in its beginning as in its completion God's gift." [71]

## 4. *Ethics and "Love"*

Granted the assumption that the Christian life is possible only because of God's grace which undergirded Augustine's ethics, how did he elaborate the practical consequences of this faith? In his comparison of Christian ethics with Manichaean ethics [72] he stated his position as follows:

> In treating of human life and morality, I do not think it necessary to inquire further than this concerning the supreme good to which all else must be referred. We have shown both by reason, to the extent this is possible, and by divine authority which goes beyond reason, that the supreme good is nothing other than God Himself. For what can be a greater good for man than the possession of that in which he finds perfect happiness? And this good is God alone to whom we can adhere only by affection *[dilectio]*, love *[amor]*, and charity *[caritas]*.
>
> If virtue leads us to the happy life, then I would not define virtue in any other way than as the perfect love *[amor]* of God.[73]

Around this understanding of virtue as the perfect love of God Augustine built his individual and social ethics. Love understood as an act of the will is the motive of the moral life. Whether this life is morally good or evil, it is always driven by love.

As indicated above the difference between good and evil depends entirely on the object of this love. He argued that human beings customarily tend to derive their ethics from the prevailing customs in their country, and he observed, "that a man will think nothing blameable except what the men of his own country and time are accustomed to condemn, and nothing worthy of praise or approval except what is sanctioned by the customs of his companions." [74] In contrast Augustine noted, "Scripture enjoins nothing except charity *(caritas)*, and condemns nothing except desire *(cupiditas)*

and in that way fashions the lives of men." [75] He defined these two
kinds of "love" as follows: "I mean by charity that affection of the
mind which aims at the enjoyment *[frui]* of God for His own sake
and then enjoyment of one's self and the neighbor for God's sake.
By desire I mean that affection of mind which aims at enjoying
*[frui]* one's self and one's neighbor, and other corporal things, without reference to God." [76] And he further distinguished, "What desire, when unsubdued, does towards one's own soul and body, is
called *vice* but what it does to injure another is called *crime*. And
these are the two classes into which all sins may be divided." [77]
Similarly he distinguished between what charity does with a view
to one's own advantage, calling it prudence *(utilitas)*;[78] and what
it does with a view to a neighbor's advantage is called benevolence
*(beneficentia)*.[79]

The centrality of love in ethics is further illustrated by the fact
that "when we ask whether someone is a good man, we are not
asking what he believes, or hopes, but what he loves." To Augustine
the alternatives are clear and mutually exclusive, "The desire of the
flesh *(carnalis cupiditas)* reigns where the charity of God *(dei caritas)* does not." [80] Commenting on 1 Timothy 6:10, he observed,
"When the Apostle Paul says that desire *(cupiditas)* is the 'root of
all evils,' he intimates to us, of course, that charity *(caritas)* may
be regarded as the root of all good things." [81]

It is noteworthy, however, that Augustine recognized the problem
of terminology as it confronted him in the Latin version of the Bible
on which he depended and that, for example, *amor* (love) and
*dilectio* (love) are indiscriminately used in Holy Scripture with
reference to both good and evil.[82] And he rejected the opinion which
he attributes to "some people" that *dilectio* (love) and *caritas* (love)
is something different from *amor* (love). While the terms themselves do not disclose the quality of the "love" the character of the
will *(voluntas)* makes the difference.

A right will is good love and a wrong will is bad love. Hence the love
that is bent on obtaining the object of its love is desire *(cupiditas)*, while
the love that possesses and enjoys its object is joy *(laetitia)*; the love that
avoids what confronts it is fear *(timor)*, and the love that feels it when it
strikes is grief *(tristitia)*. Accordingly, these emotions are bad if the love
*(amor)* is bad, and good if it is good." [83]

Augustine pointed out that even desire *(concupiscentia)* can be good and supported his claim with reference to many passages in his Latin Bible.[84] He admitted that if the Latin terms for desire, *cupiditas* and *concupiscentia*, are used without any specification of the object desired, they can be taken only in a bad sense. But he was convinced that love *(dilectio)* cannot be inactive.

What else but love *(amor)* makes a human being do evil? Show me an inactive love *(amor)* which does nothing. Vices *(flagitia)*, murders, every kind of excess *(luxuria)*, are they not the result of love *(amor)*. Purge your love, divert the water that flows into the sewer into the garden. The passion for the world turns toward the creator of the world. Am I saying to you—don't love anything? Of course not. You would be dull, dead, detestable and miserable if you loved nothing. Love, but watch what you love.[85]

The love of God and of the neighbor is charity, the love of the world and of this age is desire. But for Augustine there was no doubt about the source of this charity: "Whence, therefore, arises this love *(dilectio)*, that is to say, this charity *(caritas)* by which faith works, if not from the source whence faith itself obtained it. For it would not be within us, to what extent it is in us, if it were not diffused in our hearts by the Holy Ghost who is given to us." [86] But once the source of love is clearly perceived Augustine's ethics centered completely in this love. The cardinal virtues were subsumed under love. Virtue consists in nothing else but in loving what is worthy of love; it is prudence *(prudentia)* to choose this, fortitude *(fortitudo)* to be turned from it by no obstacles, temperance *(temperantia)* to be enticed by no allurements, justice *(justitia)* to be diverted by no pride.[87] And a little later he continued:

By means of these virtues which have been divinely imparted to us by the grace of the Man Jesus Christ, the mediator of God between the Father and us, through whom we are reconciled to God in the spirit of charity *(in spiritu caritatis)* after the hostility of our sin, by means of these virtues, I repeat, which are divinely imparted to us, we now live the good life, and afterward receive its reward, the life of happiness, which must necessarily be eternal. In this life those virtues are seen in action in the next in their effect; here they are at work, there they are our reward; here their function there their final end.[88]

This emphasis on an ethics of love whose value is entirely determined by the objects of love makes it impossible to judge human actions by their outward appearance. The motive is all-important.

What a human being does is not the thing to be considered; but with what mind and will he does it. We find God the Father in the same deed in which we find Judas; both delivering up *(traditio)* the son; the Father we bless, Judas we detest. Why do we bless the Father and detest Judas? We bless charity, detest iniquity. How great a good was conferred upon mankind by the delivering up of Christ! Had Judas that in his thought when he delivered Him up? God had in his thoughts our salvation by which we were redeemed; Judas had in his thoughts the price for which he sold the Lord . . . *the diverse intention therefore makes the things done diverse.* Though the thing be one, yet if we measure it by the diverse intentions, we find the one a thing to be loved, the other to be condemned; the one we find a thing to be glorified, the other to be detested. Such is the force of charity. See that it alone discriminates, it alone distinguishes the deeds of human beings.[89]

But this principle of discrimination applies not only where the deeds done are similar. It applies also where they are patently different. Augustine observed that a person can be made fierce by charity and charming by iniquity. A father may whip a boy, a homosexual pimp may gently caress him. Caresses seem on the surface more "loving" than blows but the ethical significance of human actions can only be discerned by the root of charity *(radix caritatis).* In this context, while explaining 1 John 4:4-12, Augustine makes the frequently quoted recommendation: "Love and do what you will" *(dilige, et quo vis fac).* It is the love described and experienced as coming from God and being passed on by men and women which for Augustine is the root of Christian ethics. He summarized the importance of love for ethics at the end of his *Enchiridion* by saying:

All the commandments of God, then, are embraced in charity, of which the apostle says: "Now the end of the commandment is charity, out of a pure heart, and of a good conscience, and of faith unfeigned" (1 Tim. 1:5). Thus the end *(finis)* of every commandment is charity, that is, every commandment relates to charity. But whatever is done either through fear of punishment or from some other carnal motive, and does not relate to that charity "which the Holy Spirit sheds abroad in our hearts" (Rom. 5:5)—however it may appear outwardly it is not yet done as it should be done. In this context, charity, of course, includes both God and the neighbor and indeed "on these two commandments hang all the Law and the Prophets" (Matt. 22:40)—and we may add the Gospel and the Apostles, for it is from these that we hear this voice, "The end of the commandment is charity" (1 Tim. 1:5) and "God is charity" (1 John 4:16).[90]

## 5. *The World as Temptation and Christian Challenge*

Granted the pivotal significance of charity/love for Augustine's ethics, how did he describe the shape of the Christian life? It is a pilgrimage. Men and women are wanderers in a strange country unable to live happily away from their fatherland. They want to return home. In order to do so they must make use of some conveyance. But as they travel, the beauty of the country through which they pass and even the means of transportation they use on their journey begin to delight them, "And," he added, "turning these things we ought to use *(uti)* into objects of enjoyment *(frui)* we become unwilling to hasten the end of our journey and becoming engrossed in a perverse delight we are estranged from that fatherland whose delights would make us truly happy." [91]

To reach our final destination we must learn to *use* the world not to *enjoy* it. Significantly, Augustine did not advocate the absolute rejection of the world but its proper use. If one is aware of the ultimate purpose of the created universe, the final destination of the human journey in God's plan, one may indeed use all things for the sake of the goal. "For the human being is never in so good a state as when his whole life is a journey toward the unchangeable life, and his affections are entirely fixed upon that." [92] On this journey "right reason" is the guide available to humans. It is the same as virtue [93] as it applies to religion obtainable only from God through faith.[94] Human beings are to use the material world "as one would use a plank in a flood which one does not discard but which one does not fully trust either." [95]

It is precisely Augustine's appreciation of the wonders of human culture which made him fear the temptations of the journey more than somebody less sensitive to his environment might. Describing the cultural achievements of human beings as made possible by the specifically human soul, given to the race by God, he extolled memory as a recorder of numberless facts. He listed agriculture, the art of the craftsman, the ability to build cities, the various marvels of construction. He talked about symbol systems using letters, words, gestures, sounds, painting, and carvings. He mentioned the languages of all peoples, their practices and institutions both old and new, their books and other monuments to preserve the past.[96] He saw the various kinds of duties, powers, and honors in the different areas of human life, family and state, peace and war, civil and ecclesiastical administration as the cultural products of the human soul. So are the ability to reason and think, eloquence, poetry, the thousand forms of play and humor, music, measurements, the study of numerical relations and speculation about the past and the future from the present. And he added, "This is all impressive and altogether human." [97]

Not only in his early writings did Augustine wax eloquent in the description of human cultural achievements, but much later in his life in the *Homilies on the Gospel of John* he wrote:

Direct now thy consideration to the soul of man, on which God has bestowed understanding to know its Creator, to discern and distinguish between good and evil, that is, between right and wrong: see how many things it does through the body! Observe this whole world arranged in the same human commonwealth, with what administration, with what orderly degrees of authority, with what conditions of citizenship, with what laws, manners, arts! The whole of this is brought about by the soul.[98]

With such achievements available it is easy to become engrossed in this beautiful world and dawdle on the pilgrimage. But if one analyzes the human situation, men and women on their journey through time, it becomes apparent that:

Notwithstanding the many great nations that live throughout the world with different religious and moral practices, distinguished by a rich variety of languages, arms and dress, nevertheless there have arisen no more than two classes, as it were, of human society. Following our Scriptures, we may well speak of them as two cities. For there is one city of men who choose to live carnally, and another of those who choose to live spiritually, each aiming at its own kind of peace, and when they achieve their respective purposes, they live such lives, each in its own kind of peace.[99]

Augustine insisted that those who live "carnally" are not merely philosophers, like the Epicureans, who have placed the highest good (*summum bonum*) in bodily pleasure, or ordinary hedonists who in their quest for pleasure do not even reflect about their ultimate destiny. Aware that Scripture does not use the term "flesh" only of the body but subsumes under the works of the flesh all kinds of activities of the mind, he observed, "In the case of idolatry, sorcery, enmity, strife, jealousy, anger, dissension, party spirit and envy, surely no one doubts that we have here defects of the mind rather than of the body." [100] Indeed it is quite possible that a person may seem to check and curb what are commonly considered carnal desires quite effectively because he worships false gods. Augustine stated plainly, "that the cause of sin proceeded from the soul not from the flesh," [101] for "the head and source of all the evils is pride." [102]

The problem of the human race is not the existence of a beautiful world but its own evil will which results in the wrong attitude toward creation and which has no efficient cause outside itself. "An evil will is the efficient cause of an evil deed, but nothing is the efficient cause of an evil will." [103] Avarice, Augustine observed, is not a defect of gold but a defect of the person who misguidedly loves gold and thus deserts righteousness, which should have been immeasurably preferred to gold.[104]

And he asserted the same about lust *(luxuria)* which is not a vice of beautiful and delightful bodies but rather a defect of the soul that discards the virtue of moderation. And he concluded: "Nor finally is pride a defect of Him who gives power or even power itself but a defect of the soul that misguidedly loves its own power while it despises the more righteous power of a higher Power." [105]

This selfish love of power is not the result of the existence of power any more than avarice is the result of the existence of gold. For Augustine it was not power that corrupts, but the "appetite of the soul to have other souls in subjection." [106]

Human beings may, indeed, subject animals, for this the divine law permits, but not rational souls, that is neighbors, companions and partners under the same law.[107]

## 6. Ethics and Community

Because of the centrality of pride *(superbia)* as a perverse love of power in Augustine's understanding of the human predicament and the isolating effect of such pride, it is not surprising that the problems of ethics are not solved individualistically but through participation or incorporation in the community, the city of those who live spiritually. This community transcends time and space and includes the holy angels, "For with them we form one city of God, the city of whom it is said in the Psalm: 'Glorious things are spoken of thee, O City of God'" (Psalm 87:3).[108] Those who belong to the part of the heavenly city that lives in the midst of the earthly city are constantly supported by that part which consists of those who have already achieved their goal, "that city on high where God's will, intelligible and immutable, is the law."[109]

When describing the two cities and the contrast between the city of God and the other city which opposes it in this world, he said:

> The two cities then were created by two kinds of love: the earthly city by a love of self carried even to the point of contempt for God, the heavenly city by love of God carried even to the point of contempt for self. Consequently, the earthly city glories in itself while the other glories in the Lord. For the former seeks glory from men, but the latter finds its greatest glory in God, the witness of our conscience. The earthly city lifts up its head in its own glory; the heavenly city says to its God: "My glory and the lifter of my head." In the one, the lust *(libido)* for dominion has dominion over its princes as well as over the nations that it subdues; in the other, both those put in charge and those placed under them serve one another in love *(caritas)*, the former by their counsel, the latter by their obedience. The earthly city loves its own strength *(virtus)*, as revealed in its men of power; the heavenly city says to its God: "I will love thee, O Lord, my strength."[110]

Both communities generate their specific ethical systems. In the earthly city even the wise live according to human interests and pursue the welfare of their bodies or of their minds or of both together. In the heavenly city the only wisdom of human beings is godliness which guides them rightly to worship the true God: "And awaits as its reward in the fellowship of saints not only human but also angelic, this goal, 'that God may be all in all'" (1 Cor. 15:23).[111]

Augustine did not hesitate to differentiate among the penultimate virtues of the ultimately doomed earthly city. "It is incorrect to say that the goods that this (earthly) city covets are not good; since through them even the city itself is better after its own human fashion."[112] It is desirable that those be the rulers who champion the relatively more righteous causes. In the struggles and conflicts of the earthly city actual goods are involved. These goods, such as peace, are even in the earthly city gifts of God. "But there are higher goods that belong to the city above, in which victory will be untroubled in everlasting and ultimate peace." [113]

False priorities are the problem of the earthly city. If the goods of the heavenly city are neglected while those of the earthly city, valuable as they may be, are coveted because they are believed to be the only real goods, the inevitable consequence will be human misery.[114]

The experience of Adam and Eve is paradigmatic. Their problem was not that they were human, physical and spiritual beings living in a physical and spiritual garden that supplied the good things for the body as well as the mind.[115] They were allowed and encouraged to *enjoy* [116] their garden spiritually and physically. Since God had planted this garden the fruit was good. The problem was disobedience. For Augustine, obedience is the virtue which in a rational creature is "the mother and guardian of all other virtues." The trivial cause of Adam and Eve's disobedience, the ease with which God's command could have been obeyed, made the offense more serious: "The crime of violating the command was all the greater in proportion to the ease with which it could have been heeded and upheld." [117]

The insignificant act of eating the forbidden fruit was the result of a profound pride, the start of all sin. It is "a craving for perverse elevation. For it is perverse elevation to forsake the ground in which the mind ought to be rooted and to become and be, in a sense, grounded in oneself." [118] Adam's self-satisfied isolation from God was the cause of his disobedience. The evil act was committed by those who were already evil.[119]

Yet the human being "did not lapse so completely as to lose all being, but by turning to himself he ended by having less true being than he had when he was rooted in him who has the highest being." [120]

Evil results from isolation, from turning inward, and effects further isolation. While obeying God produces community, disobedience brings about loss of being and loneliness. "The life of the saints is social."[121] "To leave God and to have being in oneself, that is, to follow one's own pleasure, is not to be nothing already but to come nearer to being nothing." [122] Pride was so crucial a sin for

Augustine because it destroys the community that holds life together. "Strange as it may seem," Augustine observed, "there is something in humility to uplift the mind, and there is something in exaltation to abase the mind. While it seems a paradox that exaltation abases and humility uplifts it makes sense if indeed 'the life of the saints is social.'" Augustine stated that Adam and Eve "could better have come to be [as gods] if they through obedience had adhered to their highest and true ground and not through pride set themselves up as their own ground." [123] Participation in the true God is life. "Striving for more diminishes a person, who by choosing to be sufficient unto himself suffers a deficiency in lapsing from the one who is truly sufficient for him." [124]

Thus the two cities are distinguished by the focus of their life. "In one city love of God came first; in the other, love of self." [125] Yet because both cities are "interwoven and blended together in this transitory age," [126] no hasty and final distinctions should be made by humans. It is important to remember as long as history lasts, that among the very enemy are hidden some who will eventually become citizens of the heavenly city. Conversely, among those who are now joined to the city of God while on this pilgrimage in the world and sharing the sacraments are "some who will not be with her to share eternally in the lot of the saints." [127]

Both cities are forced to live together and share many of God's gifts. In some way they actually support each other, while time lasts. Both cities share the use of the earth.[128] Both cities "alike in this life either enjoy good things or suffer evil." [129] Both have to fulfill certain duties on this earth, as, for example, the duty to reproduce the race.[130] The difference is in the way both cities deal with these common possessions, experiences and obligations; in other words the difference is ethical. In each case the false priorities of the earthly city result in false responses to the challenges of this life. "A household of human beings whose life is not governed by faith pursues an earthly peace by means of the good things and conveniences of this temporal life, while a household of those who live by faith looks to the everlasting blessings that are promised for the future, using like one in a strange land any earthly and temporal things." [131]

Similarly the identical good events and identical evils that are experienced by the citizens of the two cities, are enjoyed and suffered, "with diverse faith, diverse hope and diverse love." [132]

Even the duty to reproduce the race is shared by the citizens of both cities—except that the way they fulfill the duty is radically different.[133]

Indeed, the relationship of the two cities is not merely historical in the sense that the tension between them originated in the time since the creation of humanity, rather it has its model in the earlier conflict of the two dissimilar and opposite communities of angels. "One is both naturally good and willingly upright, while the other is naturally good, it is true, but willfully perverse." [134]

Thus the conflict of the two cities in human history is the result of a much more basic and transcendent conflict and tension between them reflects this larger struggle. Both types of angelic powers are involved in the present encounter of the two communities, "the one being a community of godly humans, the other a community of the ungodly, *each with the angels that belong to it*." [135]

But in spite of this radical difference between the two cities, Augustine was eloquent in his description and commendation of the relative possibilities for peace even in the earthly city. About the wretched he said, "though they are not indeed united with the blessed yet it is by a law of order that they are separated from them." [136] While they cannot obtain ultimate peace they can have among them peace, which is far better than not to have any peace at all.

> Wherefore, as the life of the flesh is the soul, so the blessed life of man is God, of whom the sacred scriptures of the Hebrews declare: "Blessed is the people whose God is the Lord" (Psalm 144:15). Wretched, therefore, is the people that is alienated from that God. Yet even this people loves a peace of its own, which must not be rejected; but it will not possess it in the end, because it does not make good use of it before the end. But that it should possess this peace meanwhile in this life is important for us, too, since so long as the two cities are intermingled we also profit by the peace of Babylon; and the people of God is by faith so freed from it as meanwhile to be but strangers passing through.[137]

He insists that both kinds of human groups and of households use alike the things that are necessary for this mortal life; but each has its own very different purpose in using them.[138]

While this heavenly city, therefore, goes its way as a stranger on earth, it summons citizens from all peoples, and gathers an alien society of all languages, caring naught what difference may be in manners, laws and institutions, by which earthly peace is gained or maintained, abolishing and destroying nothing of the sort, nay rather preserving and following them (for however different they may be among different nations, they aim at one and the same end, earthly peace), provided that there is no hindrance to the religion that teaches the obligation to worship one most high and true God. Even the heavenly city, therefore, in this its pilgrimage makes use of the earthly peace, and guards and seeks the merging of human wills in regard to the things that are useful for man's mortal nature, so far as sound piety and religion permit, and makes the earthly peace minister to the heavenly peace, which is so truly peace that it must be deemed and called the only peace, at least of a rational creature, being, as it is, the best ordered and most harmonious fellowship in the enjoyment of God and of one another in God.[139]

The dominant image which determines Augustine's ethics is always the pilgrimage of God's people through this world to a goal that still lies ahead. On that pilgrimage they depend to a degree on the earthly peace provided by the rulers of this world but above all on the "learned and pious men of the Catholic Church which open up the Scriptures to the willing and worthy." [140] This "most true mother of Christians" [141] provides:

training and teaching childlike for children, forcible for youths, peaceful for the aged, taking into account the age of the mind as well as of the body. Thou subjectest women to their husbands in chaste and faithful obedience, not to gratify passion, but for the propagation of offspring, and for domestic society. Thou givest to men authority over their wives, not to mock the weaker sex, but in the laws of unfeigned love. Thou dost subordinate children to their parents in a kind of free bondage, and dost set parents over their children in a godly rule. Thou bindest brothers to brothers in a religious tie stronger and closer than that of blood. Without violation of the connections of nature and of choice, thou bringest within the bond of mutual love every alliance of affinity. Thou teachest servants to cleave to their masters from delight in their task rather than from the necessity of their position. Thou renderest masters forbearing to their servants, from a regard to God their common Master, and more disposed to advise than to compel. Thou unitest citizen to citizen, nation to nation, yea, man to man, from the recollection of their first parents, not only in society but in fraternity. Thou teachest kings to seek the good of their peoples; thou counsellest peoples to be subject to their kings. Thou teachest carefully to whom honor is due, to whom regard, to whom reverence, to whom fear, to whom consolation, to whom admonition, to whom encouragement, to whom discipline, to whom rebuke, to whom punishment; showing both how all are not due to all, and how to all love is due, and how injury is due to none.[142]

Life on this earth is made tolerable for Christians by living in the community and under the guidance of this church. Indeed, the church is so important that it must be seen in conjunction with the Holy Trinity. For Augustine it is the house where the Trinity dwells, the temple God occupies, it is the city he has built.[143] Of course, the church here described is "not that part only which wanders as a stranger on the earth . . . but that part also which has always from its creation remained steadfast to God in heaven and has never experienced the misery consequent upon a fall." [144]

Here again the reference is to the host of angels which not only praises God but makes the Christian life possible by rendering assistance to that part of the church which is still wandering among strangers. This entire church, militant and triumphant, is the temple of God and the term cannot be applied unambiguously to the pilgrim church in exile on this earth.

## 7. *Ethics as Hope*

Unlike many of his Christian predecessors, Augustine had lost confidence in the transformation of this earth and its culture into the kingdom of God. In historical time the two cities do not merge; they are always intermingled yet remain ultimately distinct. Those citizens of the City of God who are living in this world live a life in which peace is at best precarious. Their righteousness in this life "consists rather in the forgiveness of sins than in the perfection of virtues." [145] Divine justice is hidden from them, "For we know not," Augustine says, "by what judgment this good man is poor and that wicked man is rich; why a man whose abandoned character seems to us to deserve the torment of grief is merry, while another whose praiseworthy life seems to deserve a merry life is full of gloom." [146] The questions are endless. Juvenile delinquents enjoy the best of health, while mere infants who have hurt nobody even with a word suffer from horrible diseases. A person who is useful to society is carried off by premature death, while another who in our opinion ought never to have been born lives on and on.[147] And all this occurs without any consistency or predictability whatsoever. "But as it is, not only are some good men in evil plight and some bad men in prosperity, which seems unjust, yet it is also true as a rule, that bad men come to a bad end and good men are visited by good results. We have the more reason to find God's judgments "inscrutable and his ways past finding out'" (Rom. 11:33).[148]

Christian hope cannot be based on the data of human history as they are observed in this life. Only through the final judgment will God's justice be vindicated when Christ shall come from heaven to judge the living and the dead.[149]

As Augustine had learned early in his life from Ambrose, in the affairs of this world victory goes to the strong. The very history of Rome is determined by military power not by justice.[150]

Indeed, Augustine knew periods when he rejoiced in what appeared to him the triumph of Christianity over paganism. Around A.D. 400 he spoke of "those few pagans who have remained such" who fail to note the victory of the God of Israel.[151] And he exulted, "that the God of Israel, the true God who made heaven and earth, and who administers human affairs justly and mercifully . . . was not overcome Himself when His Hebrew people suffered their overthrow. . . . And by Christ the King He has brought into subjection to His own name that Roman empire by which Israel was overcome."[152] He could also say, "The whole world is now the chorus of Christ. The chorus of Christ soundeth harmoniously from east to west."[153] But even at such times Augustine never lost sight of the pilgrim character of the church. Commenting on the same psalm, he observed: "Now we are pilgrims; we sigh, we groan."[154] And, "Let those, then, who being in this life, groan and long for their country run by love, not by bodily feet; let them seek not ships but wings, let them lay hold of the two wings of love."[155] These wings of love that help the Christian escape to the true Zion are again explicitly the love of God and our neighbor.[156]

Augustine's occasionally positive remarks concerning the political organizations of his times are attributable to his view that the two cities will last until the end of history. Since they are so inextricably mixed up with each other, people who really belong to "Babylon" administer the affairs of "Jerusalem" and vice versa. He observed that every earthly commonwealth—though destined to perish and though its rule is only transitory—is in fact administered by some of "our citizens." As a result the situation is better than might be expected. "For how many faithful, how many good people are magistrates in their cities as well as judges, generals, counts, and kings? They do service in the city which shall pass away. But while time lasts the teachers of the holy city have ordered the citizens of the city of God to serve faithfully and to their best abilities in the affairs of this world."

Enunciating a clear notion of a Christian vocation in this sinful world, he says, "The citizens of Babylon are commanded to be endured by the citizens of Jerusalem, showing even more attentions than if they were citizens of the same Babylon, as though fulfilling the precept, 'He that shall have exacted of thee a mile, go with him the twain.'" [157] Yet while Christians serve in the earthly city this does not make that city Christian. As Markus rightly observes, "Outside dissenting or schismatic circles Augustine was the only thinker of any stature who was deeply disturbed by the developments of the fourth century towards a sacral conception of the Empire." [158] Augustine knows only too well:

> Sometimes they are good powers, and fear God; sometimes they fear not God. Julian was an infidel Emperor, an apostate, a wicked man, an idolator; Christian soldiers served an infidel Emperor; when they came to the cause of Christ, they acknowledged Him only who was in heaven. If he called upon them at any time to worship idols, to offer incense, they preferred God to him: but whenever he commanded them to deploy into line, to march against this or that nation, they at once obeyed. They distinguished their everlasting from their temporal master; and yet they were, for the sake of their everlasting Master, submissive to the temporal master. [159]

And to those who asked, "Will this always be the case, that the ungodly have power over the righteous," he replies:

> It will not be so. The rod of the ungodly is felt for a season upon the lot of the righteous; but it is not left there, it will not be there for ever. A time will come, when Christ, appearing in his glory, shall gather all nations before Him. [160]

But this is clearly an "eschatological" answer. The kingdom of God is a future kingdom.

Under the influence of Ambrose's conflicts with the empire as

Augustine had observed it during his early days in Milan, and impressed by the vicissitudes that had shaken the empire in later years, he had come to the conclusion that Christian hope cannot be based on the uncertain destiny of any empire. The church uses the services of the available political structures. Augustine, indeed, could go very far in advising Christian rulers to apply force to those he thought might per chance be saved from heresy and for the Catholic church by the use of repressive measures.[161] But all these efforts while they may save individuals from eternal hell are not going to establish the City of God on earth. These days are *tempora christiana,* a Christian era,[162] because Christ is being proclaimed and men and women are continuously incorporated into the body of Christ—not because the state or even the government is being transformed into the kingdom of God. Christian ethics has to be lived out in a world which is seen by Augustine as full of temptations both carnal and spiritual which will not cease until "Christ appearing in his glory shall gather all nations before Him."

Thus at the end of the ancient church stands a bishop and theologian who no longer believes that the adoption of Christianity by the empire has created a radically new situation for the Christian movement and who is unwilling to tie the church to any form of political organization. There is, indeed, a certain historical agnosticism [163] in Augustine which makes it impossible for him to discern the divine purpose in the events of the day. He knows *that* the Lord will come—he refuses to speculate *when* he shall come.[164] For Augustine's ethics this meant that it was far more critical of the "Christian" answers offered in his time, even those he himself suggested, than most of his immediate predecessors or successors. Augustine's thinking proved seminal for the entire history of Christian ethics which was to follow because he was better at raising questions than giving answers. In a variety of ways the ethical systems developed in the centuries that followed were efforts to answer the questions Augustine had posed.

# Notes

## Introduction

1. Peter Berger, *The Sacred Canopy: Elements of a Sociological Theory of Religion* (Garden City, N.Y.: Doubleday, 1967), p. 41. Berger states: "The religious legitimations, or at least most of them, make little sense if one conceives of them as productions of theoreticians that are then applied *ex post facto* to particular complexes of activity. The need for legitimation arises in the course of the activity. Typically, this is in the consciousness of the actors before that of the theoreticians. And, of course, while all members of society are actors within it, only very few are theoreticians (mystagogues, theologians, and the like). The degree of theoretical elaboration of the religious legitimations will vary with a large number of historical factors, but it would lead to grave misunderstanding if only the more sophisticated legitimations were taken into consideration. To put it simply, most men in history have felt the need for religious legitimation—only very few have been interested in the development of religious 'ideas.'"

## CHAPTER I: New Testament Ethics

1. Joseph H. Hertz, *The Authorized Daily Prayer Book* (New York: Bloch, 1961), pp. 145f.
2. Rudolf Bultmann, *Primitive Christianity in Its Contemporary Setting*, trans. R. H. Fuller (New York: Meridian, 1956), p. 81.

3. Cf. Eduard Lohse, *Umwelt des Neuen Testaments* (Göttingen: Vandenhoeck u. Ruprecht, 1971), pp. 137ff.

4. Ibid., p. 140: "As varied as the views of the Messiah and the time of salvation might be, they had one thing in common, God's anointed would appear as ruler and judge who would end the lowliness of Israel, drive out the gentiles and establish the kingdom of glory."

5. To the above see also *Theological Dictionary of the New Testament,* ed. G. Kittel, trans. G. Bromiley (Grand Rapids, Mich.: Eerdmans, 1964-1974), 1:758ff.

6. Ibid., 4:803.

7. Apuleius, *The Golden Ass,* Addlington translation revised by S. Gasalee, The Loeb Classical Library (Cambridge, Mass.: Harvard University Press, 1965), pp. 579-581.

8. Ibid., p. 581.

9. Ibid., pp. 583ff.

10. James G. Frazer, *The Golden Bough: A Study in Magic and Religion,* Part 4: *Adonis Attis Osiris* (London: Macmillan, 1919), 1:6.

11. *Idyll* 15 in *Theocritus,* ed. and trans. A. S. F. Gow (Cambridge: University Press, 1950), 1:119-121.

12. We know, for instance, that temple prostitution connected with the worship of Adonis was still practiced at the time of Emperor Constantine in the fourth century A.D. See *Religion in Geschichte und Gegenwart: Handwörterbuch für Theologie und Religionswissenschaft,* ed. H. Gunkel and L. Zscharnack, 2d ed. (Tübingen: Mohr, 1927-31), 1:89.

13. As far as the term "mystery" is concerned it should be emphasized that "*mysterion* is a rare expression in the New Testament which betrays no relation to the mystery cults. Where there seem to be connections (e.g., in sacramental passages), the term is not used: where it is used, there are no such connections." *Theological Dictionary of the New Testament,* 4:824.

14. Cf. Oscar Cullmann, *The Christology of the New Testament,* trans. S. Guthrie and C. Hall, rev. ed. (Philadelphia: Westminster, 1959).

15. William Lillie, *Studies in New Testament Ethics* (Edinburgh: Oliver and Boyd, 1961), p. 15.

16. Cf. Herbert Preisker, *Das Ethos des Urchristentums,* 2nd ed. (Gütersloh: Bertelsmann, 1949), pp. 21ff.

17. Cf. Heinz-Dietrich Wendland, *Ethik des Neuen Testaments* (Göttingen: Vandenhoeck & Ruprecht, 1970), pp. 4ff.

18. In the history of Christendom there has been a variety of interpretations of this new ethical situation brought about by Jesus' advent and described in the Sermon on the Mount. Roman Catholic moral theology sees in these radical commandments *counsels for the perfect,* and makes the Sermon on the Mount the rule of monastic life. Classical Lutheranism sees these radical demands as binding on all

Christians and thus understands them as revealing sin and demonstrating the *theological use of the law,* which condemns us and drives us to Christ. Under the influence of idealism, Protestant liberalism sees in the ethics of the Sermon on the Mount an *ethics of intention,* which demands not obedience to the law but rather the right intent, the good will. Against this interpretation, Johannes Weiss and Albert Schweitzer interpreted the Sermon on the Mount ethics as *interim ethics* valid for the exceptional situation of the last days of this world. Finally, various enthusiastic groups prominent during the sixteenth-century Reformation and in more recent times finding eloquent spokesmen in Count Leo Tolstoy and some of the "Jesus people," saw in the Sermon on the Mount the *blueprint for a new Christian society,* Christ's kingdom on earth. To the above cf. ibid., pp. 17-20.

19. Rudolf Bultmann, *Glauben und Verstehen: Gesammelte Aufsätze* (Tübingen; Mohr, 1952-65), 1:234.
20. Ibid., p. 235.
21. *Ethos des Urchristentums,* p. 76.
22. Paul L. Lehmann, *Ethics in a Christian Context* (New York: Harper & Row, 1963), p. 159.
23. Ibid.
24. Joseph Fletcher, *Situation Ethics: The New Morality* (Philadelphia: Westminster, 1966), p. 68.
25. Eric H. Wahlstrom, *The New Life in Christ* (Philadelphia: Muhlenberg, 1950), p. 146.
26. Wolfgang Schrage, *Die konkreten Einzelgebote in der paulinischen Paränese: Ein Beitrag zur neutestamentlichen Ethik* (Gütersloh: Mohn, 1961), p. 9.
27. To the following cf. ibid.
28. See the literature listed in ibid., pp. 134ff.
29. Cf. Walther Bienert, *Die Arbeit nach der Lehre der Bibel: eine Grundlegung evangelischer Sozialethik* (Stuttgart: Evangelisches Verlagswerk, 1954), p. 321.
30. Schrage, p. 238.
31. Wendland, *Ethik des Neues Testaments,* p. 111. It should be pointed out, however, that the Johannine material concentrates the discussion of love on the "brethren," the fellow Christians, and the "world" seems to disappear from immediate concern (cf. 1 John 2:15ff.) even though "Christ the righteous is the expiation of our sins, and not for our sins only but also for the sins of the whole world" (1 John 2:2).
32. To the following see also Martin Dibelius, *Botschaft und Geschichte: Gesammelte Aufsätze* (Tübingen: Mohr, 1953-), 2:1-13.
33. Ibid., p. 5.
34. "Origen Against Celsus" in *The Ante-Nicene Fathers: Translations of the Writings of the Fathers Down to A.D. 325,* ed. Alexander

Roberts, American reprint of the Edinburgh edition (Grand Rapids: Eerdmans, 1963), 4:481-482. Hereafter, ANF denotes this collection.

35. Ibid., p. 484.
36. Ibid., p. 487.
37. Ibid., p. 487-488.
38. Ibid., p. 488.

## CHAPTER II: The Early Christian Fathers

1. To the following see Adolf von Harnack, *History of Dogma*, trans. N. Buchanan (New York: Russell & Russell, 1958), 2:18-93; Hans Lietzmann, *Geschichte der alten Kirche* (Berlin: de Gruyter, 1932-), vols. 1-2.
2. Lietzmann, p. 103.
3. *Against Heresies* 3.4.2 in Cyril Richardson, ed. and trans., *Early Christian Fathers*, Library of Christian Classics, vol. 1 (Philadelphia: Westminster, 1953), p. 375.
4. *The Apostolic Fathers: A New Translation and Commentary*, ed. R. Grant (New York: Nelson), 2:58.
5. Ibid., pp. 66-67.
6. Ibid., 4:44-45.
7. Ibid., 6:50.
8. Ibid., 2:126.
9. Cf. Albert C. Sundberg, *The Old Testament of the Early Church* (Cambridge, Mass.: Harvard University Press, 1964), p. 130. "Since the church did not receive a closed canon from either Palestinian or Alexandrian Judaism (but, rather, an undefined and unclosed collection of religious literature circulating throughout Judaism and varying according to local preference and language) and since the ultimate Christian Old Testament canon did not encompass the whole of this literature, it becomes evident that the church determined the extent of its Old Testament canon for itself."
10. Hans Von Campenhausen, *Die Entstehung der christlichen Bibel* (Tübingen: Mohr, 1968), p. 31.
11. Ibid., p. 32.
12. *Apostolic Fathers*, 3:85.
13. Ibid.
14. Ibid., pp. 132-133.
15. Ibid., pp. 148-150.
16. Ibid., 4:106-107.
17. Ibid., p. 106.
18. Robert M. Grant and Holt H. Graham, *The Apostolic Fathers*, (New York: Thomas Nelson, 1964-68), 6 volumes, 1 Clem. 20:1-3; II, 43.

19. 1 Clem. 21:6, *op. cit.*, II, 46.
20. 1 Clem. 37:2-3, *op. cit.*, II, 64f.
21. 1 Clem. 57:2, *op. cit.*, II, 90.
22. Ign. *Phld.*, 7:1, *op. cit.*, IV, 105.
23. Ign. *Poly.*, 6:1, *op. cit.*, IV, 134.
24. Ign. *Eph.*, 5:3, *op. cit.*, IV, 36.
25. Ign. *Trall.*, 2:1, *op. cit.*, IV, 72.
26. "Irenaeus Against Heresies" in *Early Christian Fathers*, p. 359.
27. Ibid., pp. 360-361.
28. Ibid., p. 361.
29. Cecil J. Cadoux, *The Early Church and the World: A History of the Christian Attitude to Pagan Society and the State Down to the Time of Constantine* (Edinburgh: T. & T. Clark, 1925), pp. 218-219. Cf. Herm. *Sim.* 8.3.1-2.
30. Herm. *Man.* 12.4.6.
31. Cf. Hermann Dörries, *Wort und Stunde* (Göttingen: Vandenhoeck & Ruprecht, 1966-), 2:78.
32. "Letter to Diognetus" in *Early Christian Fathers*, pp. 216-218.

**CHAPTER III: Tertullian**

1. His spectacular end was common knowledge. Tertullian writes in his essay encouraging the martyrs, "The philosophers have been outstripped—for instance Heraclitus . . . Empedocles . . . and Peregrinus, who not long ago threw himself on the funeral pile." ANF, 3:695.
2. *Lucian*, trans. A. M. Harmon, Loeb Classical Library (Cambridge, Mass.: Harvard University Press, 1936), 5:13.
3. Ibid.
4. Emperor Julian (The Apostate) wrote 200 years later after Christianity had for a time become the official religion of the empire, "For it is disgraceful that, when no Jew ever has to beg, and the impious Galileans [Christians] support not only their own poor but ours as well, all men see that our people lack aid from us." "To Asarcius, High Priest of Galatia," in *The Works of Emperor Julian*, trans. W. Wright, Loeb Classical Library (New York: Putnam, 1923), 3:71.
5. Tertullian confirms this in his introduction to *Ad Martyras*: "Blessed Martyrs Designate,—Along with the provision which our lady mother the Church from her bountiful breasts, and each brother out of his private means, makes for your bodily wants in the prison, accept also from me some contribution to your spiritual sustenance. . . ." ANF, 3:693.
6. *Lucian*, p. 15.
7. Tacitus *Annales* 15.44. See *Tacitus*, ed. and trans. C. Moore and J.

Jackson, Loeb Classical Library (Cambridge, Mass.: Harvard University Press, 1939), pp. 283-285.

8. Juvenal *Satires* 10 in *Juvenal and Persius*, ed, and trans. G. Ramsay, Loeb Classical Library (Cambridge, Mass.: Harvard University Press, 1969), p. 199.

9. From Fronto *Principia Historia*, as quoted in James Carcopino, *Daily Life in Ancient Rome: The People and the City at the Height of the Empire*, trans. E. Lorimer, ed. H. Rowell (New Haven: Yale University Press, 1940), p. 202.

10. For the measurement of 71 amphitheaters see Ludwig Friedländer, *Darstellungen aus der Sittengeschichte Roms in der Zeit von August bis zum Ausgang der Antonine*, 2d ed. (Leipzig: Herzel 1919-21), 4:239ff.

11. Seneca, *Ad Lucilium Epistulae Morales*, trans. R. Gunmere (New York: Putnam, 1925), 1:31.

12. Carcopino, *Daily Life in Ancient Rome*, p. 243.

13. Cf. Adolf von Harnack, *Geschichte der altchristlichen Literatur bis Eusebius*, 2nd ed. (Leipzig: Heinrichs, 1958), 2:667. See also Carl Becker, *Tertullians Apologeticum: Werden und Leistung* (München: Kösel-Verlag, 1954), pp. 179ff.

14. Little is actually known about Tertullian's life. The biographical information here summarized represents the "conventional wisdom." Eusebius claims that Tertullian "had an accurate knowledge of Roman law" (Eusebius *Ecclesiastical History* 2.2.4). Jerome asserted that he was a priest, a citizen of Carthage, who later left the church because of "the envy and insults of the Roman clergy" and joined the Montanists (*Catal.* 53, cf. *Chronic. ad. a.* 2224, and Augustine *De haer.* 86). Timothy David Barnes had questioned every item with important evidence in *Tertullian: A Historical and Literary Study* (Oxford: Clarendon, 1971). He renounces any attempt at a full biography, but suggests that Tertullian was born ca. A.D. 170 and died shortly after 212, belonged "both by birth and upbringing to literary circles in Carthage," and was not connected with the military or the legal profession (pp. 57-59). The story of his old age may have been a cover for an earlier martyr's death which the Catholic church did not want to report of a Montanist heretic (p. 54).

15. W. H. C. Freund, *Martyrdom and Persecution in the Early Church: A Study of Conflict from the Maccabees to Donatus* (Garden City, N.Y.: Doubleday, 1967), p. 230.

16. *De Anima* 30 in ANF, 3:210.

17. *De Spectaculis* 2 in *Tertullian-Minucius Felix*, trans. T. Glover and G. Rendall, Loeb Classical Library (New York: Putnam, 1931), p. 233.

18. Ibid., pp. 233-235.

19. *De Spectaculis* 13 in ibid., p. 267.

20. Ibid., p. 293.
21. *Apology* 40 in ANF, 3:47.
22. *De Spectaculis* 19 in *Tertullian-Minucius Felix,* p. 279.
23. *Apology* 50.15-16 in ibid., p. 227.
24. *Ad Scapulam* in ANF, 3:108.
25. Herbert Musurillo in his *The Acts of the Christian Martyrs* (Oxford: Clarendon, 1972), p. xxii, comments, "*The Acts of the Scillitan Martyrs* is our earliest dated document from the Latin church and the first to make mention of a Latin Bible. A bishop of Scillium is mentioned in 411, but the city's exact location remains a mystery." Because there is a Western tradition that Scillium was near Carthage and an Eastern (Byzantian) tradition of a *Skele* in Numidia, the suggestion may be in order that these people came from Cillium, a good-sized town in Byzacena close to the border of Numidia.
26. Tertullian mentions Saturninus in his letter to Scapula as the proconsul "who first here in Africa used the sword against us." Tertullian adds that as a result he later lost his eyesight. *Ad Scapulam* in ANF, 3:106.
27. Musurillo, *Acts of the Christian Martyrs,* p. 87.
28. See 5.1-13.5 in *Tertullian-Minucius Felix,* pp. 321-349. The following quotations are from pp. 327-329, 333-337, 349.
29. Reading *caeca* instead of *certa,* with Geral H. Rendall in the Loeb Classical Library edition.
30. *Adversus Marcionem* 2.3 *Adversus Marcionem,* ed. and trans. E. Evans (Oxford: Clarendon, 1972), 1:93.
31. Ibid.
32. 2.6 in ibid., p. 103.
33. 2.4 in ibid., p. 97.
34. 2.8 in ibid., p. 109.
35. 2.14 in ibid., p. 125.
36. *De Anima* 10.1 in ANF, 3:220.
37. Ibid.
38. Ibid., pp. 220-221.
39. Ibid., p. 221.
40. *Adv. Marc.* 2.10 in *Adversus Marcionem,* p. 119.
41. Ibid.
42. 2.13 in ibid., p. 123.
43. 2.17 in ibid., p. 135.
44. 1.10 in ibid., pp. 25-27.
45. 1.1 in ibid., p. 27.
46. Ibid.
47. 1.13 in ibid., p. 37.
48. *De Corona* 6 in ANF, 3:96.
49. *De Test. Animae* 5.1 in *Opera,* Corpus Christianorum (Turnholt, 1954), 1:180.

50. Ibid., p. 181.
51. 6.3 in ibid., p. 182.
52. *De Spectaculis* 21 in *Tertullian-Minucius Felix*, p. 283.
53. *Scorpiace* 12 in ANF, 3:645.
54. *De Patientia* 3 in ibid., pp. 708-709.
55. *Apology* 39 in ibid., p. 46.
56. *On Idolatry* 1 in ibid., p. 61.
57. Ibid.
58. Acts 15:28 f. Cf. *On Idolatry* 24 in ANF, 3:76.
59. *Opera* 2:1124.
60. *On Idolatry* 24 in ANF, 3:76.
61. 4 in ibid., p. 62.
62. 5 in ibid., p. 63.
63. 8 in ibid., pp. 64-65.
64. 9 in ibid., p. 66.
65. 20-23 in ibid., pp. 73-75.
66. 10 in ibid., p. 66.
67. Ibid.
68. Ibid., pp. 66-67.
69. *On Idolatry* 15 in ibid., p. 70.
70. Ibid.
71. Ibid., p. 71.
72. 17 in ibid.
73. To the above see, ibid., pp. 71-72.
74. Tertullian uses the word *sacramentum*, which is the military oath of allegiance (e.g., Caesar *Bellum Gallicum* 6.1 *Annales* 1.28) as describing also the Christian sacraments. For example, he calls baptism *sacramentum aquae nostrae: De Baptismo* 1.1 in *Opera* 1:277 and *ecclesiarum sacramenta* in *Adv. Marc.* 3.22.7 in ibid., p. 540.
75. *On Idolatry* 19 in ANF, 3:73 (translation slightly modified).
76. Ibid.
77. *Ad Nationes* 4 in ANF, 3:112.
78. E.g., H. Richard Niebuhr, *Christ and Culture* (New York: Harper, 1951), p. 51: "The most explicit and, apart from New Testament writers, doubtless the greatest representative in early Christianity of the 'Christ-against-culture' type was Tertullian." See also the introduction to Tertullian in *Christian Social Teachings: A Reader in Christian Social Ethics from the Bible to the Present*, ed. G. Forell (Garden City, N.Y.: Doubleday, 1966, and Minneapolis: Augsburg, 1971), p. 41.
79. To the following see Richard Klein, *Tertullian und das römische Reich* (Heidelberg: Winter, 1968).
80. *Apology* 33 in ANF, 3:43.
81. *Apology* 30 in ibid., p. 42.
82. *Apology* 5-6 in ibid., pp. 21-23. This analysis is historically inaccu-

rate, but Tertullian seems to assume that this is the way it should have been in view of the obvious self-interest of the emperors.

83. Cf. *Apology*, 35-36 in ibid., pp. 43-45.
84. *Apology* 30 in ibid., p. 42.
85. Cicero attributed the success of Rome to the gods and this attitude was the conventional wisdom Tertullian opposes. Cf. Wilhelm Kroll, *Die Kultur der ciceronischen Zeit* (Leipzig: Dieterich, 1933), 2:1ff., and Carl Koch, *Religio: Studien zu Kult und Glauben der Römer*, ed. O. Seel (Nürnberg: Carl, 1960), pp. 142ff.
86. *Apology* 25, in ANF, 3:40.
87. Ibid.

## CHAPTER IV: Clement of Alexandria

1. Cf. Salvatore R. Lilla, *Clement of Alexandria: A Study in Christian Platonism and Gnosticism* (Oxford: Oxford University Press, 1971).
2. The biographical details in R. B. Tollinton's *Clement of Alexandria: A Study in Christian Liberalism* (London: Williams and Norgate, 1914), are freely invented.
3. Cf. *The Rich Man's Salvation* 30 in *Clement of Alexandria* trans. G. W. Butterworth, Loeb Classical Library (New York: Putnam, 1919), p. 335.
4. Ottmar Dittrich, *Geschichte der Ethik: Die Systeme der Moral vom Altertum bis zur Gegenwart,* reprint of the Leipzig ed. 1923 (Aalen: Scientia, 1964), 2:259.
5. "I know your teachers, even if you would fain conceal them. You learn geometry from the Egyptians, astronomy from the Babylonians, healing incantations you obtain from the Thracians, and the Assyrians have taught you much; but as to your laws (in so far as they are true) and your belief about God, you have been helped by the Hebrews themselves. . . ." *Exhortations to the Greeks* 6.60 in *Clement of Alexandria*, p. 159.
6. *Exhortation to the Greeks* 6.61 in ibid.
7. The long passage of Sophocles which he quotes is, however, clearly of Jewish or Christian origin and falsely attributed to Sophocles. Cf. ibid., p. 165.
8. Plato *Theaetetus* 176B.
9. *Exhortation to the Greeks* 12. 94-95 in *Clement of Alexandria*, p. 263.
10. *The Instructor* 1.1 in ANF, 2:209.
11. 1.3 in ibid., p. 210.
12. 1.4 in ibid., p. 211.
13. 1.13 in ibid., p. 235.
14. Ibid.
15. 1.13 in ibid., p. 236.

16. 2.1 in ibid., p. 237.
17. Ibid.
18. 2.1 in ibid., p. 239.
19. 2.1 in ibid., p. 240.
20. 2.2 in ibid., p. 242.
21. 2.2 in ibid., p. 243.
22. Ibid.
23. Ibid. Clement refers in this context to *Ecclesiasticus* 31:25, which apparently in combination with *Proverbs* is the major biblical source for his ethics of moderation.
24. 2.2 in ibid., p. 245.
25. 2.2 in ibid., p. 246.
26. 2.3 in ibid., pp. 247-248.
27. 2.3 in ibid., p. 247.
28. 2.4 in ibid., p. 248.
29. Ibid.
30. 2.4 in ibid., p. 249.
31. 2.5 in ibid., p. 250.
32. 2.6 in ibid., p. 251.
33. 2.7 in ibid., p. 253.
34. 2.10.83. Because the editors of ANF put most of this chapter in Latin, I make reference to the particular passage as it appears in *Clemens Alexandrinus*, ed. O. Stählin, 3rd ed. (Berlin: Akadamie-Verlag, 1972).
35. It is for this reason that he engages in an extensive zoological argument about the genitals of the hyena. He denies the claim that hyenas possess both male and female sexual parts. Indeed, "nature has not allowed even the most sensual of beasts to misuse sexually the passage made for excrement"; 2.10.87.
36. Ibid.
37. 2.10.92.
38. 2.10.92.
39. 2.10.95.
40. Ibid.
41. 2.12 in ANF, 2:267.
42. 2.13 in ibid., p. 268.
43. 2.13 in ibid.
44. 3.1 in ibid., p. 271.
45. 3.1 in ibid., p. 271. The translation is modified. This Heraclitus quotation is identified by Otto Stählin, in *Clemens Alexandrinus*, p. 236, as Fragment 62 in *Die Fragmente der Vorsokratiker*, ed. H. Diels, 5th ed. (Berlin: Weidman, 1934-37), 1:164, which, however, says something quite different: "Immortals—mortals; mortals—immortals, for the life of the one is the death of the other and the death of the one is the life of the other." The Heraclitus quotation used here is not in Diels.

46. 3.1 in ANF, 2:271. Translation modified.
47. 3.1 in ibid., p. 272.
48. 3.3 in ibid., p. 275. Translation modified.
49. Ibid.
50. 3.3 in ibid., p. 276.
51. A reference to the cross of Christ.
52. 3.3 in ibid., p. 277.
53. 3.6 in ibid., p. 280.
54. 3.11 in ibid., p. 289. He uses as a proof text Leviticus 11, giving it an allegorical interpretation.
55. 3.12 in ibid., p. 293.
56. 3.12 in ibid., p. 295.
57. Ibid.
58. *Stromata* 1.1 in ibid., p. 303.
59. Ibid.
60. 1.2 in ibid., p. 304.
61. 1.5 in ibid., p. 305.
62. 2.9 in ibid., p. 357.
63. 1.6 in ibid., p. 307.
64. 2.15 in ibid., pp. 361-362. Translation modified.
65. 2.19 in ibid., p. 365.
66. 2.22 in ibid., p. 376.
67. Ibid.
68. 2.23 in ibid., p. 377.
69. Ibid.
70. It is amusing to note the different methods with which German and British scholarship of the nineteenth century handled the offensive teachings of Epiphanes. The British editors of Clement in the monumental *Ante-Nicene Christian Library: Translations of the Writings of the Fathers Down to* A.D. *325,* ed. A. Roberts, and J. Donaldson (Edinburgh: T. & T. Clark, 1869), vol. 12, part 2, translated Book III, which contains these peculiar ideas, into Latin. They say firmly in a footnote (p. 84), "After much consideration, the Editors have deemed it best to give the whole of this Book in Latin." (This is on 2:381 of ANF, the American edition of this work.) German nineteenth century scholarship dealt with the offensive Epiphanes in an even more radical fashion. Using the devices appropriate to their science, they simply abolished him by means of higher criticism. According to G. Volkmar, ("Über die Haretiker Epiphanes und Adrianus," in *Monatschrift des wissenschäftlichen Vereins in Zürich,* I (1856), pp. 276-282, there never was such a person. Clement had misinterpreted a festival to the new moon at Same, where the new moon is called Epiphanes. To the above, see John E. L. Oulton and Henry Chadwick, *Alexandrian Christianity,* Library of Christian Classics (Philadelphia: Westminster, 1954), 2:26.

71. *Alexandrian Christianity,* p. 25.
72. *Stromata* 3.2.6.1. The translation is from ibid., pp. 42-43.
73. 3.2.7.2. in ibid., p. 43.
74. 3.2.7.4. in ibid.
75. 3.2.8.1f. in ibid. p. 44.
76. 3.2.8.3. in ibid.
77. 3.2.8.4. in ibid.
78. Clement also reports how Epiphanes handled the prohibitions of the law: "One must understand the saying 'Thou shalt not covet' as if the lawgiver was making a jest, to which he added the even more comic words 'thy neighbor's goods.' For he himself, who gave the desire to sustain the race, orders that it is to be suppressed, though he removes it from no other animals. And by the words 'thy neighbour's wife' he says something even more ludicrous, since he forces what should be common property to be treated as a private possession." 3.2.9.3 in ibid.
79. 3.5.40.1f. in ibid., p. 58.
80. 3.5.43.1 in ibid., p. 59.
81. 3.6.46.1 in ibid., p. 61.
82. 3.6.46.4., in ibid.
83. 3.6.49.3f. in ibid., p. 63.
84. 3.7.57.2 in ibid., p. 66.
85. 3.7.59.1f. in ibid., p. 67.
86. 3.12.82 in ibid., p. 79.
87. 3.12.86.1 in ibid., p. 80.
88. 3.14.95.3 in ibid., p. 85.
89. 4.19 in ANF, 2:431.
90. 4.22 in ibid., p. 434.
91. Ibid.
92. 4.22 in ibid., p. 435.
93. 4.22 in ibid., p. 436.
94. Ibid.
95. 7.14 in ibid., p. 548. Translation modified.
96. 7.14 in ibid.
97. Ibid. Translation modified.
98. This is Butterworth's translation of *Exhortation to the Greeks* 11 in *Clement of Alexandria,* pp. 237-239. The phrase "through His outstretched hands" could also mean "with hands unloosened." The argument of Butterworth for his translation (footnote a, p. 238) is convincing.
99. *The Rich Man's Salvation* 23 in *Clement of Alexandria,* p. 319.
100. Ibid.
101. Ibid.
102. It is obvious that I side with Walther Völker. *Der wahre Gnostiker nach Clemens Alexandrinus* (Berlin: Akadamie-Verlag, 1952), against the efforts to make him into a "modern liberal theologian"

(e.g. John Patrick, R. S. Tollinton, and A. v. Harnack). On the other side of the argument see Lilla, *Clement of Alexandria,* pp. 3ff.
103. 6.17 in ANF, 2:515. The italics are mine.

## CHAPTER V: Origen

1. Hans Urs von Balthasar, *Origenes, Geist und Feuer: Ein Aufbau aus seinen Schriften,* 2nd ed. (Salzburg: Müller, 1938), p. 11.
2. "Origen employed the Stoic and Platonic systems of ethics as an instrument for the gradual realization of his ideal." Adolf von Harnack, *History of Dogma,* trans. N. Buchanan (New York: Russell & Russell, 1958), 2:338.
3. Anna Miura-Stange, *Celsus und Origenes: Das Gemeinsame ihrer Weltanschauung nach den acht Büchern des Origenes gegen Celsus* (Giessen: Topelmann, 1926).
4. "Origen's Metaphysics of Free Will, Fall and Salvation: A 'Divine Comedy' of the Universe" in Hans Jonas, *Philosophical Essays: From Ancient Creed to Technological Man* (Englewood Cliffs, N.J.: Prentice-Hall, 1974), p. 313.
5. Eusebius, *The Ecclesiastical History,* trans. J. E. L. Oulton, Loeb Classical Library (London: Heinemann, 1932), 2:9-23, 27-31, 49-95.
6. *Eccl. Hist.* 6.2 in ibid., p. 11.
7. *Eccl. Hist.* in ibid., p. 17.
8. It has been questioned whether the catechetical school of Alexandria was actually in existence at that time and whether Origen was a student of Clement. The argument is based on the conviction that precocious *Wunderkinder* like Origen do not exist. Manfred Hornschuh, "Das Leben des Origenes und die Entstehung der Alexandrinischen Schule," *Zeitschrift für Kirchengeschichte,* LXXI (1960), pp. 1-25 and 193-214.
9. *Eccl. Hist.* 6.8 in the translation of Oulton, 2:29.
10. Cf. *Geschichte der Ethik,* 2:249f.
11. Cf. Deuteronomy 23:1: "He whose testicles are crushed or whose male member is cut off shall not enter the assembly of the Lord." See also *Canon. Apost.* 47.22 in ANF, 7:501. "Let not him who has disabled himself be made a clergyman; for he is a self-murderer and an enemy of the creation of God."
12. Quoted in Eusebius, *Eccl. Hist.* 6.19 in the translation by Oulton, 2:57f.
13. Ibid.
14. Ibid.
15. Origines Werke, ed. P. Koetschau, *Die griechischen christlichen Schriftsteller der ersten drei Jahrhunderte* (Leipzig, 1913).

16. *Origen on First Principles,* trans. G. W. Butterworth (London: SPCK, 1936).
17. Ibid., p. 1.
18. Ibid.
19. Ibid., p. 34. See, however, p. 117 where all rational creatures are said to receive a share of the Holy Spirit. Butterworth suggests in footnote 1, "The Spirit is given potentially to all, but his effective working is confined to the saints of Old and New Testament alike."
20. Ibid.
21. Ibid., p. 35.
22. Ibid.
23. Ibid.
24. Ibid., cf. Luke 17:20-21.
25. Ibid., p. 51.
26. Ibid., p. 70.
27. Ibid., p. 71.
28. Ibid.
29. Ibid., p. 72.
30. Ibid., p. 72-73.
31. Ibid., p. 73.
32. Ibid.
33. Quoted in Jerome *Ep. ad Avitum* 4; cf. ibid., p. 74, footnote 2. For a discussion of the meaning of *Dogmata* in the usage of Origen, see also Frans Heinrich Kettler, *Der ursprüngliche Sinn der Dogmatik des Origenes* (Berlin: Töpelmann, 1966), pp. 17ff.
34. *Origen on First Principles,* pp. 163f.
35. Ibid., p. 169.
36. Ibid., p. 228.
37. Ibid., p. 199.
38. Ibid.
39. Ibid., p. 17.
40. Ibid., pp. 250f.
41. Hans Jonas, *Philosophical Essays,* p. 313f.
42. Origen, *Against Celsus* 3.78 in ANF, 4:495.
43. *Against Celsus* 1.9 in ibid., p. 400.
44. 6.68 in ibid., p. 604.
45. Ibid.
46. 7.41 in ibid., p. 627.
47. 1.63 in ibid., p. 425.
48. 1.67 in ibid., p. 427.
49. 1.67 in ibid.
50. 2.8 in ibid., p. 432.
51. 2.40 in ibid., p. 447.
52. Ibid.
53. 1.68 in ibid., p. 427. Translation slightly modified.

54. 2.79 in ibid., p. 464.
55. 7.48 in ibid., p. 630.
56. 3.49 in ibid., p. 484.
57. 3.46 in ibid., p. 483.
58. 3.46 in ibid., p. 482.
59. 3.49 in ibid., p. 484.
60. 3.54 in ibid., p. 485.
61. 3.54 in ibid.
62. 3.66 in ibid., p. 490.
63. 3.68 in ibid., p. 491.
64. 3.69 in ibid., p. 491.
65. Ibid.
66. Ibid.
67. 7.42 in ibid., p. 628.
68. Ibid.
69. 6.2 in ibid., p. 573.
70. 6.6 in ibid., p. 575. See also 8.47 in ibid., p. 657: "It is incredible that the apostles of Jesus Christ, who were unlettered men of humble life, could have been emboldened to preach Christian truth to men by anything else than the power which was conferred upon them, and the grace which accompanied their words and rendered them effective. . . . "
71. 4.63 in ibid., pp. 525-526.
72. 5.37 in ibid., pp. 559-560.
73. 5.37 in ibid., p. 560.
74. 5.37 in ibid.
75. 5.37 in ibid.
76. 7.59 in ibid., p. 634.
77. 6.3 in ibid., p. 574.
78. 5.42 in ibid., p. 562.
79. 5.43 in ibid.
80. Ibid.
81. Ibid.
82. 5.50 in ibid., p. 565.
83. Cf. 7.18 in ibid., pp. 617-618.
84. 7.18 in ibid., p. 618.
85. 7.21 in ibid., p. 619.
86. 7.22 in ibid.
87. 7.26 in ibid., p. 621.
88. 7.25 in ibid. Here Origen is concerned to show the continuity between the Old and New Testaments even on the literal level, by pointing to the similarity between Lamentations 3:27-30 and Matthew 5:34.
89. 5.34 in ibid., p. 558.
90. Ibid.
91. 5.35 in ibid., p. 559.

92. 5.39 in ibid., p. 561.
93. Ibid.
94. 8.35 in ibid., p. 652.
95. Ibid.
96. 4.81 in ibid., p. 533.
97. Ibid.
98. 4.83 in ibid., p. 534.
99. 4.85 in ibid., p. 535.
100. Ibid.
101. 4.83 in ibid., p. 534.
102. Ibid.
103. 8.68 in ibid., p. 660.
104. 8.70 in ibid., p. 666.
105. 8.73 in ibid., p. 668.
106. Ibid.
107. 8.75 in ibid.
108. 8.73 in ibid.
109. *Origen on First Principles,* p. 57.
110. To the following: W. Völker, *Das Vollkommenheitsideal des Orig-enes: Eine Untersuchung zur Geschichte der Frömmigkeit und zu den Anfängen christlicher Mystik* (Tübingen: Mohr, 1931), pp. 197ff.
111. Origen, *On Prayer* 10.2 in *Alexandrian Christianity,* p. 258.
112. Ibid.
113. 12.1 in ibid., p. 261.
114. 25.1 in ibid., p. 289.
115. 27.2 in ibid., p. 296.
116. 22.4 in ibid., p. 282.
117. Ibid.
118. Origen, *Exhortation to Martyrdom* 12 in ibid., p. 401.
119. *Exhortation* 40 in ibid., pp. 422-423.
120. Origen, *Dialogue with Heraclides* 172 in ibid., p. 454.
121. Ibid.
122. 172 in ibid., p. 455.
123. Origen, *Against Celsus,* 8.52 in ANF, 4:659.
124. 8.52 in ibid.
125. Ibid.
126. Ibid.
127. Ibid.

**CHAPTER VI: The Fourth Century**

1. Hans Lietzmann, *A History of the Early Church* (New York: Meridian Books, 1961), 3:19.
2. Ibid., p. 20.

3. Section 6 in ANF, 7:303.
4. Eusebius, *The Ecclesiastical History* 8.1 in the translation of J. E. L. Oulton, 2:251.
5. 8.9 in ibid., pp. 279, 287.
6. 8.1 in ibid., p. 253.
7. 8.1 in ibid., p. 255.
8. 8.1 in ibid., p. 253.
9. To the following see: A. H. M. Jones, "The Social Background of the Struggle Between Paganism and Christianity" in Arnaldo Momigliano, *The Conflict Between Paganism and Christianity in the Fourth Century: Essays* (Oxford: Clarendon, 1963), pp. 17-37.
10. "It has been pointed out that in both countries pagan dedications at rural shrines came to an abrupt end in the middle of the third century." Ibid., p. 18.
11. To the following see Richard H. Connolly, *Didascalia Apostolorum: The Syriac Version Translated and Accompanied by the Verona Latin Fragments* (Oxford: Clarendon, 1969). Originally in Greek, the complete text has survived only in an early Syriac translation.
12. Ibid., p. 2.
13. Ibid.
14. Ibid.
15. Ibid., p. 4.
16. Ibid.
17. Ibid., pp. 8-10.
18. Ibid.
19. Ibid., p. 11.
20. Ibid.
21. Ibid., p. 12.
22. Ibid.
23. Ibid., p. 14.
24. Ibid.
25. Ibid., pp. 20-28.
26. Ibid., p. 28.
27. Ibid.
28. Ibid., p. 30.
29. Ibid.
30. Ibid., p. 32.
31. Ibid., pp. 32-34.
32. Ibid., p. 34.
33. Ibid., p. 36.
34. Ibid., p. 38.
35. Ibid., p. 40.
36. Ibid., p. 64.
37. Ibid.
38. Ibid., p. 78.

39. Ibid., p. 86.
40. Ibid., p. 88.
41. Ibid., p. 86.
42. Ibid., pp. 86-88.
43. Ibid., p. 88.
44. Ibid.
45. Ibid.
46. Ibid., p. 98.
47. Ibid., pp. 98-100.
48. Ibid., p. 112.
49. Ibid., p. 119.
50. Ibid., p. 122.
51. Ibid., pp. 122-124.
52. Ibid., p. 132.
53. Ibid., p. 142.
54. Ibid., p. 146.
55. Ibid., pp. 147f.
56. Ibid., p. 154.
57. Ibid., pp. 158f.
58. Samuel Laeuchli, *Power and Sexuality, The Emergence of Canon Law at the Synod of Elvira* (Philadelphia: Temple University Press, 1972).
59. Of course we do not know whether these laws were actually enforced. They do, however, reflect the prevailing attitudes among the leadership of the Christian movement a few years before the so-called Edict of Milan in 313, which granted religious freedom to the Christians.
60. Canon 8: "Women who, without any preceding cause, leave their husbands and take up with other men are not to receive communion even at the end." Laeuchli, *Power and Sexuality,* p. 127.
61. Canon 47, ibid., p. 131.
62. Canon 71, ibid., p. 134.
63. Canon 16, ibid., p. 128.
64. Canon 15, ibid.
65. Canon 18, ibid., p. 128.
66. Canon 21, ibid., p. 129.
67. Canon 41, ibid., p. 131.
68. Canon 59, ibid., p. 133.
69. Canon 56, ibid., p. 132.
70. Canon 60, ibid., p. 133.
71. Canon 62, ibid.
72. Canon 79, ibid., p. 135.
73. Canon 44, ibid., p. 131.
74. Canon 42, ibid.
75, Eusebius, *Ecclesiastical History* 7.15 in the translation by Oulton, 2:171f.

76. 8.2 in ibid., p. 259.
77. Ibid.
78. 8.6 in ibid., p. 269.
79. See e.g. N. H. Baynes, "The Great Persecution" in *The Cambridge Ancient History* (Cambridge: Cambridge University Press, 1939), 12:667f. On the other hand, K. Stade, *Der Politiker Diokletian und die letzte grosse Christenverfolgung* (Frankfurt, 1926), considers Diocletian responsible.
80. Lietzmann, *History of the Early Church*, p. 65.
81. Ibid.
82. Cf. Lactantius, *The Manner in Which the Persecutors Died* 34 in ANF, 7:13.
83. Eusebius, *Ecclesiastical History* 9.1 in the translation by Oulton, 2:331.
84. To the following see: Hermann Dörries, *Constantine the Great*, trans. R. Bainton (New York: Harper & Row, 1972).
85. Ibid., pp. 29ff.
86. Eusebius, *Ecclesiastical History* 9.9 in the translation by Oulton, 2:359.
87. Jacob Burckhardt, *The Age of Constantine the Great*, trans. M. Hadas (London: Routledge and Kegan, Paul, 1949), p. 292.
88. Ibid., p. 293.
89. Dörries, *Constantine the Great*, p. 40. Cf. also J. Straub, "Konstantins Verzicht auf den Gang zum Kapitol," *Historia* IV (1955), pp. 297-313.
90. Quoted in Lactantius, *The Manner in Which the Persecutors Died* 48 in ANF, 7:320. Cf. Eusebius, *Ecclesiastical History* 10.5 in the translation by Oulton, pp. 447f.
91. Dörries, *Constantine the Great*, pp. 36f.
92. Eusebius, *Life of Constantine the Great* 2.24 in *A Select Library of Nicene and Post-Nicene Fathers of the Christian Church*, Second Series (Grand Rapids, Mich.: Eerdmans, 1952), 1:506.
93. The authenticity of this document is now generally recognized. See Dörries, *Constantine*, p. 59, and J. Winkelmann, "Die Textbezeugung der Vita Constantini," *Texte und Untersuchungen*, LXXXIV (1962).
94. Eusebius, *Life of Constantine* 2.25 in *Nicene and Post-Nicene Fathers*, 1:506.
95. 2.26 in ibid., p. 507.
96. 2.28 in ibid.
97. 2.33 in ibid., p. 508.
98. 2.44 in ibid., p. 511.
99. Dörries, *Constantine the Great*, p. 160.
100. Eusebius, *Ecclesiastical History* 9.8 in the translation by Oulton, 2:357.
101. For the relationship of Constantine and Lactantius see Eberhard

Heck, *Die dualistischen Zusätze und die Kaiseranreden bei Lactan-tius* (Heidelberg: Winter, 1972), especially pp. 158-170. Here also is a discussion of the "addresses" to Constantine in the text and their authenticity as assumed in the material below.

102. Lactantius, *The Divine Institutes* 6.2 in ANF, 7:174.
103. Ibid.
104. Ibid., pp. 174-175.
105. Ibid., p. 175.
106. Ibid.
107. Ibid.
108. Ibid.
109. Ibid.
110. 7.12 in ibid., pp. 175-176.
111. Ibid., p. 176.
112. Ibid., pp. 176-177.
113. Ibid., p. 178.
114. 1.1 in ibid., p. 10.
115. 7.26 in ibid., p. 221.
116. Ibid., pp. 221-222.
117. Geffcken, *Church and State: Their Relations Historically Developed,* trans. and ed. E. Taylor (London: Longmans, 1877), 1:111f.
118. *The Theodosian Code* 9.40.2 in *The Theodosian Code and Novels and the Sirmondian Constitutions: A Translation with Commentary, Glossary and Bibliography,* trans. C. Pharr (Princeton University Press, 1952), p. 255.
119. 3.3.1 in ibid., p. 65.
120. 16.5.1 in ibid., p. 450.

## CHAPTER VII: Basil

1. Basil described this search in Letter 223, written in 375. Cf. Saint Basil, *The Letters,* trans. R. Deferrari, Loeb Classical Library (New York: Putnam, 1926), 3:293.
2. Saint Basil, letter 2 in ibid., 1:9.
3. Ibid., p. 11.
4. Ibid., p. 15.
5. Ibid., p. 19. The influence of certain of the Athenian philosophers is quite apparent in some of the suggestions: "The humble and abject spirit is attended by a gloomy and downcast eye, neglected appearance, unkempt hair, and dirty clothes; consequently the characteristics which mourners effect designedly are found in us as a matter of course" (p. 21). That dirtiness is next to godliness was simply assumed.
6. Cf. Berthold Altaner, *Patrologie: Leben, Schriften und Lehre der Kirchenväter,* 5th ed. (Freiburg: Herder, 1958), p. 260.

7. Socrates Scholasticus, *The Ecclesiastical History* 4.23 in *A Select Library of Nicene and Post-Nicene Fathers of the Christian Church,* ed. P. Schaff and H. Wace, 14 vols., 2nd series (Grand Rapids, Mich.: Eerdmans, 1952), 2:108. This series is hereafter designated NPNF.
8. Basil, Letter 22 in *The Letters,* 1:129.
9. The biblical references Basil had in mind are here added.
10. Basil, *The Letters,* 1:131.
11. Letter 2 in ibid., 1:15.
12. Ibid., 1:17.
13. Ibid.
14. Ibid.
15. W. K. L. Clarke suggests that this work was written about 362-365. His reason is significant: "Rule 72, 1 which lays down the regulation that listeners must test what their teachers say and reject what is contrary to Scripture, is appropriate to the years 362-365. It would be less fitting from the pen of the masterful archbishop of 370-379." trans. W. K. L. Clarke (London: SPCK, 1925), p. 16.
16. Basil, *The Morals,* in ibid., pp. 101-131.
17. *The Morals* 1.1-2 in ibid., p. 101.
18. 3.1 in ibid., p. 102.
19. 43.1-3 in ibid., p. 112.
20. 48 in ibid., pp. 113f.
21. 49 in ibid., p. 114.
22. 63 in ibid., p. 125.
23. 75.1 in ibid., p. 126.
24. 75.2 in ibid.
25. 76.1-2 in ibid., p. 127.
26. 78.1 in ibid.
27. 79.1 in ibid.
28. 80.1 in ibid.
29. W. K. L. Clarke suggests that Basil is thinking of the Arian argument that the Son as "son" must be posterior to the Father. See ibid., p. 129, footnote 2.
30. 80.22 in ibid.
31. 80.22 in ibid., p. 130.
32. Ibid.
33. Ibid.
34. Ibid.
35. Letter 366 in Saint Basil, *The Letters,* 4:353.
36. Ibid.
37. *The Morals,* 70.22 in *Ascetic Works of Saint Basil,* p. 131.
38. In Homily 3.1 of the *Hexameron* he states: "I know that many artisans, belonging to mechanical trades, are crowding around me. A day's labour hardly suffices to maintain them; therefore I am com-

pelled to abridge my discourse, so as not to keep them from their work"; in NPNF, 8:65.

39. Basil, *Hexameron* 9.3 in ibid., p. 103.
40. Ibid.
41. 9.4 in ibid.
42. 9.4 in ibid.
43. Ibid.
44. Basil, Homily on Luke 12 in *Patrologiae Cursus Completus,* ed. J. P. V. Migne, Series Graeca, 176 vols. (Paris: Garnier, 1857-1912), 31:267f.
45. Ibid., p. 278.
46. Ibid.
47. E.g., ibid., pp. 278-303.
48. Cf. Letter 223 in *The Letters,* 3:293.
49. Basil wrote to a tax official to prevent an increase in the assessment of his foster brother's property, because part of this property was held in trust for Basil's support. Cf. Letter 38 in *The Letters,* 1.193f.
50. Sozomen, *The Ecclesiastical History* 6.16 in NPNF, 2:356.
51. Ibid.
52. In *Patrologiae Cursus Completus,* 29:266ff.
53. *Homilia in Divites* in ibid., 31:285f., as translated in NPNF, 8:lxiif.
54. In *Patrologiae Cursus Completus,* 31:285.
55. Ibid., p. 288.
56. Ibid.
57. Letter 45 in *The Letters,* 1:279.
58. Ibid., p. 283.
59. Letter 46 in ibid., 1:309.
60. Letter 73 in ibid., 2:65.
61. Letter 84 in ibid., 2:103-109.
62. Letters 107 and 108 in ibid., 2:203-207.
63. Letter 101 in ibid., 2:187-189; 206 in 3:177-181.
64. Letter 99 in ibid., 2:171-183.
65. Letter 188 in ibid., 3:21. This is a reference to the three stages of development of the foetus, its endowment first with a vegetative, then with a sensitive, and finally with a rational soul. Only after the rational soul is infused did one speak of a formed foetus. The reason Basil gave for considering abortion always murder was that the drugs intended to cause the abortion frequently killed the mother. The concern is at least as much for the health of the mother as for the life of the embryo.
66. Ibid., p. 23.
67. Ibid., pp. 29-31.
68. Ibid., p. 33.
69. Cf. John the Baptist's advice to soldiers in Luke 3:14.
70. Letter 106 in *The Letters,* 2:203.
71. Letter 155 in ibid., 2:383.

Notes / 203

72. Letter 116 in ibid., 2:233-235.
73. Letter 217 in ibid., 3:247.
74. Ibid., pp. 249-255.
75. Laeuchli, *Power and Sexuality*, p. 88.
76. Basil was aware and seemed to disapprove of the double morality in sexual matters. He asserted that rules in regard to divorce should logically apply to both sexes alike. But he observed, "custom does not so obtain" (Letter 188.9 in *The Letters* 3:35f.; see also letter 199.21 in 3:113: "However, he who has committed fornication shall not be excluded from living with his wife. Therefore the wife will receive her husband when he returns from fornication, but the husband will dismiss the polluted woman from his house. But the reasoning in these matters is also not easy. But the custom has so obtained.") That is, Roman law recognized the husband's right to divorce an adulterous wife, but did not permit a wife to divorce an adulterous husband. A woman's only valid cause for divorce was that her husband was a murderer, sorcerer, or a destroyer of tombs. For a man the wife's adultery, sorcery, and procuring were considered valid grounds. Cf. *The Theodosian Code*, ed. and trans. Clyde Pharr (Princeton: Princeton University Press, 1952), pp. 76-77.
77. *Theodosian Code*, pp. 217-218.
78. Ibid., p. 246.
79. Ibid., pp. 74-75.
80. Ibid., p. 70.
81. Werner Jaeger, *Early Christianity and Greek Paideia* (Cambridge, Mass.: Harvard University Press, 1965), pp. 83-84.
82. Ibid., p. 75.
83. *Patrologiae Cursus Completus*, 31:564-589.
84. Jaeger, *Early Christianity*, p. 81.
85. *Patrologiae*, p. 572.
86. Ibid., pp. 576-577.
87. Ibid., p. 584. "He who does not want to be buried in the slime *(borboros)* of sensual lust must despise the body, i.e., respect it only in so far as the body aids, in the words of Plato, in the striving for wisdom. Plato says here the same as Paul."
88. Gregory Nazianzen, *The Panegyric on S. Basil*, NPNF, 7:407.
89. Ibid.
90. Ibid., p. 416.
91. Theodoret, *The Ecclesiastical History* 4.16, NPNF, 3:120.
92. Gregory Nazianzen, *Panegyric on S. Basil*, 44f., NPNF, 7:410-412; see also Sozomen, *The Ecclesiastical History* 6.16, NPNF, 2:353-354.
93. Gregory Nazianzen, *Panegyric on S. Basil*, NPNF, 7:411.
94. Ibid., 7:416.
95. Basil, Letter 94 in *The Letters*, 2:151.
96. Letters 142 and 143 in ibid., 2:345, 347.

97. Cf. Demetrios J. Constantelos, *Byzantine Philanthropy and Social Welfare* (New Brunswick, N.J.: Rutgers University Press, 1968), p. 18:

> Today philanthropy implies prophylactic and therapeutic welfare, concern for the general public, and charity properly so called, directed toward alleviation of individual suffering. But in the thought and life of the Byzantines, *philanthropia* was: first, a philosophical and theological abstraction; second, a political attribute; third, charity directed to the individual in want; and fourth, philanthropy properly so called and expressed in organized institutions.

## CHAPTER VIII: John Chrysostom

1. This date has been questioned, and dates as early as 344 have been suggested. The arguments in C. Baur, *John Chrysostom and His Time*, trans. M. Gonzaga (Westminster, Maryland: Newman, 1959-60), 1:3, in support of 354 are convincing.
2. Ibid., 29.
3. Ibid., 16.
4. Chrysostom, *On the Priesthood* I, 5; NPNF, I, 9:34.
5. Socrates, *Church History*, IV, 26, NPNF, II, 2:110f.
6. Ibid., VI, 3; NPNF, II, 2:139.
7. The remark occurs in a context which throws some light not only on Chrysostom's opinion of Libanius but also on his attitude toward his mother: "For once when I was still a young man I know that the sophist who taught me (and he exceeded all men in his reverence for the gods) expressed admiration for my mother before a large company. For enquiring, as was his wont, of those who sat beside him who I was, and some one having said that I was the son of a woman who was a widow, he asked me the age of my mother and the duration of her widowhood, and when I told him that she was forty years of age of which twenty had elapsed since she lost my father, he was astonished and uttered a loud exclamation, and turning to those present 'Heavens!' cried he, 'what women there are amongst the Christians.' So great is the admiration and praise enjoyed by widowhood not only amongst ourselves, but also amongst those who are outside the Church." Chrysostom, *Letters to a Young Widow*, 2; NPNF, 9:122. For the identification of "the sophist who taught me" as Libanius, cf. Baur, *Chrysostom*, 1:23.
8. Libanios, *Discours Moraux*, Societe D'edition "Les Belles Lettres," Editor Bernard Schouler (Paris 1973).
9. Gerhard Kittel, *Theological Dictionary of the New Testament*, ed. Gerhard Friedrich (Grand Rapids: Eerdmans) 9:112.

10. Julian, "Against the Gallileans," *Works,* trans. Wilmer Cave Wright, 3 vols. (New York: Putnam, 1923), 3:318ff.
11. Julian, "Letter to a Priest," *Works,* 2:337.
12. Ibid.
13. Ibid., 2:299.
14. E.g., Libanius' oration to Emperor Theodosius, "On the Prisoners":
   Then, Sire, let your humanity [philanthropia] reveal itself here too. That you have enacted a law to help people under arrest as regards the length of detention, and that this does serve to protect them, I know. But I also know that the same sort of practices have been current after passing of the law as would have occurred if it was not in force. When magistrates willing to enforce them are non-existent, the laws are mere scraps of paper and do not provide assistance to the victims by allowing them to get the better of their oppressors through their results. Libanius, *Works,* II:191.
15. Baur, *John Chrysostom,* I:26.
16. Chrysostom, *On the Priesthood* I, 3; NPNF, I, 9:33.
17. Ibid.
18. Cf. Julian, "Letter to Photinus," *Works,* 3:189.
19. A. Harnack, *History of Dogma,* 4:165.
20. Baur, *John Chrysostom,* I:93.
21. Ibid., I:96.
22. Chrysostom, "Letters to the Fallen Theodore," II, 5; NPNF, I, 9:115.
23. Cf. Chrysostom, *On the Priesthood,* I, 5; NPNF, I, 9:34.
24. Palladius, *Dialogue Concerning the Life of Chrysostom,* ed. H. Moore, SPCK, London, 1921, p. 40.
25. C. Baur, *John Chrysostom,* II:3.
26. Ibid., "When about the year 439 the people of Constantinople applauded their prefect Cyrus at the racecourse louder than the Emperor, the unfortunate man was quickly relieved of his office and deprived of all his property, and dared only regard it as a favor that he was appointed Bishop of Smyrna by force. Of course this was not a special mark of favor, for his four direct predecessors in the shepherd's seat at Smyrna had been murdered one after another by their own mangy sheep."
27. Ibid., II:13.
28. Cf. Chrysostom, *Letters to the Fallen Theodore,* I, 9, 10, 11; NPNF, I, 9:97-100.
29. Chrysostom, *Letter to a Young Widow,* 3; NPNF, I, 9:123f.
30. Chrysostom, *Instructions to Catechumens,* I, 3; NPNF, 9:161.
31. Ibid.
32. Ibid., 162.
33. Ibid., 167.
34. Ibid.

35. Chrysostom, *Resisting the Temptations of the Devil*, NPNF, I, 9:191f.
36. To the above, cf. Chrysostom, *II Timothy* VIII, NPNF, I, 13:507f.
37. Baur, *Chrysostom*, I:373.
38. Chrysostom, *Homilies on St. John*, XXXI, 1; NPNF, I, 14:106.
39. Ibid., LXXXIV, 3; NPNF, I, 14:315.
40. Chrysostom, *St. Matthew* LXIV, 4; NPNF, I, 10:395.
41. Chrysostom, *Ephesians* I, 4; NPNF, I, 13:51.
42. Cf. Ibid., footnote.
43. Chrysostom, *St. Matthew* III, 6; NPNF, I, 10:17f.
44. Ibid.
45. Chrysostom, *Philippians* XII, 1; NPNF, I, 13:238.
46. Ibid., p. 239.
47. Chrysostom, *Hebrews* VII, 11; NPNF, I, 14:402.
48. Ibid.
49. Cf. Chrysostom, *De Virginitate*, in Migne, *Patrologiae Graecae*, 48:533-596.
50. Chrysostom, *Hebrews* VII, 11; NPNF, I, 14:402.
51. Chrysostom, *Adversus Oppugnatores Vitae Monast.* III, 14; Migne, *Patrologiae*, 47:373.
52. Chrysostom, *De Virginitate* 10; Migne, *Patrologiae*, 48:540.
53. Ibid., 41; Migne, *Patrologiae*, 48:564.
54. Chrysostom, *The Gospel of Matthew*, XLVI, 5; NPNF, I, 10:295.
55. These were sermons resulting from the riots of the population of Antioch against imperial taxes during which the statues of the emperor Theodosius had been overturned and dragged through the streets. The revenge of the city prefect Tisamenus, still a pagan, who feared that he would be held responsible by the emperor for the unrest, created days of terror. Rich and poor, old and young were executed. Cf. Baur, *Chrysostom*, I:259-283.
56. Chrysostom, *Concerning the Statues* XII, 9; NPNF, I, 9:421.
57. Ibid., p. 422.
58. Ibid.
59. Ibid.
60. Chrysostom, *Romans* V, 2:15; NPNF, I, 11:365.
61. Chrysostom, *Genesis* II, 8; Migne, *Patrologiae*, 53:144f.
62. Chrysostom, *Concerning the Statues* XII, 10; NPNF, I, 9:422.
63. The reference is to Ham (Gen. 9:22f.), yet Noah's curse is against Canaan, Ham's son.
64. Chrysostom, *In Genesim*, V, i; Migne, 54:599.
65. Ibid.
66. Ibid.
67. Migne, *Patrologiae*, 53:275.
68. Chrysostom, *Romans*, 5:17, NPNF, I, 11:403.
69. Chrysostom, *Matthew*, 19, 6; NPNF, I, 10:134.
70. Ibid. (Italics added).

71. Ibid., 135.
72. Ibid.
73. Ibid.
74. Ibid.
75. Ibid.
76. Ibid.
77. Ibid., 137.
78. Chrysostom, *Matthew,* I, 10; NPNF, I, 10:4.
79. Ibid., 5.
80. Ibid.
81. Ibid., 6.
82. Chrysostom, *Contra Eos Qui Sub Introducta Habent Virgines,* Migne, *Patrologiae,* 47:495ff. Palladius, p. 44: Chrysostom "inveighed against the mode of life, whitewashed under the name of 'brotherly life,' which he called by its right name of 'evil life,' in connection with the women known as 'introduced.' He showed it to be worse, if a choice of evils had to be made, than that of brothel-keepers; for they live far from the surgery, and keep the disease to themselves, for those who desire it, while the 'brothers' live within the workshop of salvation, and invite healthy people to come and catch the disease. This caused great indignation to those among the clergy who were without the love of God, and blazing with passion."
83. Cf. Baur, *Chrysostom,* II:63.
84. At the Synod of the Oak this sale of marble belonging to a church was used against him, Baur, *Chrysostom,* II:58.
85. Palladius, *Life of Chrysostom,* 46.
86. Chrysostom, *Philippians,* I; NPNF, I, 13:187.
87. Chrysostom, *De Lazaro* I, 12; Migne, *Patrologiae,* 48:980.
88. Chrysostom, *Psalm XLVIII,* 3; Migne, *Patrologiae,* 55:515f.
89. Ibid.
90. Ibid., 517.
91. Ibid., 518.
92. Chrysostom, *I Corinthians,* XXXIV, 8; NPNF, I, 12:205f.
93. Ibid.
94. Robert von Pöhlmann, *Geschichte Der Sozialen Frage und Des Sozialismus in Der Antiken Welt* (München: Beck, 1925), II:479.
95. Chrysostom, *Acts of the Apostles* VII, NPNF, I, 11:45-47.
96. Chrysostom, *I Timothy,* XII, NPNF, I, 13:447.
97. Ibid., 447, where the quotation, however, is incorrectly identified.
98. Ibid.
99. Ibid., 448.
100. Ibid.
101. Ibid.
102. Chrysostom, *Acts,* VII, *NPNF,* I, 11:48.
103. Chrysostom, *Colossians,* IV; NPNF, I, 13:279.
104. Chrysostom, *I Timothy,* XI, NPNF, I, 13:443.

105. Ibid.
106. Ibid.
107. Chrysostom, *Ephesians* XIII, NPNF, I, 13:116.
108. Chrysostom, *Matthew* XLIII, NPNF, I, 10:277.
109. Ibid., 278.
110. Ibid.
111. Chrysostom, *Romans*, XXIII; NPNF, I, 11:511. This distinction between authority *in abstracto* and *in concreto* disturbed George B. Stevens of Yale University, the nineteenth century editor of the NPNF edition, who commented, "The question of obeying unjust rulers and supporting the 'powers' in unjust measures, the apostle does not raise."
112. Ibid., 512.
113. Ibid., 513.
114. Ibid.
115. Ibid.
116. Cf. Otto Seeck, *Geschichte Des Untergangs Der Antiken Welt* (Stuttgart, 1920), V:337ff. "If a bishop opposed all heresies unmercifully it was considered to be to his credit, but if he opposed real sins and excoriated them in his sermons he was bound to come in conflict with the people of a profoundly corrupt age. Such criticism they were not willing to forgive. Nevertheless the high idealism which filled his mighty personality remained effective even beyond his exile but not to the benefit of empire or church."

## CHAPTER IX: Augustine

1. His alleged first name Aurelius "occurs neither in the *Confessions,* nor in the salutations to correspondence, nor in the earliest life by Possidus." Saint Augustine, *The City of God Against the Pagans,* trans. George E. McCracken (Cambridge, Mass.: Harvard University Press, 1957), 1:vii.
2. Cf. O. Perler, "Les voyages de saint Augustin" in *Recherches Augustiennes* (Paris: Etudes Augustiniennes, 1958), 1:23. Against Peter Brown, *Augustine of Hippo* (Berkeley: University of California Press, 1967), p. 20, who would have Thagaste 200 miles from the sea.
3. Brown, *Augustine,* p. 24.
4. Augustine, *Confessions,* II; 3, 5f., trans. and ed. Albert Outler, *Library of Christian Classics*—hereafter written LCC—(Philadelphia: Westminster, 1955), 7:52.
5. Ibid.
6. Ibid.
7. Augustine, *Confessions,* IX, 9, 22 in LCC, p. 192.
8. Augustine, *Confessions,* I, 11, 17 in ibid., pp. 404.

9. Augustine, *Confessions*, III, 4, 8 in ibid., pp. 64ff.
10. Augustine, *Confessions*, I, 12, 19ff. in ibid., pp. 41ff.
11. Augustine, *Confessions*, I, 16, 26 in ibid., p. 45.
12. Brown, *Augustine*, p. 65.
13. Augustine, *Confessions*, III, 3, 6 in ibid., p. 64.
14. Augustine, *Confessions*, III, 5, 9 in ibid., p. 66.
15. Augustine, *Confessions*, IX, 6, 14 in ibid., p. 186.
16. Augustine, *Confessions*, VI, 15, 25 in ibid., p. 132.
17. Augustine, *On the Profit of Believing*, 2; NPNF, I, 3:348.
18. Ibid.
19. *Ennarationes in Psalmos*, LIV, 20 in *Corpus Christianorum Series Latina* (Turnholt, 1956), 39, 672. The illuminating discussion of the Donatist attitude is unfortunately omitted in the English translation in NPNF, I, 8, 216.
20. *On the Profit of Believing*, 2; NPNF, I, 3:348.
21. *Confessions*, V, 8, 14 in LCC, p. 103.
22. It was this Q. Aurelius Symmachus, "the most famous writer and rhetorician Rome then had" [H. Campenhausen, *Men Who Shaped the Western Church* (New York: Harper, 1965), p. 105], who wrote the petition asking for the return of the altar of the goddess of victory to the senate building and presented it in 384 to Emperor Valentinian II. To the above see Richard Klein, *Der Streit um den Victoriaaltar* (Darmstadt: Wissenschaftliche Buchgesellschaft, 1972).
23. *Confessions*, V, 13, 23 in LCC, p. 110f.
24. Ibid.
25. *Confessions*, V, 14 in ibid., p. 111. See also H. Campenhausen, *Men Who Shaped the Western Church*, p. 94.
26. *Confessions*, V, 14, 25 in ibid., p. 112.
27. Campenhausen, *Men Who Shaped the Western Church*, p. 105.
28. To the following, see Campenhausen, *Men Who Shaped the Western Church*, pp. 105ff.
29. "The Memorial of Symmachus," 3; NPNF, 10:414.
30. Ibid., p. 415.
31. Ambrose, Letter XVIII, NPNF, II, 10:417.
32. Ibid.
33. Ibid., p. 418.
34. Ibid.
35. Campenhausen observes that this approach was also quite different from Ambrose's usual arguments, "Ambrose naturally also protested against the superstitions conjuring up of an alleged anger of the gods and declares, *contrary to his usual manner* [italics mine] that political successes or disasters are completely independent of the question of religion. In an interesting historical and theological excursus, he describes progress as the actual power that moves nature and history, and he mocks the nostalgic complaints of the

Roman senate." Campenhausen, *Men Who Shaped the Western Church*, p. 107.

36. E.g. The conflict between Constantine and Maxentius had been described by Eusebius entirely in terms of "true faith" and "superstition." Eusebius, *The Ecclesiastical History*, trans. J. E. L. Oulton (London: Heinemann, 1932), 2:359.
37. *Confessions* VI, 13, 23 in LCC, p. 130.
38. *Confessions* VI, 15 in ibid., p. 132.
39. *Confessions* VI, 6 in ibid., p. 120.
40. Ibid.
41. Ibid.
42. *Confessions* IX, 6ff.
43. F. van der Meer, *Augustine, the Bishop*. (New York: Sheed and Ward, 1961), p. 10.
44. NPNF, II, 10:1-89.
45. E.g. Cicero, *De Officiis*, trans. Walter Miller (New York: Putnam, 1928).
46. Ambrose, *Duties*. 28; NPNF, II, 10:22f. It is noteworthy that Ambrose does not follow his source uncritically. He excludes from justice those elements suggested by Cicero (e.g. "revenge" and "private property") which he considers contrary to the authority of the Gospel.
47. Cicero, *De Officiis*, III, 28 in Miller, p. 365.
48. Ambrose, *Duties* III, NPNF, II, 10:71f.
49. Ibid.
50. Ambrose, *Luke* II, 84; Migne, *Patrologiae Latinae*, 15:1665.
51. Ibid.
52. Ambrose, *De Jacob et Vita Beata*, I, 3, 10; ibid., 14:632.
53. Ambrose, *De Jacob et Vita Beata*, I, 6, 24; ibid., 14:637.
54. To the following see: Ottmar Dittrich, *Geschichte der Ethik* (Leipzig: Scientia Verlag Aalen, 1964), 2:219ff.
55. Augustine, *Earlier Writings*, in LCC, 6:102.
56. Ibid.
57. Augustine, *On Free Will*, III, 46 in ibid., p. 199.
58. Augustine, *On Free Will*, III, 50 in ibid., p. 201.
59. Augustine, *On Rebuke and Grace*, 1; NPNF, I, 5:472.
60. Ibid.
61. Ibid.
62. Ibid.
63. Augustine, *On Rebuke and Grace*, II; in ibid., p. 472.
64. Augustine, *On Rebuke and Grace*, V, in ibid., p. 474.
65. Augustine, *On Rebuke and Grace*, X, in ibid., p. 482.
66. Augustine, *On Rebuke and Grace*, XII, in ibid., p. 485.
67. Augustine, *On Rebuke and Grace*, XIII, in ibid., p. 489. (Italics added.)
68. Augustine, *On Rebuke and Grace*, XII, in ibid., p. 485.

69. Augustine, *On Grace and Free Will*, XI, in ibid., p. 456. (Italics added.)
70. Augustine, *On Rebuke and Grace*, VII, in ibid., p. 476f.
71. Augustine, *On the Predestination of the Saints*, VIII, in ibid., p. 506.
72. Augustine, *The Catholic and Manichaean Ways of Life* XIV in *The Fathers of the Church* (Washington: Catholic University of America Press, 1964), 56:22.
73. Ibid. Translation modified.
74. Augustine, *On Christian Doctrine*, III, 10; NPNF, I, 2:561.
75. *Ibid.* Translation modified, i.e., *cupiditas* is translated as desire.
76. Ibid. It is noteworthy that Augustine here uses *frui* (enjoy) in a good and bad sense and does not change to *uti* (use) when talking about *cupiditas*.
77. Ibid. For Augustine all crimes are sins. He does not raise the possibility that an act may be a crime according to the "positive laws" of the country—yet not a sin before God.
78. The NPNF translation of *utilitas* as "prudence" is not very precise, but preferable to the more literal meanings of the word.
79. Augustine, *On Christian Doctrine* III, 10; NPNF, I, 2:561. The translation of *beneficentia* as benevolence also lacks precision since benevolence *(benevolentia)* implies *feelings* of friendliness while *beneficentia* emphasizes a kind *treatment* of others.
80. To the above, Augustine, *Enchiridion*, XXXI in LCC, 7:409. (Translation modified.)
81. Augustine, *On the Grace of Christ*, I, 19; NPNF, I, 5:224. (Translation modified.) As is the case frequently NPNF does not translate the Latin terms with any consistency. Those dependent on English translations should be aware that Augustine's precise terms are not translated with equal precision and change frequently according to the preference of the particular translator.
82. Augustine, *City of God*, XIV, 7, trans. Philip Levine (Cambridge: Harvard University Press, 1966), pp. 286ff.: "If a person's intention is to love God and also to love his neighbor even as himself, not according to man, but according to God, he is beyond any doubt called a man of good will because of this love. And although this disposition is more commonly termed "charity" *(caritas)* in holy Scripture, yet it is also designated as "love" *(amor)* according to the same sacred writings."
83. Ibid., pp. 290-291.
84. Ibid.
85. Augustine, *Ennarationes in Psalmos*, XXXI, II, 5, in *Corpus Christianorum*, Series Latina XXXVIII (Turnhold, 1956), p. 228.
86. Augustine, *On the Spirit and the Letter*, 5b; NPNF, I, 5:108. See also: Augustine, *On the Grace of Christ*, I, 27; NPNF, I, 5:227f.
87. Augustine, *Letters*, 155 (To Macedonius, A.D. 414) in *The Fathers of the Church*, 20:314.

88. Ibid., 317.
89. Augustine, *Epistle of St. John,* VII, 7; NPNF, I, 7:504. (Translation modified and italics added.)
90. Augustine, *Enchiridion,* 121; NPNF, I, 3:275f. (Translation modified.) This discussion has ignored the complex analysis of Augustine's concept of love as presented first by Karl Holl, *Gesammelte Aufsätze zur Kirchengeschichte,* Vol. I, *Luther* (Tübingen: Mohr, 1932); Hannah Arendt, *Der Liebesbegriff bei Augustin, Versuch einer philosophischen Interpretation* (Berlin: 1929); *Philosophische Forschungen,* Vol. 9; Anders Nygren, *Eros und Agape* (Gütersloh: Carl Bertelsmann, 1930/37): and its critical re-interpretation in J. Brechtken *Augustinus Doctor Caritatis* (Meisenheim: Hain, 1974), which in a variety of ways calls attention to the difficulties Augustine had in fusing the egocentric eudaimonism he had inherited from his philosophical tradition with the self-giving love of God revealed in the incarnation of Christ. While this was, indeed, a major intellectual problem for Augustine, he seemed quite aware of it. But his categories "enjoy" vs. "use" *(frui* vs. *uti)* which dominate his theoretical discussion of the human relationship to God and the world are simply inadequate. He himself observed, "And so it is the big question whether human beings should enjoy *(frui)* or use *(uti)* themselves or do both" (Augustine, *On Christian Doctrine,* I, 22; NPNF, I, 2:527; Migne, *Patrologiae,* 34, 26). He knows that this is the "big question," but the categories he forces on it are insufficient. He does become involved in incredible terminological difficulties when trying to determine whether God "enjoys" human beings or "uses" them. He asserts, "For God loves us, and Holy Scripture frequently sets before us the love He has towards us. In what way then does He love us? As objects of use or objects of enjoyment?" Because of the alternatives he has forced on the discussion, he concludes, "He does not enjoy us, but makes use of us. For if He neither enjoys us nor uses us, I am at a loss to discover in what way He can love us." (Ibid., p. 531.) He is admittedly "at a loss," but to call him for this reason "a corrupter of Christian morality" (Holl) seems unfair. In spite of the total inadequacy of his philosophical solution Augustine brought profoundly biblical insights to bear on the development of Christian ethics.
91. Augustine, *On Christian Doctrine,* I, 4; NPNF, I, 2:523. (Translation modified.)
92. Ibid., I, 22; NPNF, I, 2:527.
93. Augustine, *On the Profit of Believing,* 27; Migne, *Patrologiae,* 42:85.
94. Ibid.
95. Augustine, *De Musica,* VI; Migne, *Patrologiae,* 32:1187.
96. Augustine, *On the Greatness of the Soul,* 72 Migne, *Patrologiae,* 32:1075.
97. Ibid.

98. Augustine, *On the Gospel of St. John,* 8, 2; NPNF, I, 7:58. Nowhere has Augustine expressed his admiration for creation more
eloquently than in *City of God* XXII, 24, under the heading "Of
the Good Things With Which The Creator Has Filled Even This
Condemned Life" (Loeb, 7:327-337, e.g. 329). "What marvellous,
stupendous results has human industry achieved in the production
of clothing and buildings! What progress in agriculture and in navi-
gation! What imagination and elaboration it has employed in pro-
ducing all kinds of vases, and also in the varieties of statues and
paintings! How marvellous, in theatres, to those who sit as spectators, how incredible to those who merely hear the report, are the
compositions and performances contrived by men! What great inventions for capturing, killing and taming irrational animals! Against
even human beings all the many kinds of poison, weapons, engines
of war! And how many drugs and remedies it has discovered to
preserve and restore men's health! How many seasonings and appe-
tizers it has found to increase the pleasure of eating!

"What a number, what variety of signs for conveying thought
and persuading men, among which words and letters are most important! What ornaments of speech to delight the mind, what abundance of all kinds of poetry! What musical instruments, what modes
of song have been devised to soothe the ears! What skill in measur-
ing and reckoning! With what acuteness have the courses and laws
of the heavenly bodies been grasped! With what enormous knowledge of worldly things have men filled their minds! Who could
describe this, especially if we wished not to gather everything in one
pile, but to dwell on each separate topic?

"Finally, who could estimate the great talent of philosophers
and heretics displayed in defending errors and untruth? For we
are speaking now about the natural capacity of the human mind
with which this mortal life is endowed, not about the faith and
way of truth by which that immortal life is obtained."
99. Augustine, *City of God,* XIV, in Loeb, 4:529f.
100. Ibid., 265f.
101. Ibid., 269.
102. Ibid., 273; Augustine quoted as his prooftext for this fundamental
and ethically seminal notion Ecclesiasticus 10:12-13 in the Vulgate
translation which differs from the Septuagint where this sentence
reads, "The origin of pride is to forsake the Lord, man's heart re-
volting against his Maker; as its origin is sin, so persistence in it
brings on a deluge of depravity" (NEB).
103. Augustine, *City of God,* XIV, 6 in Loeb, 4:25.
104. Ibid., p. 37.
105. Ibid.
106. Augustine, *De Musica,* VI, 41; Migne, *Patrologiae,* 32:1185.
107. Ibid.

108. Augustine, *City of God*, X, 7 in Loeb 3:279.
109. Ibid.
110. Augustine, *City of God*, XIV, 28 in Loeb, 4:405f.
111. Ibid.
112. Augustine, *City of God*, XV, 4 in Loeb, 4:425.
113. Ibid., 427.
114. Ibid.
115. Augustine interprets the paradise story quite literally and considers absurd the notion that an allegorical interpretation of Scripture, (such as the allegorical interpretation of paradise which he also uses) must abrogate the literal meaning. *City of God*, XIII, 21 in Loeb, 4:217ff.
116. In view of the *frui/uti* distinction it is interesting to note that Augustine writes: "This paradise was not merely corporeal to supply the good things of the body without also being spiritual to supply the good things of the mind; nor was it merely spiritual for the human being *(homo)* to enjoy through his inner senses without also being corporeal for him to enjoy *(frueretur)* through his outer senses." *City of God*, XIV, 11 in Loeb, 4:328.
117. *City of God*, XIV, 12 in Loeb, 4:335.
118. Ibid., XIV, 13.
119. Ibid.
120. Ibid.
121. *City of God*, XIX, 5 in Loeb, 6:139.
122. *City of God*, XIV, 13 in Loeb, 4:339.
123. Ibid., p. 341.
124. Ibid.
125. Ibid.
126. Ibid., XI, 1 in Loeb, 3:427.
127. *City of God*, I, 35; Loeb I, 137.
128. *City of God*, XIX, 17; Loeb VI, 193f.
129. *City of God*, XVIII, 54; Loeb VI, 93.
130. *City of God*, XV, 20; Loeb IV, 525.
131. *City of God*, XIX, 17; Loeb VI, 193f.
132. *City of God*, XVIII, 54; Loeb VI, 93.
133. Cf. *City of God*, XIV, 21; Loeb IV, 371ff. "The nuptial blessing, however, whereby the pair, joined in marriage were to increase and multiply and fill the earth, remained in force even when they sinned, yet it was given before they sinned, for its purpose was to make it clear that the procreation of children is a part of the glory of marriage and not of the punishment of sin." In this context Augustine's relatively positive attitude toward the female sex may be of some interest. In contrast to some earlier Christian theologians, e.g. Origen, Augustine insisted, "The female sex is not a defect, but a natural state." In heaven, "there will be female parts, not suited to their old use, but to a new beauty, and this will not arouse the

lust *(concupiscentia)* of the beholder, for there will be no lust, but it will inspire praise of the wisdom and goodness of God." *City of God*, XXII, 17; Loeb VII, 281.

134. *City of God*, XI, 33; Loeb III, 565.
135. *City of God*, XIV, 13; Loeb IV, 341 (translation modified, italics added).
136. *City of God*, XIX, 13; Loeb VI, 175.
137. *City of God*, XIX, 26; Loeb VI, 237.
138. *City of God*, XIX, 17; Loeb VI, 195.
139. *City of God*, XIX, 17; Loeb VI, 197ff.
140. Augustine, *Morals of the Catholic Church*, 10, 16; NPNF, I, 4:46.
141. Ibid., 58.
142. Ibid.
143. Cf. Augustine, *Enchiridion*, 56; NPNF, I, 3:255.
144. Ibid.
145. *City of God*, XIX, 27; Loeb VI, 23a.
146. *City of God*, XX, 2; Loeb VI, 255.
147. Ibid.
148. *City of God*, XX, 2; Loeb VI, 256.
149. Cf. *City of God*, XX, 1; Loeb VI, 249f.
150. Augustine refers repeatedly to the significance of the fratricide of Romulus for the entire development of the history of the Roman empire: "When Romulus slew his brother, who had perpetrated no evil against him, is it the case that his mind was bent on the vindication of justice, and not on the acquisition of absolute power?" Augustine, *Harmony of the Gospels*, I, 19; NPNF, I, 6, 85. See also *City of God*, III, 6; Loeb I, 283.
151. Augustine, *Harmony of the Gospels*, I, 14; NPNF, I, 6:85.
152. *Ibid.*, 86.
153. *Ennarationes in Psalmos*, 149, 7; NPNF, I, 8:678. (In this translation the passage is given as 149, 4.)
154. Ibid.
155. Ibid.
156. Ibid. For the debate in the secondary literature about the "contradiction" between Augustine's attempt to render the history of the Roman Empire theologically neutral (e.g. Erik Peterson) and his adoption of the more conventional *Reichstheologie* (e.g. P. Brown) see Robert Markus, *Saeculum; History and Society in the Theology of Augustine* (Cambridge: University Press, 1970), pp. 22ff. Markus claims that Augustine held the triumphalist view briefly around 400 just after "the Roman armies had crushed the African revolt of Gildo" (p. 33). He soon abandoned them again. His use of the phrase *tempora christiana* does not restrict it to the period since 325 but "refers to the whole period since the Incarnation" (p. 38).
157. Augustine, *Ennarationes in Psalmos*, LXI, 8; *Corpus Christianorum*, XXXIX, Turnholt, 1956, p. 779; NPNF, I, 8:253.

158. Markus, *Saeculum*, 157.
159. *Ennarationes in Psalmos*, CXXIV, 7; NPNF, I, 8:602f.
160. Ibid.
161. A variety of studies have dealt with this problem, e.g. P. Brown, "Saint Augustine's attitude to religious coercion," *The Journal of Roman Studies*, Vol. LIV, 1964, pp. 107-116. R. Doly, "Saint Augustine et L'intolerance Religieuse," *Revue Belge de Philologie Et D'Histoire*, Vol. XXXIII, 2; 1955, pp. 263-294. And especially E. L. Grasmück, *Coercitio, Staat und Kirche im Donatistenstreit*, Bonn, 1964, pp. 168-250.
162. *City of God*, XVIII, 47; Loeb, VI, 53.
163. I owe this suggestion to Robert Markus, *Saeculum*, p. 161.
164. A summary of Augustine's eschatological hope is contained in his letter to Hesychius (ca. 419). He concludes with the following words: "Consequently, the one who says that the Lord will come soon speaks of what is more desirable, but he is wrong at his peril. Would that it were true, because it will be a cause of trouble if it is not true! But the one who says that the Lord's coming will be delayed, and who nevertheless believes in, hopes for, and loves His coming, is happily in error if he is wrong about His delay. He will have greater patience if it is so; greater joy if it is not. Thus for those who love the manifestation of the Lord, it is sweeter to listen to the first, safer to believe the second. But the one who admits that he does not know which of these views is true hopes for the one, is resigned to the other, is wrong in neither of them. *I beg you not to despise me for being such a one.*" Augustine, *Letters*, IV, pp. 400ff. *The Fathers of the Church*, New York, 1955. (Italics added.)

# Bibliography

Altaner, Berthold. *Patrologie: Leben, Schriften und Lehre der Kirchenväter*. Fifth ed. Freiburg: Herder, 1958.

*Ante-Nicene Fathers: Translations of the Writings of the Fathers down to A.D. 325*. Edited by Alexander Roberts. 10 vols. Grand Rapids, Mich.: Eerdmans, 1963.

Apuleius. *The Golden Ass*. Adlington Translation Revised by S. Gaselee. Loeb Classical Library. Cambridge: Harvard University Press, 1965.

Arendt, Hannah. *Der Liebesbegriff bei Augustin, Versuch einer philosophischen Interpretation*. Vol. 9 of *Philosophische Forschungen*. Berlin. 1929.

Augustine. *The Catholic and Manichaean Ways of Life*. Vol. XIV of *The Fathers of the Church*. Washington: Catholic University of America Press, 1964.

Augustine. *The City of God Against the Pagans*. Translated by George E. McCracken and others. 7 vols. Cambridge: Harvard University Press, 1957-1966.

Augustine. *Confessions*. Translated and edited by Albert Outler. Vol. VII of Library of Christian Classics. Philadelphia: Westminster, 1955.

Balthasar, Hans Urs von. *Origenes, Geist und Feuer: Ein Aufbau aus seinen Schriften*. Second ed. Salzburg: Müller, 1938.

Barnes, Timothy David. *Tertullian: A Historical and Literary Study*. Oxford: Clarendon, 1971.

Basilius, Saint. *The Ascetic Works of Saint Basil*. Translated by W. K. L. Clarke. London: SPCK, 1925.

Basilius, Saint. *The Letters*. Translated by R. Defarrari. Loeb Classical Library. New York: Putnam, 1926.

Baur, Chrysostomus. *John Chrysostom and His Time.* Two vols. Translated by Sr. M. Gonzaga. Westminster, Maryland: Newman, 1959-1960.

Baynes, N. H. "The Great Persecution." In *The Cambridge Ancient History,* Vol. 12, pp. 646-677. Cambridge: University Press, 1939.

Beach, Waldo and Niebuhr, H. R. *Christian Ethics, Sources of the Living Tradition.* New York: Ronald, 1955.

Becker, Carl. *Tertullians Apologeticum: Werden und Leistung.* München: Kösel-Verlag, 1954.

Berger, Peter. *The Sacred Canopy: Elements of a Sociological Theory of Religion.* Garden City, N.Y.: Doubleday, 1967.

Bienert, Walther. *Die Arbeit nach der Lehre der Bibel: eine Grundlegung evangelischer Sozialethik.* Stuttgart: Evangelisches Verlagswerk, 1954.

Blumenkranz, Bernhard. *Die Juden Predigt Augustins.* Basel: Helbing & Lichtenhahn, 1946.

Brechtken, J. *Augustinus Doctor Caritatis.* Meisenheim: Hain, 1974.

Brown, P. "Saint Augustine's attitude to religious coercion," *The Journal of Roman Studies,* LIV (1964), pp. 107-116.

Brown, Peter. *Augustine of Hippo.* Berkeley: University of California Press, 1967.

Bultmann, Rudolf. *Glauben und Verstehen: Gesammelte Aufsätze.* Tübingen: Mohr, 1952-65.

Bultmann, Rudolf. *Primitive Christianity in Its Contemporary Setting.* Translated by R. H. Fuller. New York: Meridian, 1956.

Burckhardt, Jacob. *The Age of Constantine the Great.* Translated by M. Hadas. London: Routledge and Kegan Paul, 1949.

Cadoux, Cecil J. *The Early Church and the World: A History of the Christian Attitude to Pagan Society and the State Down to the Time of Constantine.* Edinburgh: T. & T. Clark, 1925.

*The Cambridge Ancient History.* Cambridge: Cambridge University Press, 1939.

Campenhausen, Hans von. *Die Entstehung der christlichen Bibel.* Tübingen: Mohr, 1968.

Campenhausen, H. *Men Who Shaped the Western Church.* New York: Harper, 1965.

Carcopino, James. *Daily Life in Ancient Rome: The People and the City at the Height of the Empire.* Translated by E. Lorimer. Edited by H. Rowell. New Haven: Yale University Press, 1940.

Cicero. *De Officiis.* Translated by Walter Miller. New York: Putnam, 1928.

Clemens, Titus Flavius. *Clemens Alexandrinus.* O. Stählin, ed. 3rd ed. Berlin: Akademie-Verlag, 1972.

Clemens, Titus Flavius. *Clement of Alexandria.* Translated by G. W. Butterworth. Loeb Classical Library. New York: Putnam, 1919.

Connolly, Richard H. *Didascalia Apostolorum: The Syriac Version*

*Translated and Accompanied by the Verona Latin Fragments.* Oxford: Clarendon, 1969.

Constantelos, Demetrios J. *Byzantine Philanthropy and Social Welfare.* New Brunswick, N.J.: Rutgers University Press, 1968.

Cullmann, Oscar. *The Christology of the New Testament.* Translated by S. Guthrie and C. Hall. Revised ed. Philadelphia: Westminster, 1959.

Deman, Th. *Le Traitement Scientifique De La Morale Chretienne Selon Saint Augustine.* Paris: Libraire Philosophique J. Vrin, 1957.

Dibelius, Martin. *Botschaft und Geschichte: Gesammelte Aufsätze.* 2 vol. Tübingen: Mohr, 1953.

Diels, H., ed. *Die Fragmente der Vorsokratiker,* 5th ed. Berlin: Wiedmann, 1934-37.

Diesner, Hans-Joachim. *Studien zur Gesellschaftslehre und Sozialen Haltung Augustins.* Halle: Niemeyer, 1954.

Dittrich, Ottmar. *Geschichte der Ethik: Die System der Moral vom Altertum bis zur Gegenwart.* 5 vols. Reprint of the 1923 Leipzig ed.; Aalen: Scientia, 1964.

Dörries, Hermann. *Constantine the Great.* Translated by Roland Bainton. New York: Harper & Row, 1972.

Dörries, Hermann. *Wort und Stunde.* 2 vols. Göttingen: Vandenhoeck & Ruprecht, 1966.

Doly, R. "Saint Augustine et L'intolerance Religieuse," Revue Belge De Philologie Et D'Histoire, XXXIII, (2: 1955) pp. 263-294.

Eusebius. *The Ecclesiastical History.* Translated by J. E. L. Oulton. Loeb Classical Library. London: Heinemann, 1932.

Fletcher, Joseph. *Situation Ethics: The New Morality.* Philadelphia: Westminster, 1966.

Forell, George W., ed. *Christian Social Teachings: A Reader in Christian Social Ethics from the Bible to the Present.* Garden City, N.Y.: Doubleday, 1966; Augsburg, 1971.

Frazer, James G. *The Golden Bough: A Study in Magic and Religion.* Part 4: *Adonis Attis Osiris.* London: Macmillan, 1919.

Freund, W. H. C. *Martyrdom and Persecution in the Early Church: A Study of Conflict from the Maccabees to Donatus.* Garden City, N.Y.: Doubleday, 1967.

Friedländer, Ludwig. *Darstellungen aus der Sittengeschichte Roms in der Zeit von August bis zum Ausgang der Antonine.* 9th ed. 4 vols. Leipzig: Hirzel, 1919-21.

Geffcken, Friedrich H. *Church and State: Their Relations Historically Developed.* 2 vols. Translated by and edited by E. Taylor. London: Longmans, 1877.

Grant, Robert, ed. *The Apostolic Fathers: A New Translation and Commentary.* 6 vols. New York: Nelson, 1964-68.

Grasmück, E. L. *Coercitio, Staat und Kirche im Donatistenstreit.* Bonn, 1964.

Gunkel, H. and Zscharnack, L. *Religion in Geschichte und Gegenwart: Handwörterbuch für Theologie und Religionswissenschaft.* 2nd ed. Tübingen: Mohr, 1927-31.

Gustafson, James M. *Protestant and Roman Catholic Ethics Prospects for Rapprochement.* Chicago: University of Chicago Press, 1978.

Gustafson, James M. *Theology and Christian Ethics.* Philadelphia: Pilgrim, 1974.


Hall, Thomas C. *History of Ethics Within Organized Christianity.* New York: Scribner's, 1910.

Hand, Volkmar. *Augustin und das klassisch Römische Selbstverständnis.* Hamburg: Helmut Bushe, 1970.

Harnack, Adolf von. *Geschichte der altchristlichen Literatur bis Eusebius.* 2nd ed. 2 vols. Leipzig: Hinrichs, 1958.

Harnack, Adolf von. *History of Dogma.* Translated by N. Buchanan. New York: Russell & Russell, 1958.

Heck, Eberhard. *Die dualistischen Zusätze und die Kaiseranreden bei Lactantius.* Heidelberg: Winter, 1972.

Hertz, Joseph H. *The Authorized Daily Prayer Book.* New York: Bloch, 1961.

Holl, Karl. *Gesammelte Aufsätze zur Kirchengeschichte.* Vol. I, *Luther.* Tübingen: Mohr, 1932. Vol. II *Der Osten,* Mohr, 1928.

Hornschuh, Manfred. "Das Leben des Origenes und die Entstehung der Alexandrinischen Schule." *Zeitschrift für Kirchengeschichte.* LXXI (1960): 1-25, 193-214.


Jaeger, Werner. *Early Christianity and Greek Paideia.* Cambridge, Mass.: Harvard University Press, 1965.

Jonas, Hans. *Augustin und das Paulinische Freiheitsproblem.* Göttingen: Vandenhoeck & Ruprecht, 1965.

Jonas, Hans. *Philosophical Essays: From Ancient Creed to Technological Man.* Englewood Cliffs, N.J.: Prentice-Hall, 1974.

Jones, A. H. M. "The Social Background of the Struggle Between Paganism and Christianity." In *The Conflict Between Paganism and Christianity in the Fourth Century: Essays,* pp. 17-37. Edited by Arnaldo Momigliano. Oxford: Clarendon, 1963.

Julianus. *The Works of Emperor Julian.* Translated by W. Wright. Loeb Classical Library. New York: Putnam, 1923.

*Juvenal and Persius.* Edited and translated by G. Ramsay. Loeb Classical Library. Cambridge, Mass.: Harvard University Press, 1969.

Kettler, Frans Heinrich. *Der ursprüngliche Sinn der Dogmatik des Origenes.* Berlin: Töpelmann, 1966.

Kittel, Gerhard, ed. *Theological Dictionary of the New Testament.* Translated by G. Bromiley. Grand Rapids, Mich.: Eerdmans, 1964-1974.

Klein, Richard. *Der Streit um den Victoriaaltar.* Darmstadt: Wissenschaftliche Buchgesellschaft, 1972.

Klein, Richard. *Tertullian und das römische Reich.* Heidelberg: Winter, 1968.

Koch, Carl. *Religio: Studien zu Kult und Glauben der Römer.* Edited by O. Seel. Nürnberg: Carl, 1960.

Koetschau, Paul, ed. *Origenes Werke.* In *Die griechischen christlichen Schriftsteller der ersten drei Jahrhunderte.* Leipzig, 1913.

Kroll, Wilhelm. *Die Kultur der ciceronischen Zeit.* 2 vol. Leipzig: Dieterich, 1933.

Laeuchli, Samuel. *Power and Sexuality, The Emergence of Canon Law at the Synod of Elvira.* Philadelphia: Temple University Press, 1972.

Laufs, Joachim. *Der Friedensgedanke bei Augustinus.* Wiesbaden: Steiner, 1973.

Lehmann, Paul L. *Ethics in a Christian Context.* New York: Harper & Row, 1963.

Libanius. *Discours Moraux.* Edited by Bernard Schouler. Paris: Les Belles Lettres, 1973.

Lietzmann, Hans. *Geschichte der alten Kirche.* 3 vols. Berlin: de Gruyter, 1932.

Lietzmann, Hans. *A History of the Early Church.* 3 vols. New York: Meridian, 1961.

Lilla, Salvatore R. *Clement of Alexandria: A Study in Christian Platonism and Gnosticism.* Oxford: Oxford University Press, 1971.

Lillie, William. *Studies in New Testament Ethics.* Edinburgh: Oliver and Boyd, 1961.

Lohse, Eduard. *Umwelt des Neuen Testaments.* Göttingen: Vandenhoeck & Ruprecht, 1971.

Long, Edward LeRoy. *A Survey of Christian Ethics.* New York: Oxford University Press, 1967.

Lucianus Samosatensis. *Lucian.* Translated by A. M. Harmon. Loeb Classical Library. Cambridge, Mass.: Harvard University Press, 1936.

Markus, Robert. *Saeculum: History and Society in the Theology of Augustine.* Cambridge: University Press, 1970.

Mausbach, Joseph. *Die Ethik des heiligen Augustinus.* 2nd ed. 2 vols. Freiburg: Herder, 1929.

Miura-Stange, Anna. *Celsus und Origenes: Das Gemeinsame ihrer Weltanschauung nach den acht Büchern des Origenes gegen Celsus.* Giessen: Töpelmann, 1926.

Musurillo, Herbert. *The Acts of the Christian Martyrs.* Oxford: Clarendon, 1972.

*New English Bible with the Apocrypha.* New York: Oxford University Press, 1971.
*Nicene and Post-Nicene Fathers.* Edited by Philip Schaff, First & Second series, 28 vols. Grand Rapids, Mich.: Eerdmans, 1953.
Niebuhr, H. Richard. *Christ and Culture.* New York: Harper, 1951.
Nygren, Anders. *Eros and Agape.* Gütersloh: Bertelsmann, 1930/37.

Origenes. *Origen on First Principles.* Translated by G. W. Butterworth. London: SPCK, 1936.
Oulton, John E. L. and Henry Chadwick. *Alexandrian Christianity.* Library of Christian Classics. Philadelphia: Westminster, 1954.

Palladius. *Dialogue Concerning the Life of Chrysostom.* Edited by H. Moore. London: SPCK, 1921.
*Patrologiae Cursus Completus.* Edited by J. P. Migne. Series Graeca. 176 vols. Paris: Garnier, 1857-1912.
Pelikan, Jaroslav Jan. *The Christian Tradition; A History of the Development of Doctrine.* Vol. I, *Emergence of the Catholic Tradition,* Chicago: University of Chicago Press, 1971.
Perler, Othmar. "Les voyages de saint Augustine," *Recherches Augustiennes,* Vol. I, Paris, 1958.
Pöhlmann, Robert von. *Geschichte der Sozialen Frage und des Sozialismus in der Antiken Welt.* 2 vols. München: Beck, 1925.
Preisker, Herbert. *Das Ethos des Urchristentums.* 2nd ed. Gütersloh: Bertelsmann, 1949.

Raeder, Hans. "Kaiser Julian als Philosoph und religiöser Reformator," *Classica et Mediaevalia* Vol. 6, 1944, pp. 179ff.
Richardson, Cyril, ed. and trans. *Early Christian Fathers.* Library of Christian Classics, Vol. 1. Philadelphia: Westminster, 1953.
Rief, Joseph. *Der Ordobegriff des Jungen Augustinus.* Paderborn: Ferdinand Schöningh, 1962.

Schaff, Philip, and Wace H., eds. *A Select Library of Nicene and Post-Nicene Fathers of the Christian Church.* 14 vols. 2nd Series. Grand Rapids, Mich.: Eerdmans, 1952.
Schrage, Wolfgang. *Die konkreten Eingelgebote in der paulinischen Paränese: Ein Beitrag zur neutestamentlichen Ethik.* Gütersloh: Mohn, 1961.
Seeck, Otto. *Geschichte des Untergangs der Antiken Welt.* 6 vols. Stuttgart: Metzler, 1966.
Seneca. *Ad Lucilium Epistulae Morales.* Translated by R. Gunmese. 2 vols. New York: Putnam, 1925.

Stelzenberger, Johannes. *Conscientia bei Augustinus.* Paderborn: Ferdinand Schöningh, 1959.
Stade, K. *Der Politiker Diokletian und die letzte grosse Christenverfolgung.* Frankfurt: 1926.
Straub, J. "Konstantins Verzicht auf den Gang zum Kapitol." *Historia* IV (1955): 297-313.
Sundberg, Albert C. *The Old Testament of the Early Church.* Cambridge, Mass.: Harvard University Press, 1964.

Tacitus. *Tacitus.* Edited and translated by C. Moore and J. Jackson. Loeb Classical Library. Cambridge, Mass.: Harvard University Press, 1939.
Tertullianus. *Adversus Marcionem.* Edited and translated by E. Evans. Oxford: Clarendon, 1972.
Tertullianus. *Minucius Felix.* Translated by T. Glover and G. Rendall. Loeb Classical Library. New York: Putnam, 1931.
*Theocritus.* Edited and Translated by A. S. F. Gow. Cambridge: University Press, 1950.
*The Theodosian Code and Novels and the Sirmondian Constitutions: A Translation with Commentary, Glossary and Bibliography.* Translated by C. Pharr. Princeton, N.J.: Princeton University Press, 1952.
Tollinton, Richard Bartram. *Clement of Alexandria: A Study in Christian Liberalism.* London: Williams and Norgate, 1914.
Troeltsch, Ernst. *Augustin, die Christliche Antike und das Mittelalter.* Berlin: Oldenbourg, 1915.
Troeltsch, Ernst. *The Social Teaching of the Christian Churches.* Translated by Olive Wyon. 2 vols. New York: Macmillan, 1931.

Uhlhorn, W. *Die Christliche Liebesthätigkeit in der Alten Kirche.* Stuttgart: Gundert, 1882.

VanderMeer, F. *Augustine the Bishop.* New York: Sheed and Ward, 1961.
Völker, W. *Das Vollkommenheitsideal des Origenes: Eine Untersuchung zur Geschichte der Frömmigkeit und zu den Anfängen christlicher Mystik.* Tübingen: Mohr, 1931.
Völker, Walther. *Der wahre Gnostiker nach Clemens Alexandrinus.* Berlin: Akadamie-Verlag, 1952.
Volkmar, G. "Über die Häretiker Epiphanes und Adrianus," *Monatschrift des wissenschaftlichen Vereins in Zürich* I, (1856), pp. 276-282.

Wahlstrom, Eric H. *The New Life in Christ.* Philadelphia: Muhlenberg, 1950.
Wendland, Heinz-Dietrich. *Ethik des Neuen Testaments.* Göttingen: Vandenhoeck & Ruprecht, 1970.
Winkelmann, J. "Die Textbezeugung der Vita Constantini." *Texte und Untersuchungen,* LXXXIV (1962).

# Index of Subjects

228 / *Index*

# Index of Names

# Index of
# Biblical References

# Index of
# Greek and Latin Terms

Indexes prepared by Edith Fischer-Mueller and Richard W. Schoenleber.